History Of The Gwydir Family

SIR JOHN WYNNE OF GWEDIR,

from a rare Print by Rob.t Vaughan.

London, Printed for Robert Wilkinson. N.º 125 Fenchurch Street.

THE

HISTORY

OF THE

GWYDIR FAMILY,

WRITTEN BY

SIR JOHN WYNNE, KNT. AND BART.,

UT CREDITUR, & PATET.

OSWESTRY:

WOODALL AND VENABLES, OSWALD ROAD.

1878.

WOODALL AND VENABLES, PRINTERS,

BAILEY-HEAD AND OSWALD-ROAD,

OSWESTRY.

TO THE RIGHT HONOURABLE

CLEMENTINA ELIZABETH,

(IN HER OWN RIGHT)

BARONESS WILLOUGHBY DE ERESBY,

THE REPRESENTATIVE OF THE OLD GWYDIR STOCK

AND THE OWNER OF THE ESTATE :

THE FOURTEENTH WHO HAS BORNE THAT ANCIENT BARONY:

THIS EDITION OF THE

HISTORY OF THE GWYDIR FAMILY

IS, BY PERMISSION,

RESPECTFULLY DEDICATED BY

THE PUBLISHERS.

OSWALD ROAD, OSWESTRY,
1878.

· PREFACE

OF all the works which have been written relating to the general or family history of North Wales, none have been for centuries more esteemed than the *History of the Gwydir Family*.

The Hon. Daines Barrington, in his preface to his first edition of the work, published in 1770, has well said, "The MS. hath, for above a century, been so prized in North Wales, that many in those parts have thought it worth while to make fair and complete transcripts of it."

Of these transcripts the earliest known to exist is one in the Library at Brogyntyn. It was probably written within 45 years of the death of the author; but besides that, it contains a great number of notes and additions of nearly the same date, which have never yet appeared in print.

The *History of the Gwydir Family* has been thrice published. The first edition, edited by the Hon. Daines Barrington, issued from the press in 1770. The second was published in Mr. Barrington's *Miscellanies* in 1781; the third, edited by Miss Angharad Llwyd, made its appearance in 1827.

The *History of the Gwydir Family* is the only one that gives any account of the state of society in North Wales in the 15th, and in the earlier part of the 16th centuries, but unfortunately, it is lamentably deficient in dates.

The present edition owes its existence to the long and painstaking labour of of W. W. E. Wynne, Esq., of Peniarth, who has collated his copy of Miss Llwyd's edition with the *Brogyntyn, Wynnstay,* and *Peniarth MSS.,* adding a very large collection of dates, from contemporary records, including the *Ministers' Accounts* in the Public Record Office, in London.

Mr. Wynne having very kindly placed his copy at my disposal, it has been my pleasant task during the last three or four months to superintend the issue of the present edition through the press, and I have most heartily to thank the Rev. Canon Williams, of Rhydycroesau, for his advice and assistance, without which several errors would-have passed uncorrected.

The text followed in the present edition is that of Barrington's *Miscellanies,* published in 1781, and this has been carefully compared with the other editions, the variations being pointed out in the notes. The *Memoirs* from page 90 to the end are taken from Miss Llwyd's book.

In one of the copies of the Gwydir MS. at Mostyn, there is, at the head of it, in a later handwriting than the MS. itself, " A true coppy of a manuscript written by Sʳ Joᵃ Wynne of Gwydir Kⁿᵗ and Barrᵗ ut Creditur & patet. 1607." It also contains the Latin MS. of Bishop Robinson, mentioned in note 3, page 12 of this book. The same Mostyn MS. also ends the list of the children of Meredith ap Jevan with those by his concubine, which appears as a note on page 87, taken from the Gwydir MS. at Wynnstay. A second written copy preserved at Mostyn has at its commencement the following :—" This book was transcribed from a coppy belonging to Sʳ Morris Parry[1] of Llan Elian Clerk in the year 1674, And afterwards compar'd with & corrected by two coppys, the one belonging to the Reverend Dr. Humphreys Dean of Bangor[2] the other found among the Evidences att Gweder, which last was in many places corrected & interlind, & much of it writt with the hand of Sʳ John Wynn himself the Author. 1683. THOMAS MOSTYN, of Gloddeath."

The references to other editions, in the notes to the present one, are indicated on page 11. The letter " W." is only affixed to a few of the more personal notes by Mr. Wynne; the bulk of those with no initial attached being also from his pen.

The portrait of Sir John is reproduced by photo-lithography from an old engraving, the plate of which Miss Llwyd used for her edition of 1827. The portrait of Sir Richard, by Janson, is also copied by the same process from an engraving by Bartolozzi which has appeared in Pennant's *Tours* and else-where. The view of Dolwyddelan Castle is reduced from an engraving published by Buck in 1742. The somewhat rude sketch of Gwydir House, with the arms of the family, is a copy of the one mentioned on page 6 as being on the border of a county map published about 1720. There is one of the original issues of this map at Wynnstay, but unfortunately the portion containing Gwydir is damaged, and the illustration given in this book has been very faithfully copied on stone by Miss M. W. Minshall from a photograph kindly lent me by W. Wynne Ffoulkes, Esq., of Chester. The still older picture on the title page, which represents Upper Gwydir as it was in 1684, when the Duke of Beaufort in his progress through Wales lodged there, is copied from the *Beaufort Progress*, and I am indebted for the use of it to Dr. Nicholas in whose *Annals of County Families* it appeared. The copy of the monument in Dolwyddelan church illustrates a pleasant paper on that attractive district in the *Archæologia Cambrensis*, by the Rev. D. R. Thomas, to whom my thanks are due for the use of the engraving.

ASKEW ROBERTS.

Croeswylan, Oswestry.

---

[1] He was rector of Llanelian from 1660 to 1683.   [2] I suspect this to be the *Wynnstay MS.*—W.

GWYDIR MEMORIALS.

THE life of Sir John Wynn, the historian of the Gwydir Family, was so uneventful that but few records remain to form materials for a memoir. The chief incidents in his career may almost be summed up in a paragraph:—"His character has been held up as all that was worthy, and decried as everything that was crafty. He was Member of Parliament for the county of Carnarvon in 1596, one of the Council of the Marches of Wales, and created a baronet in 1611. Being 'shrewd and successful in his dealings,' people were led to believe he oppressed them, and, says Yorke in his *Royal Tribes of Wales*, 'it is the superstition of Llanrwst to this day, that the spirit of the old gentleman lies under the great waterfall Rhaiadr y Wennol, there to be punished, purged, spouted upon, and purified from the foul deeds done in his days of nature.' It is recorded that in 1615, Sir John having incurred the displeasure of the Council of the Marches, Lord Ellesmere, the Chancellor, was appealed to, but, the 'shrewd' baronet made his peace in the surest manner, by paying a bribe of £350. He was a man, evidently, who tried to make the best of both worlds, for after squaring the court with his bribe,[1] and managing to keep his name on the Commission for Carnarvonshire, he made his peace with heaven by founding a hospital, endowing a school at Llanrwst, and giving up sundry tithes to support these charities. Sir John bore one of the great standards at the funeral of Henry, Prince of Wales. He died in 1626-7, at the age of seventy-three."

Mr. Barrington, in his introduction to the *History of the Gwydir Family* (see page 7) inserts the letter of Sir John to his kinsman, Sir Hugh Myddleton, respecting the reclamation of land, where Tremadoc now stands,[2] and Mr. Halliwell, some years back, published "An Ancient Survey of Pen Maen Mawr," which is supposed to be from the pen of Sir John Wynn, and to which Bishop Gibson had access when

---

[1] The following is the "bargain" struck between the parties:—*M'd*. Yf Mr. Bernard Lyndesey Esquier Groom to his Maties. Bedchamber procure a pardon for Sir John Wynn Knight and Baronet and some of their fynes and offences inflicted upon them by the Counsell of the Marches, upon the sealing of the said pardon he is to receave from Richard Wynn Esquier sonne and heire to the said Sir Jo: Wynn the somme of three hundred and fiftye pounds. In witness of this agreement between us we have both sette our hands the sixteenth of January 1615.

Signed in the presence   B. LYNDESEY,
of me   RICH. WYNN.
     AMB. THELWALL.

[2] The following reply to the letter of Sir John, is published in the Rev. Walter Davies's *Agricul-tural Survey of North Wales :* — Honorable Sir.—I have received your kind letter. Few are the thinges done by me, for which I give God the glory. It may please you to understand, my first undertaking of publick workes was in my owne countrey, within less than a myle of the place where I hadd my first beinge, 24 or 25 years since, in seeking of coals for the towne of Denbigh. Touching the drowned lands near your lyvinge, there are manye things considerable therein. Iff to be gayned, which will hardlie be performed without great stones, which was plentiful at the Weight, as well as wood; and greate sums of monye to be spent, not hundreds but thousandes—and first of all His Majesty's intereste must be got. As for myself, I am grown into years, and full of busienesse here at the mynes, the river at London, and other places, my weeklie

he prepared his edition of Camden.   One extract from this is interesting, exhibiting as it does, a considerable mixture of superstition and simplicity in the shrewd baronet's mind.   Speaking of a carnedd on Moelfre, a smooth round hill somewhere between Llanvairvechan and the village bearing the dreadful name of Dwygyvylchi, he says :—

Neare unto this place there is a ffyne delicate hill called Moelvre, rownd by nature and mownted very highe; and in the toppe very playne and pleasant : uppon this hill there is a cyrcle marked, whereuppon stood three stones aboutes a yard and a quarter above grownd, the one redd as blood the other white, and the thyrd a litle bluer then the white stone, standynge in a triangle wiese.   What shoulde bee the reason of placynge such three stones in such a place upon soe highe and soe pleasant a mounte, and to place there stones of such colloures.   I cannott expresse otherwiese than wee have ytt by tradicion.   The tradicion is this, that God Allmighty hath wrought in this place a miracle for increasynge of our fayth, and that was thus.   Three women, aboutes such tyme as Christianity began to creepe in amongest us, uppon a Sabaoth day in the mornynge went to the toppe of this hill to wynowe there corne, and havynge spread there wynowynge sheete uppon the grownd and begunn there worke, some of there neighbours came unto them and did reprehend them for violatynge and breakynge the Lorde's commaundement by workynge uppon the Saboathe day.   These faythless women, regardynge there profytt more than the obsearvynge of God's commaundement, made slight of there neighbours admonition, and healde on in there worke ; whereuppon ytt pleased God instantly to transfourme them into three pillars of stones, and to frame these stones of the same collour as the womens clothes weare, one read, thother white, and the thyrd bluishe, and to transfourme there winowyng sheete and corne into earth, and soe to leave them there in example unto others. This is a tradicion wee have and beleeved by the oulde people in that neighbourhood, and housoever, whether ytt was soe or noe, the tradicion is wholesome, and will deterr others from workynge uppon the Sabaoth day.   These stones, beynge worth the seynge as they weare there placed, have beene digged uppe by some idle headed youthes within this sixe yeeres, and weare rowled downe the hill, and doe now lie att the foote of the hill.

If Sir John Wynn led a life of retirement, it was none the less a busy one, Besides his concern for the reclamation of land on the Carnarvonshire coast, and his survey on the Carnarvonshire mountains, he appears to have been actively engaged in other works for the benefit of his neighbours, but not at the same time forgetting himself.   The following extract points to the local manufacture of Welsh Friezes, by Irishmen ; and to mining operations in Anglesey :—

GWYDIR, 2d AUG. 1623.

. . . .   One Roper, of Roper's Rest in Ireland, beinge one of the Privie Counsel, would gladly set 300 people here a work to spin woolle, and desired your answer to know whether it might be done.   I say it may bee done ; for I have conferred with divers which do affyrme the same.   And a more fittinge tyme there cannot be than this time of necessitié : for if the tymes did amend, they will not goe out of their own countrye.   I will find them houseing upon my lands about Llanrwst and Trevriew, beinge within a myle of my house ; and all thynges necessarie for them, and monie aforehand, for it will require a great somme of monie to make them loomes and other implements fitte for the occupation, and alsoe to make mylls and tenters.

. . .   Woolle is to be had in this countrié good store, and verie cheape.   Because it is so charytable a deede, and for the goode of the countrye, I offer my furtherance with all my hearte, and the servise of my people : and I should myselfe be best able to further it of anie in this countrye, all circumstances considered.   It is fitte the gentleman should send a sufficient man here, with fulle instructions concerning his intended purpose ; and would best begin a lesse preparation aiminge at a greater. . . .

Yours, &c., JOHN WYN.

P.S.   I pray you doe your endeavoure to selle my lead oare that is at Beaumaris.   Methinks those foreiners that have received so much monie of the countrye for the corne they brought in, should be bound to leave some parte thereof for our countrye commoditie, that all the monie of the land be not carried away ; and this shoulde be done by your beinge pryme officer in your towne.   I sould always for three pounds a tonne, allowing the long hundred ; but to take monie, now I woulde sell it for somethinge lesse.

---

charge beinge above £200 ; which makth me verie unwilling to undertake anie other worke, and the least of theise, whether the drowned lands or mynes, requireth a whole man, with a large purse. Noble Sir, my desire is greate to see you, which should draw me a farr longer waie, yet such are my occasiones at this tyme here, for the settlinge of this greate worke, that I can hardlie be spared one hour in a daie.   My wiefa being also here, I cannot leave her in a strange place.   Yet my love to publicke workes, and desire to see you (if God permit), maie another tyme drawe me into those partes.   Soe with my heartie commendations I commit you and all your good desires to God.— Your assured lovinge cousin to command, HUGH MYDDLETON. Lodge, Sept. 2, 1625.

The foregoing letter was addressed to "Humph: Jones, Esq., Receiver of North Wales," and the two that follow were written to Lord Eure, President of the Marches of Wales, respecting the Copper Mines in Parys Mountain, probably some years earlier. They are all taken from the Rev. Walter Davies's *Survey of Agriculture* :—

No. 1.

. . . I sende you the myneral water of Anglesey to be tried . . . I saw when Medley made the tryal before Sir Henry Sidney, and I laid down the particulars. First—a quantitie of iron was beaten small into powder, which was put into the water in a great boiler of lead, whereof there were either half a dozen or more. Anie of these boilers, haveing flat bottoms, and not verie deep, not unlike the form of a cooller, did contain manie barrels of licker, beinge that water; which beinge boiled with an exceeding hot fire of turf to a great height, and afterwards suffered to coolle, there was congealed in that water a threefolde substance :—the one copperas, beinge greene, highest; the second alome, beinge white, in the middle; and the thirde, called the earth of iron, being yellowe in the bottome. The alome and copperas seemed both to be perfectlie good. The earth of iron, after it was fullie dried, grewe to a substance like the ruste of iron which had long been canckered, yet yellowe. Of this earth of iron I have a greate quantitie laide upon charcoale in a bricke furnace, and blowne downe and smelted like lead; and downe came a greate quantitie of iron synders intermingled here and there with copper. The 1-10th parte of that which came downe proved to be copper; whereof parte was sent to the Lo. of the Counsell that were partners in the worke, parte to others of the nobilitie; and every gentleman of qualitie there presente had parte to carrie in his pockette, who were of opinion that the work would not quitte coste; and so it proved, for that in a while it was given over. Wishinge your Lo. good successe in all your attempts, and especiallie in these your alcymycall conclusions.   I do rest yours, &c.

                                                JOHN WYN.

No. 2.

. . . . . I REMEMBER some twentie eighte years agoe that there was a greate myneral worke in Anglesey, some twentie miles beyonde me: that one Mr. Medley had undertaken by boylinge of a water, which wroughte these effectes. It made alome and copperas, and transmuted iron into copper; all which the selfe same water did perfforme, whereof the manner and particularities I have forgotten, though I have been an eye witnesse of the same;[1] for I went thyther in companie with the late Lord Treasurer Burley, the Earl of Leister, and Sir Francis Walsingham, who were partners in that worke; whereof the evente succeeded not; whether by reason of Medley's want of skill on his parte, is a questione . . .

One of the most notable events in the career of Sir John that has come down to us, is his controversy with Bishop Morgan.[2] The Bishop would not confirm a lease of church lands held by the baronet, and pleads "conscience," which, he says, "assureth me that youre request ys such, that in grauntyng yt, I shold prove my selfe an unhonest, unconsionable, and irreligiouse man; ye a sacrilegiouse robber of my church, a perfydiouse spoyler of my Diocese, and an unnaturall hyndrer of preachers and good

---

[1] There is an inconsistency in these two letters that requires explanation. In the (previous) Letter the Baronet frankly owns that he had laid down the *particulars* of Mr. Medley transmuting iron into copper;—in this (last) Letter, he says he had forgotten the manner and particularities thereof. This was Sir John's sophistry, either to save himself the trouble of giving the information required by Lord Eure; or, he wished, for private reasons, to conceal the favourable symptoms that Parys mountain contained copper. As Mr. Medley is known to have made his experiments in 1579; and as Sir John, in this last letter, says they were made "some twenty-eighte years" back;—both letters appear to be written in the same year, namely, 1607: and it is probable that this last letter was written first; and on being further pressed by Lord Eure the wary Baronet gave the information contained in letter one.—Rev. WALTER DAVIES.

[2] The Rev. Canon Williams, in his valuable *Dictionary of Eminent Welshmen*, tells us that this "incomparable man for piety and industry," was born in the parish of Penmachno, a village not far from Gwydir. He was educated at St. John's College, Cambridge, and his first preferment was the vicarage of Welshpool, to which he was instituted August 8th, 1575. After three years' residence there he was removed to the Vicarage of Llanrhaiadr-yn-Mochnant, near Oswestry, and there he finished his great undertaking of translating the Bible into the Welsh language. He soon afterwards was rewarded with more than one sinecure, after the manner of the times, and was consecrated Bishop of Llandaff in 1595, at the express command of Queen Elizabeth. He was translated to St. Asaph in September, 1601, and he died there September 10, 1604.

scholars," &c., &c. Sir John, however, as will be seen by his reply, cared little for the charge of robbery and sacrilege ; but very much for what he deemed to be his rights :—

Hominibus ingratis loquimini, lapides. The sower went out to sowe; and some of his seede fell in stonie ground, where hitt wythered, because hitt could take noe roote. The seede was good, but the land nought. I may justly say soe by you. I have in all shewed my selfe your ffreinde, in soe much as yf I had not pointed you-the waye with my finger (whereof I have yett good testimonye) you had beene styll Vycar of Llanrhayder. You pleade conscience when you should geve, and make no bones to receave curtesie of your ffreinds. But I appeale to him that searcheth the conscience of all men, whether you have used me well, and whether hitt be conscience (w^th . you ever have in your mouth) be the sole hinderance of my request. I wyll avowe and justiffie hitt before the greatest Dyvyns in England, that it hath beene, nowe ys, and ever wylbe, that a man may w^th . a salfe conscience be farmour of a lyvinge, payeing in effect for the same as much as hitt ys woorth ; and soe ys this, surmyse you the value to be as you layst. Nether was the losse of the thynge that I regard a dodkyn, but your unkinde dealinge. Hitt shall leson me to expect noe sweete fruite of a sower stocke. Your verball love I esteeme as nothinge ; and I make noe doubt (w^th . God's good favour) to lyve to be able to pleasure you, as much as you shall me, et é contrâ. You byd me thanke God for his meny benefyts towards me. God graunt me the grace ever soe to doe. In truth, I did much thanke Him in mynde to see you preferred to the place you are in, as yf you had beene my owne brother; but that I recall, for I never expect good wyll of you, nor good torne by you.

JOHN WYN,
of Gwyder.

Gwyder, the house that did you and your's good. *24th February*, 1603.
[To the Reverend Father, The Lord Busshop of St. Asaphe.]

Sir John also writes to Mr. Martyn (who appears to have been a friend of both) a long and bitter letter, in which he threatens the Bishop with his revenge. He says :—

SIR, No greefe to the greefe of unkyndnes : They rewarded me yll for good to the great dyscomfort of my sole. I may say so, and justly complaen unto you of my L. of St. Asaphe, who (besydes what hys ancestors receved by myen) ys dyversly, and in great matters, behouldynge unto me, whereof (beynge schooled by hys late letter, of w^ch . I send you a trew coppy) thoghe I expect no rent, yett yt easethe my wronged mynd muche, to lay open hys hard dealyngs towards me, and my benefyts towards hym, befor you, who are not ignorant that I delyver but a truethe, in most of them havynge been an ey wytnes.

Hyt squarethe therefor w^th . a good method in a narration to begyn w^th . my deserts, w^th . I wyll run over breefly ; w^th . I wold have you to put hym in mynd of : I. in that he protested to hys late servant Tho. Vaghan, that he remembred no more therof, then that I had lent hym my geldyngs to go to Llandda, and had sent hym a fatt oxe att hys fyrst comynge to St. Assaphe. W^ch . ys to strayne a gnatt, and swallow a camell.

Fyrst, I let hym have a Lease uppon hys farme of Wybernant, parte of the township of Doluthelan for forty years, for forty poundes in money. The farme he hathe sett att the yerly rent of twenty foure poundes per ann: and yeldethe of the Kyng's rent viijs. too pence yerly, as farre as I remember.

In measurynge the sayd farme w^th . my farme of Penannen, I let hym have, in Pant yr Helygloyn, land. to the valew of iijl. yerly ; for w^ch . my uncle Owen Wyn reprooved me muche.

I bare the hatred of Jeuan M^r dythe, and hys nephew Ed. Morice, the lawyer, durynge his lyfe ; for that I was a daysman, and agaenst hym ; I mean, Jeuan M^r dythe, and appointed my frends commyssyoners agaenst hym.

Was hyt not I that fyrst delt w^th . Mr. Boyer to make hym Bushopp, and made the bargen, S^r ? Mr Boyer was nether knowen to hym, nor he to Mr. Boyer ; ergo, yf that had not beene, he had contynued styll Vycar of Llan Rhayder. I know you do not forgett what was obiected against hym and hys wyf to stopp his last translation, and how that my certyfycatt and my frends quitted hym of that imputation, and so made hym prevayle ; for the w^ch, both they and I wear worse thoght of by those we have good cause hyghly to respect.

I labored, as yf hit had beene to save the lyf of on of my chyldren, to end the cause of dylapidations between hym and my coosin Dd. Holland ; knowynge hit wold have beene his great hynderance to be so matched att first dashe. How sufficyent a man, how well ffrended, and what a toothe-man in hys suets my cousin Holland ys, every man that knowethe hym, knowethe that also.

My L. of St. Assaphe I knew to be but poore (hys translation havynge stood him in muche) yett wylfull and heddy to run into law suets ; therefor I was as muche trobled to reclaeme hym to reson and consyderation of hys owen estate as I was to bringe the adverse part to reson and conformyty. My L. Bushopp's cheefe lyvynge was the tenthe of the Paryshe of Abergele, where my coosin Holland comandeth absolutely. Yf they had gone to suet of law, he would so have wronged him in the gatherynge of the tythe, as hit should have beene lyttell worthe unto hym. My self excepted, was ther on Jent. in the contrey wold once have shewed hym self for hym agaenst my coosin Holland? and that knew he well. But my L. can make use of Jent. when they serve hys torne, and after decarde them upon pretence of conscyence; w^ch . may appere by the coppye of hys letter[1] unto me, whereof, I avowe on my credyt this ys the trew coppye. Thus much touchynge that matter of my desert; and now touchynge my request.

Mr. Sharp, my L. Chancelor's Chaplen beynge by hys L. collated parson of Llanrwst, leased hys benefyce to on Robt. Gwyn of Chester, who appointed a ffrend of myen, on Robt. Vaughan, brother to my brother Tho. Vaughan, his under farmor. Doctor Elice, sometyme a great comander in theese quarters, in favor of Doctor Meryke (who rewarded him w^th . a townshyp of tcythe whear his mansyon house was in 'Spytty) dyd geeve lev to dysmember the parsonadge of Llan rwst of Tybrithe tythe, and to joyne hit to Corwen. Whearuppon, pyttyinge to see Llan rwst churche dysmembered by unlawfull practyse, acqueanted my L. of S^t. Assaphe, that I ment to stand for the right of Llanrwst agaenst Doctor Meryke, w^ch . with an intent to do more for that churche, as I then made knowen to my L. The suet prooved, by Doctor Meryke's weywardnes and hope in his fautors, more chardgeable and troblesom then was expected. Wheruppon I eftsons acquainted my L. Bushop, that I ment to buy Robt. Gwyn's lease into my hands, that, surrendringe hit, Mr. Sharp (in consyderation of my great chardge in the suet) myght grant me a lease of the lyvynge for iij lyves, the only mean in som part to quit my chardge ; w^ch . he promysed me to confyrme, and that hit should be the fyrst of all other that should receve confyrmation. Havynge to my chardge and troble compased Robt. Gwyn's lease of 10 ycars, and by surrender of the same gott a new lease of three lyves of Mr. Sharp, I sent hyt to be shewed my L. by my servant W_m. Lloyd ; who then seemed to myslyke hit, and answered doutfully touchynge the confyrmation, w^th . all chidd Mr. Sharp in suche sort, as givynge cause to have my lease new made, he made me pay 10l. more then was att fyrst, by reson my L. Bushop had chidd hym. In end, hearynge of a Chapter appointed for the confyrmation of the other leases, I sent myen also by my son Mostyn, and my letter to my L. the contents whearof you shall fynd in my Lord's answer. To w^ch . I received this answer ; w^ch . whether hit be fyttynge my desert ys your's to judge, as also to expostulat w^th . hym, beynge oure ffrend, common to us bothe.

I am not of nature to put up wronge ; for as I have studyed for hys good, and wrought the same, so lett my L. be assured of me as bytter an enemye (yf he dryve me to hit) as ever I was a steadfast frend ; nether ys he com to that heyght, or wantethe enemyes, that he may say, Major sum, quám cui possit fortuna nocere. For as Honores mutant mores, so mores mutant honores. I am ashamed for hym, that he hathe geeven herby cause to his enemyes and myen to descant of his ungrate dysposition ever aggravated towards hym. Hys answer att lardge I pray you retorne me, yf nothynge els.

Your lovynge ffrend
JOHN WYN,
of Gwyder.

Gwyrmm, this xiljth of Marhe, 1608.

He promysed me an advowson of the lyvynge by Tho. Robts, when 'he denyed the confyrmation. I sent unto hym the same man, wch in too dayes after for the same, and my coosin Elice Vaghan wth all ; and he denyed me eny, sayinge he had provyded no preferment for his wife, and that he myght overlyve Sharpe, and have that lyvynge in Comendam. So, to conclude, I must have nothynge but a scornefull, chetynge letter, in leu of all my good indeavors.

In allusion to the taunt of patronage in the letter of Sir John Wynn to him, the Bishop, in confesse to Mr. Martyn, says :—" I confesse that Mr. Wyn thearein shewed greate love (as then I thought) to me ; but (as nowe I fynde) to hym selfe, hopynge to make a stave of me to dryve preacher's patrydges to his hys netts."

The baronet of Gwydir evidently had very little veneration for the clerical office, and his directions to his Chaplain on his manner of life and behaviour, is a curiosity. The poor man is thus counselled :—

FIRST. You shall have the chamber, I shewed you in my gate,[2] private to yourself, with lock and key, and all necessaries.

In the morning I expect you should rise, and say prayers in my hall, to my houshhold below, before they go to work, and when they come in at nygt—that you call before you all the workmen, specially the yowth, and take accompt of them of their belief, and of what Sir Meredith taught them. I beg you to continue for the more part in the lower house : you are to have onlye what is done there, that you may informe me of any misorder there. There is a baylyf of husbandry, and a porter, who will be comanded by you.

---

[1] The letters from the Bishop to Sir John and to Mr. Martyn will be found in the Appendix to Yorke's Royal Tribes of Wales.

[2] This chamber, and a gloomy one it is, still stands at the entrance to Gwydir, from the Bettws-y-coed road. The gateway (which has the arms and initials of Sir John over it) is perhaps the oldest portion of the place remaining.

The morninge after you be up, and have said prayers, as afore, I wo⁴ you to bestow in study, or any commendable exercise of your body.

Before dinner you are to com up and attend grace, or prayers, if there be any publicke; and to set up, if there be not greater strangers, above the chyldren—who you are to teach in your own chamber.

When the table, from half downwards, is taken up, then are you to rise, and to walk in the alleys near at hand, until grace time; and to come in then for that purpose.

After dinner, if I be busy, you may go to bowles, shuffel bord, or any other honest decent recreation, until I go abroad. If you see me voyd of business, and go to ride abroad, you shall comand a geldinge to te be made ready by the grooms of the stable, and to go with me. If I go to bowles, or shuffel bord, I shall lyke of your company, if the place be not made up with strangers.

I would have you go every *Sunday* in the year to some church hereabouts, to preache, giving warnynge to the parish to bring the yowths at atter noon to the church to be catekysed; in which poynt is my greatest care that you be paynfull and dylygent.

Avoyd the alehowse, to sytt and keepe drunkards company ther, being the greatest discredit your function can have.

That such an active and energetic country gentleman as Sir John Wynn would be busy at election times, no one can doubt, and the following letter, which has been preserved in manuscript, probably refers to a contest in Carnarvonshire[1] in 1620 :—

Sr. the experience of yoʳ love in this late ellection hath made me to thinke myself infinitelie bound vnto yoʷ : I pray yoʷ continewe yt to the end, the rather for that yoʳ owne reputacon lieth att stake aswell as myne, and in requitall yoʷ shall find me to answeare yoʳ kindnes in matters of greater ymportance. Co'mending me very kindlie vnto yoʷ, and yoʳ good Ladie, and my good Cosyn Mⁱˢ Ann Brynkir, doe rest Yoʳ assured Loving Cosyn

     Gwyder, the 19th   JOHN WYNN
         of December 1620.   of
                                                             Gwydei.

     To the right Worˡ my very Loving Cosyn Sʳ William Maurice Knight.[2]

The last record of Sir John we are able to present to our readers, is an Inventory of his Wardrobe, taken from the Appendix to Pennant's *Tours* :—

A noate of all my clothes : taken the eleventh day of *June*, 1616.

IMPRIMIS. i tawnie klothe cloake, lined thoroughe with blacke velvett; one other black cloake of clothe, lined thouroughe with blacke velvett; another blacke cloake of velvett, lined with blacke taffeta.

Item. ii ridinge coates of the same colour, laced with silke and golde lace; i hood and basses of the same; one other olde paire of basses.

Item. ii blacke velvett jerkins; two clothe jerkins laced with goulde lace, of the same colour.

Item. One white satten doublett, and blacke satten breeches; one silke grogram coloured suite; and one suite of blacke satten cutt, that came the same time from *London*.

Item. One other blacke satten suite cutt; and one blacke satten doublett, with a wroughte velvett breeches.

Item. One leather doublett, laced with blacke silke lace; one suite of *Pteropus*, laced with silke and golde lace; another suite of *Pteropus*, laced with greene silke lace.

Item. One olde blacke silke grogram suite cutt; two blacke frise jerkins.

Item. One blacke velvett coate for a footman.

Item. One redd quilte waskoote.

Item. ij pare of olde boothose, toppes lined with velvett in the topps.

Item. ij pare of blacke silke stockins; and two pare of blacke silke garters, laced.

Item. One pare of perle colour silke stockins; one pare of white *Siserop* stockins; three pare of wosted stockins.

Item. ij girdles, and one hanger, wroughte with golde; one also blacke velvett girdle; one blacke cipres scarfe.

Item. Nine blacke felte hattes, wherof fowre bee mens hattes; and five cipres hatbands.

Item. One guilte rapier and dagger, and one ridinge sworde with a scarfe, with velvett scabbards.

---

[1] Mr. Breese in his *Kalendars of Gwynedd*, under the heading of "Members for the County and Borough of Caernarvon," gives "John Griffith, jun., of Llyn, Esq.," as a Knight of the Shire, elected 27 Dec., 1620.

[2] Seal—Owen Gwynedd, and Griffith ap Conan, quarterly. In the centre of the shield, the Baronet's badge—The Shield on the Breast of an Eagle, as now borne by Sir Watkin Williams Wynn, Bart.

Item. ij pare of *Spanishe* leather shooes.
Item. One russett frise jerkin.
Item. Two pare of leather *Yamosioes*, and one of clothe.
Item. ij pare of white boots ; one pare of russett boots.
Item. iij pare of newe blacke boots, and five pare of old blacke boots.
Item. ij pare of damaske spurres, iii pare of guilte spurres.

Before we proceed to · give copies of the monumental inscriptions to the memory of the family in the Gwydir Chapel and elsewhere, there are two letters that will be interesting to readers of this book. The original of the first is at Brogyntyn. The writer was Sir John Wynn, Knight, eldest son of Sir John Wynn of Gwydir, Bart. He died before his father :—

S! According to my promise, I have sent to you hearby what I receaved of late from London as newes. The Prince [1] as I heare died not of any wronge doen him by the Physitians, as was hertofore receaved for truth, but of a surfett : during his disease which was not long, he patiently gave God thanks by prayer for his visitacoen. The kinge being desirous to see him in his perplexitie, was persuaded therefrom by the Counsell, who besought him to ride to Theobalds, ther to continewe for a while, which he did accordinglie, till the tyme of his departure which was within three dayes after—he ys generally Lamented of all. My father ys stayed by my Lord Chamberlain to continewe for ten dayes after the tearme, to be a mourner. These do mourne but Earles and Barrons, & Barronetts.

My cosin Pierse Gruffithes [2] cause ys dismissed the Court of wardes, & the possession of the land in question settled in the adverse partie. Sir John Egerton's cause was heard in the Court of wardes, & a case made of hitt which longe will not be vndecided. Mr. Needham is like to be dismissed that Courte, & I feare to be undoen, for as yt ys thought there is noe hope for him to Prevaile.

This ys all the last news I heard which I could not choose (seeinge I have mett with so convenient a messenger) but write to you, although I was in hast to meet a gent. this morninge, and ready to take horse. Comending me very kindly to yourself your good Lady & the rest of your good Companie at Carnarvon do ever rest your loving cosin & ffrinde assured to vse,

JOHN WYNN.

Llanvrothen the
xxvi.th of Nov. 1612.

Whether the mariadge goe forward or not, I know not, neather have I receaved thereof any thinge. The Palgraves stile ys this—The high & mihty Prince FREDERICKE the fift, by the grace of God, Counte Pallatyn of the Rhein, Duke of Bavaria, Elector, & Arch sewer of the sacred Romaine Empire, & in Vacancie of the same, Vicar thereof &c: Born at Amberge in his upper Pallatinat the 16 of August 1596. This did I finde intituled above his pickture—farwell in great hast. J. W.

The other one—or rather the one from which only an extract is taken—is from Owen Wynn, afterwards Sir Owen Wynn, Bart., to Sir Wm. Maurice of Clenenney, and is dated 5 July 1622 :—

My Lo.[3] hath not bought Penrhyn[4] as yet, nor likelie to buy it for ought I heare, so as the Treavours must find out another to buy it, except they let it at that rate which it is worthe—my Lo. hath offered 8000 pound for it beinge fullie as much as it is woorthe, which they have refused, & as I doe heare now they truly repent them of their refusal.

My lo. Cookes great Cause in the Courte of wardes is heard, & ended this tearme, & he hath the glorie of the day, which I am sure you wilbe glad of beeinge such a speciall ffriend of yours.

The greate cause in Chauncerie, for the burninge of the chauncerie office, betweene M! Tothill, one of the six clearkes, & Sir Robert Riche, is also heard & determyned, this terme : there is a decree in that cause by which everie man is ordered to set by his owne losse, & be quiett, for the certayntie where the fire began could not be knowne.

There is noe newes woorth the writing of—the generall want of money maketh all the officers both of the starrechamber & of other courtes sitt ydle, for want of employment, & long may they be ydle for anie goodnes they have.[5]

----

[1] Henry, Prince of Wales, son of King James I.

[2] Of Penrhyn.

[3] John Williams, Archbishop of York.

[4] The great estate of Penrhyn, in Carnarvonshire, which the Archbishop afterwards bought.

[5] The seal to this letter bears an impression of the arms of the Wynns of Gwydir—the 3 eagles—first and fourth ; second and third, a chevron between 3 fleurs-de-lys. In the centre of the shield, a crescent for difference.

The memory of Meredith ap Ievan, who may be called the founder of the Family at Gwydir, is commemorated by a brass in Dolwyddelan Church, a facsimile of which, reduced in size, is given below.[1] The Rev. D. R. Thomas, in the paper alluded to in the preface, incorporates the following description of this brass, from the pen of Mr. Bloxam :—

The effigy, represented as kneeling, is bare-headed, with the hair clubbed in the fashion which prevailed in the early part of the reign of Henry VIII. Round the neck is worn a collar of mail. The body-armour consists of a globular breastplate with angular-shaped tuilles attached to the shirt, and beneath these is an apron of mail of that peculiar kind represented on Welsh sepulchral effigies. On the shoulders are pass-guards, the arms above and below the elbows are protected by epaulieries and vambraces, the elbows by coudes, the hands are uncovered; the thighs are protected by cuisses, the knees by genouilleres, the legs by jambs, the feet by sollerets, broad-toed, and apparently laminated,—a fashion as to broad-toed which prevailed not before the reign of Henry VIII. On the left side is a sword, on the right a dagger; the hands are conjoined, as in prayer. The peculiarity in this effigy consists in the representation of the collar and apron of mail. In this and other sepulchral effigies in Wales, the mail-armour appears very different to that description of armour in England. Was it so in fact? This is a problem to be solved. Mail-armour, though restricted in use to cover certain portions only of the body, as in this instance the neck and loins, was worn so late as the middle of the sixteenth century. I have a pair of splints (armour so called), viz., a breast- and back-plate *temp*. Philip and Mary, *circa* 1555. To the breast-plate is attached an apron of mail. Are there any small portions of mail-armour, I do not mean Asiatic, existing in any of the inhabited castles or country houses in Wales?

(Drawn to quarter original size).

[1] I have a strong impression that the shield of arms stood originally in the centre of this monument, and that there was a brass representation of the wife of Meredith opposite to him.—W.

In the Gwydir Chapel at Llanrwst there is a marble tablet containing the following pedigree, comprising a period of Five hundred years :—

This Chappel was erected Anno Dom 1633, By Sr. *Richard Wynn*, of *Gwyder*, in the Covnty of Carnarvon, Knight & Baronet, treasvrer to the high and mightie Princess Henriette Maria, queen of England, daughter to Henry the fourth, King of France, and wife to our sovaraigne King Charles. Where lyeth buried his father, Sr. John Wynn, of Gwyder, in the Covnty of Carnarvon, Knight and Baronet, sonne and heyre to Maurice Wynn, sonne and heyre to John Wynn, sonne and heyre to Meredith ; which three lyeth buried in the Church of Dolwethelan, with tombes over them. This Meredith was sonne and heyre to Evan, sonne and heyre to Robert, sonne and heyre to Meredith, sonne and heyre to Howell, sonne & heyre to David, sonne and heyre to Griffith, sonne and heyre to Caeradock, sonne and heyre to Thomas, sonne and heyre to Rodericke, lord of Anglisey, sonne to Owen Gwyneth, prince of Wales ; and younger brother to David prince of Wales ; who married E'me Plantaginet, sister to King Henry the second. There succeeded this David three princes : his nephew Leolinus Magnvs, who married Ione, daughter to King John ; David his sonne, nephew to King Henry the third ; and Leolyn, the last prince of Wales of that house and line, who lived in King Edward the first's time. Sr. Iohn Wynn married Sidney, who lyeth buried here, the daughter of Sir William Gerrard, Knight, lord chancellor of Ireland, by whom he had issue, Sr. Iohn Wynn, who died at Lvca, in Italy ; Sr. Richard Wynn, now living ; Thomas Wynn, who lyeth here ; Owen Wynn, now living ; Robert Wynn, who lyeth here ; Roger Wynn, who lyeth here ; William Wynn, now living ; Maurice Wynn, now living ; Ellis Wynn, who lyeth buried att Whitford, in the covnty of Flynt ; Henry Wynn, now living ; Roger Wynn, who lyeth here ; and two daughters ; Mary, now living, married to Sr. Roger Mostyn, in the Covnty of Flynt, Knight ; and Elizabeth, now living, married to Sr. Iohn Bodvill, in the Covnty of Carnarvon, Knight.

This Chapel is referred to on page 9 as being probably from designs by Inigo Jones. Some years ago a local printer issued a handbill purporting to be a description of the building, and giving copies of the monumental inscriptions. Partly availing ourselves of this handbill (a copy of which hangs in the chapel, and, we are told is often transcribed by visitors), but restoring the inscriptions to their original language and spelling, the following is its substance :—A brass, fixed on the wall, beneath the Tablet, is described as "a superb engraving of Dame Sarah Wynne . . executed by one William Vaughan in a style of elegance hardly to be met with." Beneath the figure there is the following inscription :—

> Here lyeth the body of Dame Sarah Wynne wife to the Honoured Sr. Richard Wynne of Gwyddur Barronet and one of the daughters of Sr. Thomas Middleton of Chirke Castle Knight Shee departed this life the 16th day of Iune, 1671.
> [Guil : Vaughan, Sculpsit].

On each side of the Tablet are brasses (with the heads finely engraved) bearing the following inscriptions :—

Here lyeth the body of John Wynn of Gwedvr Kt. and Baronet who died first of March 1626.

Here lyeth ye body of ye La. Sydney Wynn [1] wife of Sir John Wynn of Gwedvr Kt & Baronet who died ye eight of Ivne 1632,

Beneath a table which stands in front of the reading desk, (and which contains some figures in old oak, of the eagle and griffin), there is a marble monument, ruthlessly marred by the initials of the vulgar ; on which reclines the quaint figure of a child, with a raised shield of arms on each side, and underneath, this inscription :—

---

[1] The following letter by this lady is from an autograph formerly in the possession of Maurice Wynne, L.L.D., Rector of Bangor Iscoed. Sir Richard, to whom it was addressed, was, by birth, second son of Sir John, but the elder son John, who was also a Knight, died without issue, at Lucca, and Richard succeeded to the Baronetcy. He was Groom of the Bed-chamber to Charles Prince of Wales, afterwards King Charles I., and accompanied him and Buckingham, in the Prince's matrimonial expedition to Spain in 1623. Sir Richard wrote an account of that expedition, which is published in Hearne's *Historia Vitæ et Regni Ricardi II.*, Vol. I, page 297.

Good Sonne Richard,
I am glad to hear of yor safe retourne out of Spayne, and that yow have yor health well (wch god continue) for I much feared the same, and prayed very heartily for you. Thus having nothing els to write vnto you but my best wishes and Loue vnto my Daughter yor Wife recommended, with my prayers to God to blesse you, I rest
Yor Louing Mother,
SYDNEY WYNN.
Gwydder June 16
1623.
To my very Louing Sonne Sr Richard Wynn, Kt.

Here lieth the Bodie of Sidney Wyn davghter to Owin Wyn Esqr. which was borne the 6th of September & departed this life the eight of Octobr, following, Anno D'ni
1639.

"On the South side," says the handbill, "are two stately Pyramidal Columns of variegated Marble, decorated with Martial Insignias, one to the memory of Meredith Wynn, the other to Sir John Wynn, and Sydney his wife: on their Pedestals are Latin inscriptions on black Marble":—

Meredith Wyn a'r. Oweni Gwynedd qvondam Cambriæ Principis progenies fælicibus avspicijs fvndavit domvm Gvyder ffanvm S'ti Gwyddelan transtulit et reedificavit in expeditione Tornatensi 5° H. 8. ffortissimvs dvx fato cessit Mense Marcij 1525.

Iohnnes Wyn de Gwyder Miles & baronettus Cvm Sydneia filia Wm. Gerrardi [1] Militis regni Hyberniæ cancellarij, vnica et ivventvtis conivge, cvi peperit filios vndecem et filias dvas hic Iacent Christi adventvm in Gloria expectante.

Between the "Pyramidal Columns" there is a tablet to the memory of John Wynn ap Meredith, with this inscription:—

Iohannes Wyn de Gwyder filivs Meredith ar' paternæ virtvtis emvlvs vir ivstvs et pivs, Cvi Elena vxor eivs peperit qvinqve filios et dvas filias. Obijt. 9° Ivlij A° Dom.
1559.

On the floor is a stone effigy in armour, with the feet resting on a lion couchant, of Howel Coetmore ap Gruffith Vychan ap Griffith David Goch, natural son to David Prince of Wales, from whose descendants, according to tradition, Gwydir was purchased by the Wynns. "Near to the effigy of Howel is the underpart of a stone coffin in which Llewelyn ap Iorwerth, surnamed The Great, the son-in-law of King John, was buried at the Abbey of Conwy." On a brass attached to this the fact is recorded that—

This is the coffin of Leoninus Magnus, Prince of Wales, who was buried at the Abbey of Conwy, which upon the dissolution was removed thence.

"On going from the chapel to the church you pass over a large square flag of freestone, having on its sides a Latin inscription":—

Monvment. Filior. Io: Wyn de Gwyder milit. et baronet. qvi. obierunt, svperstite patre. Io: Eques avrat. sepvlt. Lvccæ Italiæ civitate Libera, A° æta, 30 A°D 1613. Robert. in Art. Ma. Sacris Iniciat. A° Eta, 24, Do. 1612. Tho. Rog. et Rog. in Minori etate. Fvnvs Fvmvs Fvimvs Ecce.

In addition to the foregoing there are two brasses on the same wall as the Tablet but to the right of the window, with inscriptions as follow:—

Fili'eius natu secund. Iohes Mostyn Armiger mærens posuit an'o Dom 1658.

Obijt 25 die Febr. anno domini 1653.

Conditum · in · hoc · tumulo · Iacit · corpus · eximiæ · admodum · dnæ · dnæ · Mariæ · Mostyn · conivgis · Rog: Mostyn de Mos: in com: Flin. eq: Avrati · primogenitœ · Io: Wynne de gue: com: car: eq: et: bar: fili · ejus · natu · secundæ · Iohes · Mostyn · armig' · mærens · posuit. Ano' dni' 1657.

Both these brasses have heads engraved on them, and the one to the right bears the name of the artist;—"Silvanus Crue, sculp." A smaller brass, with only an inscription, records that "Here resteth the body of Sr. Owen Wynne of Gwedvr Baronet, who dyed the 15 of August 1660, aged 68." And, on the opposite wall, there is also a brass (with female figure engraved on it) to the memory of "Katherine Lewis, eldest davghter of Maurice Lewis, of Festyniog, Esq.," who died at the age of 16, in 1669. The heiress of the Lewises was married to one of the Wynns, which will account for the presence of the brass in the Gwydir Chapel.

---

[1] There is a monument to "Sir William Gerrard, Knight, Lord Chancellor of Ireland, one of Her Majesty's Most Honourable Council in the Marches of Wales, &c·," in St. Oswald's Church, Chester. He died 1 May 1581, and was one of the Welsh Judges, and Recorder of Chester.

GWYDIR MEMORIALS.

In Pennant's time (1781) these brasses[1] were "trampled under feet," and there is yet another inscription in the chapel that shows to whose care it was that the place has been restored to order :—"Pet: Rob: Drvmmond Willovghby Dom: de Eresby et Gvydir Restitvit A.D. MDCCCXXXV."

The inscriptions on two of the monuments to members of the Gwydir family are given on pages 4 and 9, the former being that to the memory of Sir Richard at Wimbledon, and the latter to Henry, tenth son of Sir John Wynn, in the Temple Church, London. In Pennant's *History of the Parish of Whitford* (1796) the following inscription is given from a monument in the church of that place :—

> Here lyeth interred the body of Ellici Wynn, the 9th son of Sir John Wynne of Gwydyr, Knight and Baronet, aged xx, who died the xxth of 9ber, and was buried the xxiii. of the said month. Ao Domini 1619. Omnis caro fœnum.

And there is yet another monumental inscription which was formerly amongst those in the Chapel at Llanrwst :—

> Moricius Wyn de Gwydder ar: hic jacet pacis et Justiciæ Acerrimus assertor cui prima conjux Jana fil. Rici' Bulkley Venedocie camerarii. Secunda Anna fil. Edw. Grevyll de Mycot[3] militis. Tertia Katharina fil. et hæres Tuderi ap Rob'ti Ar: x⁴ die augusti mortuus. 1580.

Local tradition asserts that Sir John Wynn was one of the first to obtain a hint of the existence of the Gunpowder Plot, and that he did so through his cousin Dr. Thomas Williams of Trevriw, a zealous Roman Catholic. The story goes that this cousin sent the baronet an enigmatical letter foretelling some dire catastrophe, and recommending him to absent himself from Parliament. Sir John took the warning with him to London, and found a member who had also received anonymous advice to the same effect. Of course a secret held by two soon became no secret at all, and the plot was frustrated as history tells us.* But Sir John was too shrewd to betray a secret, so his kinsman's name was never mentioned to Protestant or Papist.

One interesting incident in the family history is its connection with so celebrated a figure in Welsh annals as Catherine de Berain. It will be seen on Table III. (opposite page 48) that "Mam Gwalia"—as she was popularly called—was the third wife of Morris Wynn. Her portrait, taken in old age, was exhibited by the Rev. R. H. Howard, at the North Wales Exhibition, held at Wrexham in 1876; and there is, in Yorke's *Royal Tribes*, the copy of a portrait of her when a young and blooming woman. "We are told that Catherine had for her first husband, Salisbury, heir of Lleweni, and by him had a son, Thomas, who was executed for Babington's plot in Sep., 1587. Her second son, 'Sir John Salisbury, The Strong,' succeeded at Lleweni. Her Beren estate followed the heiress of the Lleweni house into the Combermere family. Her second husband was Sir Richard Clough; by him she had two daughters; one married Wynn of Melai, and the other Salisbury of Bachegraig, and from this marriage descended Dr. Johnson's friend Mrs. Thrale. Catherine's third husband was Maurice Wynn of Gwydir. Her fourth husband, who survived her, was Edward Thelwall, a widower, and his son, by a former marriage, married the daughter of Catherine by Maurice Wynn. . . 'Mam Gwalia' is said by Yorke to have been a 'singular character,' but in what her singularity consisted—further than she had four husbands—we are not informed. The story goes that

---

[1] Mr. Pennant, writing of the brass in memory of Dame Sarah, says it was "by far the most beautiful engraving he ever saw, yet neither the names of this (Vaughan) or the foregoing artist (Crew) are on the records of the fine arts." It is also singular that there should have been *two* Vaughans—William and Robert—of whom nothing is definitely known. The latter (see page 3), who engraved the very rare print of Sir John Wynn, was supposed by Mr. Barrington to be the Antiquary of Hengwrt, but Mr. W. W. E. Wynne is sure that this is an error.

[3] Milcote in Warwickshire.

she lost no time in courting.   After the funeral of her first husband she left
the church in company of Maurice Wynne, who, it is said, ' proposed ' to her.
He was too late, Sir Richard Clough having done so, and been accepted, as the
funeral procession wended its way to the grave yard.   However, she promised
Maurice that, in case there should be another opening, he should be her third.
And he was !" [1]
    The first Sir Richard, who was buried at Wimbledon, died without issue.   He
was succeeded by his brother Sir Owen,[2] whose son Sir Richard is stated to have
been chamberlain to Catherine, queen of Charles the Second, and to have presented to
her majesty a pearl from the river Conwy, which is said at one time to have been a conspicuous object in the royal crown.   The pearl fisheries in those days seem to have been
more productive off Trevriw than nearer the mouth of the river, and singular stories
are still told in the district, of fortunate discoveries of these gems, now never
to be met with.   A box containing a great number of large Conwy pearls was in
the possession of the last Sir R. W. Vaughan, Bart.   One of them was given to Mr.
Wynne, and is now at Peniarth.   The only daughter of the second Sir Richard became
the wife of Lord Willoughby, the first duke of Ancaster.
    The Baronetage of Gwydir " continued and ended in Sir John Wynn of
Wynnstay, the grandson of Sir John of Gwydir, by his tenth son Henry and
the heiress of Rhiw Goch.   Sir John of Wynnstay married the heiress of
Watstay.   He changed the name, as nearer his own, to Wynnstay. . . He
died at the age of ninety-one, and lies buried at Rhuabon. . . He left
Wynnstay, and his other estates of great value, to his kinsman Watkin Williams,
afterwards Sir Watkin Williams Wynn."[3]
    Gwydir, it is said, derives its name from gwy = water, and tir = land ; or from gwaed
dir = the bloody land, in allusion to the battle fought there by Llywarch Hên about the
year 610.   Mr. Cradock, in his Welsh Tour, says, " the word Gwedir is supposed to
signify glass, and the Wynne family was probably the first who, in these parts, had a
house with glazed windows."

---

[1] See *Bys-gones* 1876, pp. 132-3.

[2] We have already given one letter by Owen,
afterwards Sir Owen Wynn, Bart.   The following
from him, relative to the manuscripts of Dr. Davies
of Mallwyd, is from the original at Peniarth :—
    Coosen Vaughan,
        I writte heertofore by John Thomas of
Dolegelle vnto you to entreate you to thynke of
some way to preserve the Welshe manuscriptes of
M[r] doctor Davyes gatherynge then in possession of
his wydow (wheether yow received the letter or noe
I know not,) & wth all I did signifie vnto yow (as I
remember) that I would ioyne wth yow to buy them
out of her handes yf they weare to be sould.
    I doe herebie second that my request about the
selfe same busynes, & though I well know, that it

is now noe tyme to thynke of those kynd of
busynes, yet I beleive it is great negligence & a
fault in anie of vs that be wellwishers either to the
partie deceassed or to the Antiquities of the Country, to lett all his paynes come to nothing, if they
may be preserved by anie of vs.
    This is all I have to say at this tyme, & wth my
love to you & yours, I end, & rest
                                Your loving Coosen
        [addressed]   OWEN WYNN.
To my worthie good Coosen
    Robert Vaughan
        at Henecourt neere
            Dolegelley
            d'd' these.

[3] See Yorke's *Royal Tribes*, p. 10.

LIST OF SUBSCRIBERS.

Adnitt, H. W., Esq., Lystonville, Shrewsbury.
Anwyl, R. C., Esq., Llugwy, Merioneth.

Barnes, Jas. R., Esq., Brookside, Chirk.
Beedham, B., Esq., Ashfield House, Kimbolton.
Bennett, N., Esq., Glan-yr-afon, Caersws.
Blaikie, Robert, Esq., Oswestry.
Breese, E., Esq., F.S.A., Morva Lodge, Portmadoc.
Bridgeman, the Rev. Hon. Canon, Wigan Hall.
Burrell, the Honourable Willoughby, 11, Merrion Square East, Dublin.

Cholmondeley, the Most Noble the Marquess of, 1, Hyde Park, London, W.
Chester, Col. Joseph Lemuel, LL.D., Linden Villas, 124, Blue Anchor Road, Bermondsey, London.
Coombs, Howard, Esq., Elmley House, Worcester.

Davies, David, Esq., M.P., Broneirion, Llandinam.
Davies, Henry, Esq., Castle House, Oswestry.
Davies, J. Sides, Esq., The Poplars, Oswestry.
Davies, John, Esq., 103, London-road, Southwark.
Davies, J. Pryce, Esq., Bronfelen.
Davies, John, Esq., Treasury, London.
Davies, James, Esq., Plasnewydd, Llanrhaiadr.
Dovaston, J., Esq., Westfelton.
Davies, Rev. J., St. David's Vicarage, Blaenau.
Davies, Rev. James, Prebendary of Hereford, Moor Court, Kington, Herefordshire.
Downing, W., Esq., 74, New-street, Birmingham.

Edwards, Mr. J. G., Llangedwyn.
Edwards, Mr. Richard, Sefton-street, Litherland.
Edwards, R., Esq., The Cottage, Llanbrynmair.
Evans, Joseph, Esq., Haydock Grange, St. Helens.
Evans, Owen, Esq., Broom Hall, near Pwllheli.
Evans, Rev. W. Howell, Vicarage, Oswestry.
Evans, Rev. Thomas Henry, Llanwddyn Vicarage.
Evans, Rev. Edward, Llanfihangel Rectory.
Evans, Rev. D. Silvan, B.D., Llanwrin Rectory.
Evans, S., Esq., Llanfair, Welshpool.
Evans, Stephen, Esq., Bryntirion, Hornsey Lane, London, N. (two copies.)

Ffoulkes, W. Wynne, Esq., M.A., Judge of County Courts, Old Northgate House, Chester (two copies.)

Fletcher, P. Lloyd, Esq., Nerquis Hall, Mold.
Fuller, Dr., Oswestry.

Gillart, Richard, Esq., Llynlloedd, Machynlleth.
Girardot, Mrs., Rose Hill, Rhuabon.
Griffith, J. Lloyd, Esq., M.A., Frondeg, Holyhead.
Guest, Dr., Master of Caius College, Cambridge.
Gwylim Davydd, 77, Everton Terrace, Liverpool.

Hanmer, the Rt. Hon. Lord, Bettisfield (two copies.)
Harlech, the Rt. Hon. Lord, Brogyntyn, Oswestry.
Hamilton, Sir E. A., Chorlton, Malpas.
Hancock, Mr. T. W., 5, Furnival's Inn, London.
Howell, David, Esq., Machynlleth.
Hughes, R. H., Esq., Lord Lieutenant of Flintshire. Kinmel Park, Abergele.
Hughes, Thomas, Esq., F.S.A., The Groves, Chester.
Hughes, Mr. Wm., Tanner, Oswestry.

James, Rev. T., M.A., LL.D., F.S.A., Netherthong Vicarage, Huddersfield (two copies.)
Jebb, A. T. Esq., The Lyth, Ellesmere.
Jenkins, R. H., Esq., 16, Abchurch-lane, London.
Jeudwine, Rev. Wm., Chicheley Vicarage, Newport-Pagnel.
Jones, E. P., Esq., Diphwys Casson Co., Festiniog.
Jones, John, Esq., St. John's, Wrexham.
Jones, Mr. T. G., Llansantffraid, Oswestry.
Jones, Mr. Jacob, Cambrian House, Bala.
Jones, Rev. R., B.D., Editor [of 'Y Cymmrodor, Vicar of All Saints', Rotherhithe, London.
Jones, J., Esq., Ashlands, Oswestry.
Jones, John. Esq., Ynysfor, Penrhyndeudraeth.
Jones, Morris C., Esq., F.S.A., Gungrog, Welshpool.
Jones, R. E., Esq., Cefn-Bryntalch, Abermule.
Jones, Rev. John, M.A., Rector of Llanaber.
Jones, Rev. Richard, The Rectory, Llanfrothen.
Jones, R. Watkins, Esq., Wesleyan Coll., Didsbury.
Jones, W. Eccles, Esq., Tynyllan, Llansilin.

Kenyon, Hon. George T., Llanerch Panna.
Kenyon, J. R., Esq., Q.C., Pradoe, West Felton.
Kirkham, Rev. J. W., M.A., Rector of Llanbryn mair, Rural Dean of Cyfeiliog and Mawddwy.

Lee, Rev. M. H., Hanmer.
Leighton, Rev. W. Allport, Shrewsbury.

Leighton, Stanley, Esq., M.P., Sweeney Hall.
Lewis, Dr. James, 50, Broad-street, Oxford.
Lewis, Geo., Esq., Frankton Grange.
Lewis, Rev. Evan, Dolgelley.
Lewis, Rev. David, Rector of Llangyniew.
Liverpool Free Public Library, William Brown-street, Mr. P. Cowell, Librarian.
Lloyd, Alfred, Esq., 28, Park-road, Haverstock Hill, London, N.W.
Lloyd, Edward Evans, Esq., Moelygarnedd, Bala.
Lloyd, Howel W., Esq., 22, Scarsdale Villas, Kensington,
Lloyd, John, Esq., Queen's Hotel, Oswestry.
Lloyd, J. Y. Wm., Esq., Clochfaen, Llangurig (two copies.)
Lloyd, Rev. T. H., Vicar of Nerquis.
Loxdale, James, Esq., Castle Hill, Aberystwyth.

Mostyn, the Right Hon. Lord, Mostyn, Flintshire.
Mainwaring, Salusbury Kynaston, Esq., Oteley.
Mainwaring, Townshend, Esq., Galltfaenan.
Markey, George, Esq., Oswestry.
Matkin, Mrs., Gwydir Castle, Llanrwst.
McIntyre, Peter, Esq., Agent, Llanrwst.
Middleton, John, Esq., Westholme, Cheltenham.
Minshall, Charles, Esq., Beechfield, Oswestry.
Minshall, Miss M. Wynne, Castle View, Oswestry.
Minshall, P. H., Esq., Oswestry.
Morgan, Rev. D., Vicarage, Penrhyndeudraeth.
Morris, E. R., Esq., Homestay, Newtown.
Morris, Henry, Esq., 392, Strand, London, W.C.
Moses, Mr., Trevor Issa, Rhosymedre, Rhuabon.

Nicholl, G. W., Esq., The Ham, Cowbridge.
Nicholas, Thomas, Ph.D., M.A., F.G.S., 156, Cromwell Road, South Kensington, S.W.
Nunnerley, John, Esq., the Priory, Warrington.

Owen, A. C. Humphreys, Esq., Glansevern.
Owen, Rev. Elias, M.A., Diocesan Inspector of Schools, Ruthin.
Owen, D. C. Lloyd, Esq., Birmingham.
Owen, Rev. R. Trevor, Llangedwyn (two copies.)
Owen, George, Esq., Park Issa, Oswestry.
Owen, Morris, Esq., Solicitor, Carnarvon.

Powis, the Rt. Hon. the Earl of, Lord Lieutenant of Montgomeryshire, Powis Castle, Welshpool.
Pamplin, Wm., Esq., Llandderfel, Merionethshire.
Parkins, Wm. Trevor, Esq., Glasfryn, Gresford.
Payne, William, Esq., Woodleigh, Southsea.
Penson, R. Kyrke, Esq., F.S.A., Ludlow.
Pierce, Mr. Ellis, Bookseller, Dolwyddelan.
Pierce, Mrs., Sherbourne House, Leamington.
Pryce, Elijah, Esq., Trederwen House, Llansantffraid.
Pryce, Rev. Shadrach, M.A., Penymorfa, Carmarthen.

Quaritch, Bernard, Esq., 15, Piccadilly, London,

Reid, Augustus H., Esq., Temple Row, Wrexham.
Richards, Captain E., Morben Hall, Machynlleth.
Roberts, Mr. D., Willow-street, Oswestry.
Roberts, Mr. Tom, M.R.C.V.S., Oswestry.
Roberts, Thomas, Esq., C.E., Portmadoc.
Rochdale Free Library, Mr. G. Hanson, Librarian.

Rowland, William, Esq., The Oak Hotel, Welshpool.
Rylands, J. Paul, Esq., F.S.A., Highfields, Thelwall, near Warrington.

Sandbach, Henry R., Esq., Hafudunos, Abergele.
Salisbury, E. R. G., Esq., Glan Aber, Chester.
Salusbury, Philip H. B., Esq., do.
Savin, John, Esq., Bodegroes, Pwllheli.
Scott, Mrs., Peniarth Ucha, Towyn.
Southern, Francis R., Esq., Ludlow,
Southwell, T. Martin, Esq., The Woodlands, Bridgnorth.
Smith, Hubert, Esq., Belmont, Bridgnorth,
Stuart, Major, Betton Strange, Shrewsbury.
St. David's College, Lampeter.

Taylor, Edw. James, Esq., F.S.A., Newc., Bishopswearmouth.
Temple, Rev. R., M.A., Glanbrogan, Oswestry.
Thomas, Howel, Esq., Local Government Board, London.
Thomas, John, Esq. (Pencerdd Gwalia), 53, Welbeck-street, Cavendish Square, London.
Thomas, John, Esq., Slate Wharf, Portmadoc.
Thomas, John, Esq., Castle Buildings, Oswestry.
Thomas, Rev. D. R., M.A., F.R.H.S., Editor of Archæologia Cambrensis, Meifod Vicarage.
Thomas, Rev. Llewelyn, Jesus College, Oxford.
Thomas, Mr., The Buildings, Baschurch.
Thursfield, T. H., Esq., Barrow, Broseley, Salop.
Tomkies, John, Esq., Copenhagen Terrace, Georgestreet, Cheetham Hill, Manchester (two copies.)
Treherne, George M., Esq., St. Hilary, Cowbridge.
Tucker, Stephen, Esq., Rouge Croix, Heralds' College, London.

Vaughan, Henry F. J., Esq., B.A., S.C.L., 30 Edwardes-square, Kensington, W.
Verney, Captain Edmund H., Rhianva, Bangor.
Venables, Rowland Geo., Esq., Oakhurst, Oswestry.

Willoughby de Eresby, the Baroness, Grimsthorpe, Bourne, Lincolnshire (four copies.)
Webb, T., Esq., Talworth House, Cardiff.
West, W. Cornwallis, Esq., Lord Lieutenant of Denbighshire, Ruthin Castle, Ruthin.
Wheldon, Rev. T. J., B.A., Bethania, Carnarvon.
Williams, Edward Esq., Broomhall, Oswestry.
Williams, J. Ignatius, Esq., Goldsmith Buildings, Temple, London.
Williams, Pryce, Esq., Holly House, Bristol.
Williams, Richard, Esq., Celynog, Newtown.
Williams, Rev. Canon R., Rhydycroesau Rectory.
Williams, Rev. Canon, Llanfyllin.
Williams, Rev. H. E., Vicarage, Dolwyddelan.
Williams, Rev. W. Wynn, Menaifron, Anglesey.
Williams, Stephen, Esq., Penralley, Rhayader.
Williams, T. Humphrey, Esq., Llwyn, Dolgelley.
Wilkins, Charles, Esq., Springfield, Merthyr Tydvil.
Wood, R. H., Esq., F.S.A., Pantglas, Trawsfynydd, Merionethshire.
Wynn, Sir Watkin Williams, Bt., M.P., Wynnstay.
Wynne, Wm. W. E., Esq., Peniarth, Towyn-Merioneth (two copies.)
Wynne, Wm. R. M., Esq.   do.
Wynne, Owen S., Esq., Plas-Newydd, Rhuabon.
Wynne, J., Kendrick, Esq., Eccleshall, Staff.
Wynne, Robert Vaughan, Esq., Eccleshall, Staff.

Corn. Johnson pinx.t

F. Bartolozzi Rd.t.y sculp.t

SIR RICHARD WYNNE

Printed for Robert Wilkinson, 106 Fenchurch Street.

THE HISTORY OF THE GWEDIR FAMILY,

BY SIR JOHN WYNNE,

The first Baronet of that Name, who was born in 1553.

INTRODUCTION.[1]

IT may not be improper to give the reader some account of what he is, or is not, to expect from the present publication, as well as to throw together what few particulars can be now collected with regard to its author.

The MS. hath, for above a century, been so prized in North Wales, that many in those parts have thought it worth while to make fair and complete transcripts of it. One of these Carte had consulted, and he refers to it as his authority for the Welsh Bards having been massacred by Edward the First[2]. This circumstance alone may stamp a most intrinsic value on the MS., as it hath given rise to an ode which will be admired by our latest posterity. The whole passage relative to this tradition is also cited by the Rev. Mr. Evans, in his Specimens of Welsh Poetry, and it appears that he had made the extract from a copy in the collection of Sir Roger Mostyn, Bart.[3]

---

[1] This history of the Gwedir family was first published in octavo, 1770; but the impression having been sold, it hath for some years been in considerable request and is therefore here [1781] reprinted, with some additional notes.—B. It was again reprinted, in 1827, with additional notes by Miss Angharad Llwyd.

[2] See Carte, vol. II. p. 196, where it is entitled *Sir John Wynne's History of the Gwedir family.*—B.

[3] See Jones's *History of Breconshire,* and Stephens's *Literature of the Cymry,* for a complete refutation of Sir John's statement about the Massacre of the Bards.

It is believed likewise that there is another transcript[1] in · the possession of Mr. Panton, of Plasgwyn in Anglesey, who, together with Mr. Holland, of Conway, and the Rev. Mr. Jones (late Vicar of Llanrwst), have been so obliging as to communicate many particulars with regard to the Gwedir family.

The author was indeed a general collector of what related not only to his own ancestors, but the antiquities of the Principality[2], as Rowland cites an Extent[3] or Survey of North Wales, illustrated by useful remarks of Sir John Wynne.

There was some difficulty in settling the time of the author's birth and death, till Mr. Granger's Biographical Dictionary was consulted, who gives the following inscription under a copy made by Vertue, from an engraving of the author by Vaughan :—[4]

"Johannes Wynn de Gwedir in Com. Carnarvon Eques & Baronettus[5]; obiit 1mo die Martii, 1626, æt. 73."[6]

The accuracy of these dates seemed at first to be very suspicious, as there is an account of a voyage to Spain by Sir *Richard Wynne, of Gwedir, Baronet*, in 1623, which is prefixed to that volume of Hearne's Tracts that begins with the Life of Richard the second. Application was however made to the late Mr. West, Pr. R. S., for leave to examine the original print, in his very valuable and curious collection. Mr. Granger's dates are thereby most exactly confirmed, and it may not be improper here to add the inscription under the engraving :

[1] The present publication is also from a copy that belonged to Capt. Joseph Williams of Glanravon, which he kindly communicated.—B.

[2] See *Mon. Antiq.* p. 123.

[3] This extent or survey of North Wales is now in the *Harleian Collection.* It is a very fine MS. in Folio, and appears to have been made in the 26th year of Edward the Third. It relates only to the counties of Anglesey, Carnarvon, and Merioneth.—B. A MS. amongst Dr. Foulkes's papers says that this extent was begun in Edward the first's time, and continued by Edward the second, and finished the 26th of Edward the third. It is called the " Record of Caernarvon," in the *Harleian Collection.* It relates only to the counties of Môn, Caernarvon, and Meirionydd. No. 4776.—L.

[4] One of the prints of Sir John Wynn, by Vaughan, sold, many years ago, in London, for about £14. There is one at Wynnstay, and another at Peniarth.

[5] He was created Baronet in 1611. (See Gwillim's *Heraldry*, 6th ed.)—B.

[6] The words "nec timet nec tumet" are inscribed on Sir John Wynn's picture at Mostyn.—L.

"Vera effigies Domini Clarissimi Johannis Wynn de Gwedir in Com. Carnarvon, Equitis & Baronetti.

"Obiit primo die Martii 1626, ætat. 73.[1]

"Honoris ipsius causâ Rob. Vaughan sculpsit, prolique D.D."

This was possibly Robert Vaughan of Hengwrt the great antiquary, who was a particular friend of Sir John Wynn, as also of his son Sir Richard, to whom he dedicated his book entitled "British Antiquities revived." I find also by the letter subjoined, that Mr. Robert Vaughan of Hengwrt engraved himself, and that the expression of *sculpsit* therefore is strictly accurate.

"SIR,

"I wold intreate you to send me certayne directions, whether itt shold be three Egletts in a Scutcheon, or one Eagle on a Wreath; for to doe it in a Scutcheon with one Eagle is contrary to the rules of heraldry, and not your cote: likewise whether itt shold not have a Labell for the distinction of an elder brother, during the life-time of his father, in this manner; If you please to send by the weekly post I will answer you by the next convenient messenger. When these troubles began I had drawne the pedigree of Sir Richard from Owen Gwynedd line- ally to himselfe; now in my absence from London both the copper plate which I had began to 'grave and the draught was embezzeld from me: now I am resolved (God willing) this vacation time to sett it a foote agayne. I onely want the names of your ancestors from Owen Gwynedd to your selfe, of which you are the 15th (leaving out young Sir John and Sir Richard) because they died issueless. For the faces I am at my own fancy till I come to Sir John Wyn your father; for the rest that are beyond him I thinke you have no true pictures of them extant. This (if I have your fayre leave) I wold dedicate to posterity, in some small measure, to expresse my duty I owe to your honor'd family; and during life remayne,

"Your evervowed servant

"London, June 22, 1650.   "ROBERT VAUGHAN.[2]

"To the Hon. Sir Owen Wynne, Knt.

"Baronet at Gwedur,

"These, with his service, present."

[Communicated by Paul Panton, Esq.]

[1] He died, at Gwydir, on Thursday, March 1, 1626-7, and, as was said, was buried at Llanrwst the next day. (See *Arch. Camb.* Oct., 1864, p. 322.)

[2] Mr. W. W. E. Wynne is quite certain that this was not Robert Vaughan of Hengwrt.

It seems improbable that the engraver could be inaccurate in the dates of Sir John Wynne's birth and death, when the print is dedicated to his family.

The title therefore given by Hearne to a voyage of Sir Richard Wynne[1] of Gwedir, Baronet, in 1623, when he only became so in 1627, must have arisen from his being a Baronet when he, perhaps, made a more fair and complete copy of his Travels.

If this could want any confirmation, it may receive it from two commissions in Rymer[2]; in the first of which, dated in 1626, mention is made of Sir *John* Wynne, Baronet; and in the second, dated in 1627[3], of Sir *Richard* Wynne, Baronet.

Though Mr. Granger therefore seems to· be accurate, with re-· gard to the birth and death of the first Baronet, yet, from a similarity of names, he hath made a mistake in ascribing the republication of " Dr. Powel's History of Wales from Cadwalader to Llewelyn, by W. Wynne, A.M.," to this Baronet.

The author, who was born in 1553, seems to have lived chiefly in retirement, during which period no very interesting particulars can be expected.[4]

The building a new house is an event of some consequence in such a life; he began Upper Gwedir[5] in 1604, as appears by an inscription over the entrance.

[1] An inscription in Wimbleton church.—Hic jacet Ric: Wyn de Gwedir in Com: de Caernar: Mil: et Baron: thesaurarius nec non conciliarius Honoratissimus Principis et Henriette Mariæ reginæ qui lineâ parentali et illustri illa Famillâ et antiquissima Stirpe Britanica North Walliæ Principum Oriundus Denatus 19 die Julii 1649 Ætatis 61.—L.

[2] See Rymer's *Fœd.* vol. VIII. part ii. p. 145 and 233. Hague ed.—B.

[3] Sir John Wynn probably died on March 3 1626.—B. (See note 1 page 3).

[4] It should seem, that he had travelled in his younger days, as Archbishop Williams (then tutor to his sons at St. John's College, Cambridge) speaks of him as a man, Multorum mores hominum qui vidit, & urbes. [MS. Letter penes Paul Panton, Esq.]—Which circumstance is perhaps confirmed by his son having visited Italy when young, as fathers generally wish that their sons should be educated in the same manner with themselves. B. A letter in Mr. Panton's possession from Mr. Williams, afterwards Archbishop of York, speaks of Sir J. Wynne's sons as very promising scholars. By No. 2129 of *Harleian* MSS., it appears that there was a room within the hall at Gwydir painted with the arms and descent of the family.—L.

[5] The house, called Lower Gwedir, he mentions in this MS. to have been built by his great grandfather. As for Upper Gwedir, it was covered almost with inscriptions in different languages; scarcely any of which remain, as the wainscot hath

It was considered as one of the best houses in the Principality, because there is a tradition that it was calculated to receive any of the Royal Family, who might have occasion to go to Ireland [1].

As in the year 1604 none of the blood Royal could probably think of such a journey, it may rather be supposed that it was destined for the reception of the Lords Deputies of Ireland, as it is little out of the road to Holyhead, if at this time they did not go from Chester to Dublin.

Be this as it may, some reason for any mention being made of this house arises from a possibility of its having been designed by Inigo Jones, in his first manner, before he had been in Italy, as this great architect was protected by Sir John Wynne.

The name of Jones sufficiently proves him to have been of Welsh extraction; to which it may be added, that his cast of

---

been lately used in repairing farm-houses on other parts of the estate. The Pigeon-house appears by the date to have. been built in 1597. There is an engraving of Lower Gwedir in a map of Denbigh and Flintshire, which was published 40 or 50 years ago, by William Williams. A Welsh inscription, which is still legible, over the entrance, is here subjoined:

Bryn Gwydir gwelir golau adeilad,
Uwch dolydd a chaerau,
Bryn gwych adail yn ail ne,
Bron wen henllys brenhinlle.

Hugh bach ap Howell ap Shenkin a ganodd yr Englyn uchod, ddeng mlynedd cyn amcanu gwneuthur yr adeilad hon.

" ' A conspicuous edifice on Gwydir hill, towering over the adjacent land, a well chosen situation, a second paradise, a fair bank, a palace of royalty.

" This *Englyn* was written by little Hugh Shenkin, *ten years before the building was designed.*" [It should seem from this, that little Hugh Shenkin was a prophet, as well as poet.]—B.

The late reverend Mr. Jones, vicar of Llanrwst, was so obliging as to copy the above inscription and to accompany it with the translation here given. He also observes, that this Welsh composition is a sort of jingle, for which he knows no English name, or any similar metre.—B.

Gwydir Summer House bears date 1673.—L.

[1] A correspondent of his son Sir Richard Wynne speaks thus of Gwedir, in 1661.

" DEARE SIR,
" I Know not how in part to acquit myselfe of the obligation you have layd on me, without giving my acknowledgement to your excellent lady whom I have taken the boldness to visit, and find her in the happy condition I desired, being very well, and upon inquiry, continuing in the hopeful way you left her to increase your family. Really upon my view and consideration of the seate of Gwidder, I conclude it to be the best place in Wales, and inferiour to few in England. I need not urge those things to hasten your returne; but I should judge very weakly of those that have such conveniencys, and will not enjoy them, if not detained by very great consider-. ations. In fine, I am in the buttery, just taking leave, and drinking your health, bidding adieu to your house, and the like at this time to your-selfe.

" Your most humble servant,
" And obliged Cosen,
" THOMAS BULKELY."

" Gwydder, this 27th May, 1661.
[Present this to the Hon. Sir Richard Wynne, Bart.]
" John Win ap Meredith dwellith at Gweder at two bows shots above *Conway* town, on the *ripe* of Conway River: it is a praty place." Lel. *Itin.* vol. V. p. 40. Leland here most evidently mistakes Conway for Llanrwst.—B.

features, as represented in Hollar's engraving of his portrait, seems
to show that he must have been an inhabitant of the Principality.

All traditions have generally some foundation, and it is commonly believed in the neighbourhood of Llanrwst, that Jones
was born either at that town, or Dolwyddelan, which is equally
situated near considerable estates of the Gwedir family. The tradition is also so circumstantial, as to suppose that he was
christened by the name of *Ynyr*,[1] which, after his travels into
Italy, he exchanged for *Inigo* as sounding better.[2] It is part likewise of the same tradition, that he was patronised by the Wynnes
of Gwedir, and that he built Plastêg, belonging to the Trevor
family, on the road from Wrexham to Mold.[3]

As every particular which relates to this great architect is interesting, it may not be improper also to observe, that Jones, who
went a second time to Italy in 1612, might possibly have travelled[4]
under the protection of the author's eldest son, John, who died
at Lucca in that year. As for his being patronised by the Earl
of Pembroke at this time, it seems to be very justly doubted by
Mr. Walpole.[5]

[1] I think with much more probability, that it was
Inco, which I find was a name not very uncom-
mon in those times, and there is a house not
far from Llanrwst which is called to this day
" Pen-craig Inco." P. B. Williams.—L.

[2] Thus Cooper (master for the Viol da Gamba
to Charles the First) after he had been in Italy
changed his name to Coperario. Hawkins's
History of Music, vol. IV. He also altered his
Christian name, stiling himself Giovanni instead
of John. *Ibid.* vol. IV. p. 55. Thus likewise
Peter Philips, another musician, who had been
much in Italy, stiled himself Pietro Philippi. *Ibid.*
v. III. p. 327. Jones was branded by Ben
Jonson for his vanity, as one of the latter's
epigrams is addressed to Inigo Marquis *would
be*. Jones indeed contrived the scenes for Jonson's masques, which being perhaps more admired than the poetry, excited Jonson's envy.
It is remarkable also that one of these scenes
represents *Craig Eryri*, or the rocks of Snowdon,

under which Jones was born, if a native of Llanrwst.—B. [By Snowdon is here meant, what was
anciently included in the forest of that name.—B.]
Davydd Rhys, changed his surname into Rizzio;
his father, Dr. John Davydd Rhys studied Physic
in the University of Sienna, in 1555.—L.

[3] There is an engraving of the front of this
house on the side of a large map of Denbighshire and Flintshire, which was published about
forty or fifty years ago.—B.

[4] The university of Oxford, A.D. 1605, upon
King James visiting it, hired one Mr. Jones, a
great traveller, who undertook to further them
much, and furnish them with rare devices, but
performed very little, to that which was expected,
though paid £50. for his service. Addition to
the second volume of Lel. *Collect.* p. 646.—B.

[5] *Anecdotes of Painting* in England (article
JONES); where notice is likewise taken, that this
great architect was possibly protected by the Earl

It is not improbable likewise that Jones might have obtained the considerable station he afterwards rose to from the patronage of this family, which considered him as a promising genius, that did particular honour to Gwedir and its neighbourhood. But to return to what more immediately concerns the author of these Memoirs, and his family.

In 1610 Sir John Wynne erected at Llanrwst some almshouses (to which he gave the name of Jesus Hospital) for the reception of twelve poor men, and drew up regulations for the management of his benefaction. He also endowed this charity very liberally with the rectorial tithes of Eglwys Fach, which are now valued at £200. per annum.

In 1615 he had incurred the displeasure of the Council of the Marches, as the then Chancellor (Lord Ellesmere) is informed, that Sir John Wynne, Knight and Baronet, is improper to be continued a member thereof, and also that his name should not remain in the commission of the peace for Carnarvonshire.[1]

The year before his death he was desirous of promoting a considerable embankment on the confines of Carnarvon and Merionethshire;[2] as appears by the following letter :

" Right worthee SIR, my good Cousyn, and one of the greate Honours of Veneration,

" I Understand of a greate work that you have performed in the Isle of Wight, in gaininge two thousand acres from the sea: I may saie to you as the Jewes said to Christ; we have heard of thy great workes done abroad, doe somewhat in thine owne Countrey.

" There are two wayis in Merionythshire whereon some parte of my living[3] lieth,

---

of Arundel.—B. Inigo Jones was employed by Q. Eliz. in repairing one of the piers of London Bridge, which gained him repute, after being recommended to that Queen by Sir John Wynne. This anecdote the late Rev. John Lloyd, Rector of Caerwys, received from Mr. Stoddart, of Llandderfel, who had it from the late Mr. Wynn, of Bodscallen, who was possessed of several anecdotes relative to Inigo Jones.—L.

[1] MS. Letter, penes Mr. Panton.—B.

[2] Engineers have lately made their reports in favour of this undertaking; but hitherto no workmen have been employed.—B. Readers of the present edition of this book will scarcely need to be informed that by the embankment made by Mr. Madocks early in this century, nearly 3,000 acres of land have been reclaimed.

[3] Anciently used for an *estate*, thus, " I have a little *living* in this town."—The *London Prodigal* ascribed to Shakespeare.—B.

called Traethmawr and Traethbychan, of a greate extent of ground, and entringe into the sea by one Issue, which ys not a mile broade at full sea and verie shallow: the fresh currents that run into the sea, are both vehement and greate, and carrie with them much sand, beside the southerly winde, which bloweth to the haven's mouth, carrieth with it so much sand that it hath overwhelmed a greate quantitie of the ground adjacent. There are also in the boarderinge countreys abundance of wood, brush, and other materials fit to make mounts, to be had at a verie cheape rate, and easilie brought to the place, which I hear they do in Lincolnshire to repell the sea. My skill ys little, and my experience none at all in such matters; yet I ever had a desire to further my country in such actions as might be for their profit, and leave a remembrance of my endeavours; but hindered with other matters, I have onelie wished well and done nothinge.

"Now seinge yt pleased God to bringe you into this countrey, I am to desire you to take a view of the place, not beinge above a daie's journey from you; and yf you doe see things fit to be undertaken, I ame content to adventure a brace of hundreth pounds to joine with you in the worke.

"I have leade oare on my ground in greate store,[1] and other minerals neere my house, yf it please you to come hither, being not above two daies journey from you, you shall be most kindely welcome; yt may be you shall find here that will tend to your commoditie and myne; yf I did knowe the day certaine when you would come to view Traithmawr, my sonne Owen Wynn shall attend you there, and conduct you thence along to my house. Commending me verie kindely unto you, doe rest,

"Your loving Cousyn and Friend,

"Gwyder, Sept. 1, 1625.   "John Wynne."

To the Hon. Sir Hugh Myddleton,
        Knight and Baronet.

[A coppie of a letter to Sir Hugh Myddleton, Knight and Baronet, at the Silver Mines[2] in Cardiganshire.]

In 1626, at the age of seventy-three, he died much lamented both by his family and neighbourhood, which may be inferred from the engraving by Vaughan already mentioned, as in those times few had such respect shewn to their memories, who were not very singularly esteemed.

---

[1] These mines have been lately worked, and I am told with some success.—B.

[2] There is so much silver in some of the lead mines not far from Aberystwith, that they have been stiled the Welsh Potosi; I have been in-

formed also that money hath been coined from them.—B. This was done by Mr. Bushel in the time of Charles 1st. See the grant to him for that purpose in Rymer's *Fœdera*.

LLANRWST BRIDGE IN 1781.

How many of Sir John Wynne's children were living at his
death cannot now be accurately known; he had, however, by
Sidney, daughter of Sir William Gerard, chancellor of Ireland,
eleven sons and two daughters.[1]

Sir Richard Wynne, who became the eldest son upon the death
of his brother John, was one of the Grooms of the bedchamber to
Charles the First when Prince of Wales, and was appointed
afterwards Treasurer to Queen Henrietta.

In 1633 Sir Richard built the chapel at Llanrwst, which is supposed by tradition to have been planned by Jones, and in 1636 the
bridge over the Conway at the end of the town was completed.
This bridge is also considered as a work of Jones's, and is so
elegant a structure that it sufficiently speaks itself to be the plan
of a masterly architect.[2]

Having stated the few circumstances which could be collected
with regard to the author, it may not be improper to mention,
that no liberties have been taken in improving his orthography or
style, except now and then by breaking a very long and compli-
cated period into two, so as to make it more perspicuous and intelligible.

[1] This appears by the inscription over the
author's tomb at Llanrwst. A letter from Archbishop Williams states, that some of his elder sons
were promising scholars.—B.

In the Temple Church is a monument to Henry
Wynn, one of the eleven sons of Sir John Wynn
of Gwedir, Bart. This Henry Wynn married
Catherine, the daughter and heiress of Ellis
Lloyd, Esq., of Rugoch in Merioneth. He was
Judge of the Marshalsea, Prothonotary of the
N.W. Circuit, and Secretary to the Court of
the Marches. He died in 1671. See also No.
2129. p. 148 & seq. of the *Harleian MSS.* for
many inscriptions on the tomb-stones of the
author's ancestors in Llanrwst church, which
seem to have been copied about a century ago,
and many of which are now scarcely legible.—B.
Henry Wynn was father to Sir J. Wynn, of Wynnstay, Bart. who, having no children, left his estates
to Sir William Williams, Bart. of Llanvorda, the
husband of Jane, grandaughter and heiress to
William Wynn, of Garthgynnan, who was the
fourth son of Sir J. Wynn, of Gwydyr, upon
condition of his taking the name and arms of
Wynn. The present Sir W. W. Wynn is the lineal
descendant, and representative of Sir William
Williams.—L. It was to Mr. Watkin Williams,
the eldest son of Sir William, that Sir John Wynn
left the estates.

[2] Mr. Panton hath informed me, from the records
of the Quarter Sessions for Denbighshire, that
this bridge was directed to be rebuilt in the 9th
of Car. I. by a letter from the Privy Council,
Jones being then surveyor of the works, and,
having therefore probably procured this order in
favour of the place of his nativity. The estimate
amounted to £1000. which was to be levied
on the two counties of Denbigh and Carnarvon.
[A modern lawyer would probably dispute the
legality of such a requisition.]—B.

C

It is not pretended that the present publication is entitled to any merit of this sort, as it appears to have been compiled merely for the author's information, and that of his descendants.

His intention in these memoirs of his family was to deduce his pedigree from Owen Gwynedd[1], Prince of N. Wales in 1138. So long therefore as his ancestors continued to be some of the *reguli* of that country, it may be considered as a history, or rather brief chronicle of the Principality. Imperfect however as it is, yet it may be entitled to some degree of value, in the light of a supplement to Dr. Powel's *Chronicle of Wales*.

It appears by this MS. that the author was furnished with some materials, which neither Powel, nor Wynne, the only other historian of Wales, had ever seen.

In different parts of these memoirs he cites as his authorities, The copy of a Fragment of a Welsh Chronicle, in the possession of his cousin Sir Thomas Williams of Trefriw; Welsh Pedigrees; The records kept in Carnarvon Castle; Records copied for him at the Tower by J. Broughton, Esq., then Justice of N. Wales; as also the tradition of the country.

What seems to be most interesting in the work, are some anecdotes and circumstances which relate to the more immediate ancestors of the author, as they are strongly characteristick of the manners and way of living in the Principality during that period.

As the places mentioned are often nothing more than farms, and in a part of Wales not much known probably to English Readers, it hath been thought proper to subjoin in a note some account of their situations.

If this had been done, however, in every instance, it would have greatly increased the size of the publication; it therefore may not be improper to premise, that the scene chiefly lies in

---

[1] Owen Gwynedd succeeded his father Griff. ab Cynan, in the Principality of North Wales, in the year 1137, and reigned 32 years.—L.

Eifionydd[1], Dolwyddelan[2], and Gwedir, all of which are in Carnarvonshire.

I conceive it to be much to the credit of these Family Memoirs that the very learned and ingenious Dr. Percy (Dean of Carlisle) hath perused them with such attention as to have drawn out four genealogical tables,[3] as also to have added some notes, for the illustration of certain parts, and more particularly with regard to the pedigrees. I am proud to insert these, and the reader will find them under the mark of P. I have likewise added some observations for which I am indebted to the Rev. Mr. Evan Evans, translator of some specimens of ancient Welsh Poetry, published for Dodsley, in quarto : these are marked E.[4]

[1] Evionydd is a tract of country lying between the promontory of Lleyn and the mountainous region of Snowdon. It was formerly a comot of the cantrev, or hundred of Dunodig; the other comot was Ardudwy, now a part of Meirionyddshire, between Harddlech and Barmouth. Walter Davies.—L.

[2] Dolwyddelan, a parish near Capel Curig.—L.

[3] These tables were largely augmented in the edition issued by Miss Angharad Llwyd in 1827;

and in the present edition they are further augmented by Mr. W. W. E. Wynne.

[4] In the present edition these initials are retained, and the other notes in the two editions issued by the Hon. Daines Barrington have the letter B. attached to them. Those for which Miss Llwyd is responsible are marked L. The most important notes now added (including all the references to the existing copies of the Gwydir MS., and most of the dates from other sources) are the work of W. W. E. Wynne, Esq., of Peniarth.—A.R.

Written by Sir JOHN WYNNE of Gwyder, Knt. and Baronet,
Ut creditur, & patet.

GRUFFITH ap Conan,[1] Prince of Wales, had by his wife
Anghared, the daughter of Owen ap Edwyn, Lord of
Englefield, Owen Gwynedd, Cadwalader and Cadwallon, who
was slaine before his father's death: he reigned over Wales fifty
years. His troublesome life and famouse actes are compiled by a
most aunceint frier or monke of Wales: this was found by the
posterity of the said Gruffith ap Conan in the house of Gwedir[2]
in North Wales, and at the request of Morice Wynne, Esq.
(who had the same written in a most ancient booke and was
lineally descended from him) was translated into Latine by Nicholas Robinson, Bishop of Bangor.[3]

[1] Gruffith ap Conan died in 1137. In the MS.
copy of the Gwydir History at Wynnstay, the
arms of the wife of Griffith ap 'Conan are given
as, Sable, a chevron between 3 roses, argent, and
those of the wife of his son, Owen Gwynedd, as
argent, a cross ingrailed, flory, sable; between 3
Cornish choughs, proper.

[2] There are two houses so called at present
very near each other, the one Lower *Gwydir*
and the other *Upper*; they are both in Carnarvonshire, on the western side of the Conway
opposite to the town of Llanrwst. One of these
houses is so ancient as to be mentioned in
Saxton's map of Carnarvonshire, which was engraved in 1578.—B. Evan Evans Cler. derives
the name of Gwydir from Gwy (water) and tir
(land), and Mr. Lloyd of Cowden, from Gwaed tir,
or the Bloody Land, there having been a great
battle there, &c. It is certain, that in the above
life of Gruff. ap Cynan, there is an account of a
bloody battle between him and Trahayarn ab Cara-
dog, fought at a place from thence denominated,
Gwaed-erw, or tir gwaedlyd, alias gwaedir; I
believe from the circumstances of that battle,
that it was fought upon this spot. The foregoing

remarks upon the etymology of the word Gwydir
bear the stamp of high authority; at the same
time, it is not improbable, when the peculiar
situation of the house and lands is considered,
being on the banks of the Conway, from which
probably the latter was originally recovered, that
Gwy dir, or water land, is the true one. Gwy or
Wy is the ancient word for water, still found in
the names of rivers, i. e. Cynwy the first or chief
river, Elwy, or Ailwy, the second river, and Wye,
the river by way of eminence.—L.

[3] The late Rev. Mr. Lloyd of Cowden, in
Sussex, informed me that he saw this MS. of
Bishop Robinson, at the Rev Mr. Hugh Hughes's
late vicar of Bangor, whose father and eldest
brother were stewards after him at Gwedir.—B.
The Life of Griffith ab Cynan was written in
Welsh, and translated by Bishop Robinson into
Latin. This translation, in his own handwriting,
is preserved at Peniarth, and a transcript of the
Welsh Text, and of the Latin, was made by the
Rev. Canon Williams, of Rhydycroesau, and pub-
lished in the *Archæologia Cambrensis* in 1866.

The MS. said to have been at Wig, Llandegai,
is as follows: Sciant tam præsentes quam futuri

TABLE No. I.

TABLE I.

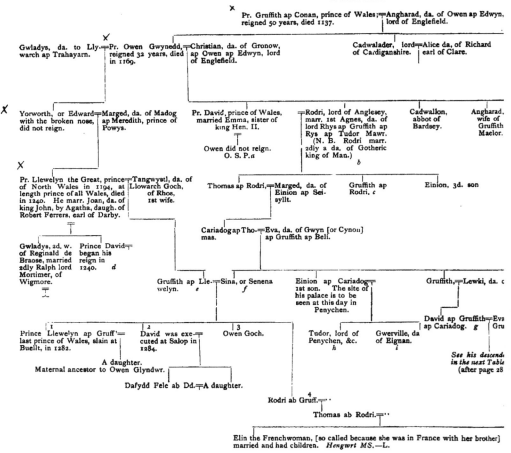

Pr. Gruffith ap Conan, prince of Wales;=Angharad, da. of Owen ap Edwyn, reigned 50 years, died 1137. | lord of Englefield.

Gwladys, da. to Lly-=Pr. Owen Gwynedd,=Christian, da. of Gronow,   Cadwalader, lord=Alice da, of Richard
warch ap Trahayarn. | reigned 32 years, died | ap Owen ap Edwyn, lord   of Cardiganshire. | earl of Clare.
                     | in 1169. | of Englefield.

Yorworth, or Edward=Marged, da. of Madog   Pr. David, prince of Wales,   =Rodri, lord of Anglesey,   Cadwallon,   Angharad,
with the broken nose, | ap Meredith, prince of   married Emma, sister of   marr. 1st Agnes, da. of   abbot of   wife of
did not reign. | Powys.   king Hen. II.   lord Rhys ap Gruffith ap   Bardsey.   Gruffith
                                                  Rys ap Tudor Mawr.   Maelor.
                          Owen did not reign.   (N. B. Rodri marr.
                          O. S. P. a   2dly a da. of Gotheric
                                            king of Man.) b

Pr. Llewelyn the Great, prince=Tangwystl, da. of   Thomas ap Rodri,=Marged, da. of   Gruffith ap   Einion, 3d. son
of North Wales in 1194, at | Llowarch Goch,   Einion ap Sei-   Rodri, c
length prince of all Wales, died | of Rhos,   syllt.
in 1240. He marr. Joan, da. of | 1st wife.
king John, by Agatha, daugh. of
Robert Ferrers, earl of Darby.

Gwladys, 2d. w.   Prince David=   Cariadog ap Tho-=Eva, da. of Gwyn [or Cynon]
of Reginald de | began his   mas.   ap Gruffith ap Beli.
Braose, married | reign in
2dly Ralph lord | 1240. d
Mortimer, of
Wigmore.

                  Gruffith ap Lle-=Sina, or Senena   Einion ap Cariadog=   Gruffith,=Lewki, da. c
                  welyn. e   f   1st son. The site of |
                                        his palace is to be
                                        seen at this day in
                                        Penychen.   David ap Gruffith=Eva
                                                                            ap Cariadog. g | Gru

Prince Llewelyn ap Gruff'=   David was exe-=   Owen Goch.   Tudor, lord of   Gwerville, da   See his descend.
last prince of Wales, slain at | cuted at Salop in   3   Penychen, &c.   of Eignan.   in the next Table
Buellt, in 1282. | 1284.   h   i   (after page 28

A daughter.
Maternal ancestor to Owen Glyndwr.

Dafydd Fele ab Dd.=A daughter.

                                          4
                              Rodri ab Gruff.=·
                              Thomas ab Rodri.=··

Elin the Frenchwoman, [so called because she was in France with her brother]
married and had children. Hengwrt MS.—L.

---

* This interesting anecdote identifying Syr Jevan of Wales, (whose chivalrous exploits occupy so large a portion of Froissart's *Chronicle*
Hengwrt MSS. belonging to Gryffydd ap Howel Vaughan, Esq. of Rûg, whose kind indulgence in permitting the Editor a perusal of this valuab

Cadwallon, slain═ Gwenllian, wife of Gruff'
before his father's │ ap Rhys ap Tudor mawr,
death. │ prince of South Wales.

Natural sons by various women.

. . . .

| | |
1, Conan had | 2. Llewellyn.
part ot Merio- | 3. Meredith.
neth. He had | 4. Edward.
several sons; | 5. Rhun.
scil. | 6. Howel.
| 7. Cadelh.
| 8. Madoc.
| 9. Einion.
| 10. Cynwric.
| 11. Philip
Gruff', ob. │ Meredith, | and
1253. | other issue. | 12. Riryd.

═

│
Howell.

─────────────────────────────
Llowarch, &c. Will' Cariadog, alias Wilkock
Craidog, 3d. son marr. an in-
heretrix in Pembrokeshire.

da. and heir of
ith Vaughan.

ıts
l.

───────────────
Owen llaw gôch, or Owen with the " Bloody Hand,"
who distinguished himself in the wars of France,
temp. E. 3, & is celebrated by Sir John Froissart, in
his *Chronicles*, by the name of Syr Ievan of Wales.
Murdered by John Lamb, in 1381.*—L.

, with the son of Tomas ab Rodri, was discovered in one of the
volume is most gratefully acknowledged.—L. *j*

---

a He was living 31 Oct., 1212.

b Rodri was living in 1183.

c Living 31 Oct., 1212.

d Prince David, &c.═

Ellis ap Jer-═Agnes
werth ap
Owen Bro-
gyntyn.

e It has been generally said that Griffith was illegitimate,
but the celebrated Welsh Antiquary, Vaughan of Hengwrt
maintained a contrary opinion.

f Living A° 25 Hen. 3.

g See page 25.

h Dead in 1328. See Rolls of Parliament.

i Angharad coheiress to her brother 2 Edw. 3, 1328. Se
Rolls of Parliament.

j I strongly suspect that the following is the passage to which
Miss Angharad Llwyd refers. It is in *Hengwrt MS.* 351, the
only one she is likely to have had access to, as being at Rhûg
in Col. Vaughan's time. It is on page 865, and is a copy of a
large MS. in the autograph of Robert Vaughan the Antiquary.
Hengwrt MS. 96.

" On Loawgoch alas yn Ffrainc gan Joⁿ Lam ei was drwy
frad yn ei wely pan oed yn arfaethy dyfod i oresgyn talaith
Cymru J. B. 30, O. S. P.

"Elen Ffrances am ei bod yn Ffrainc gydai brawd ac yn
medry Ffrangeg═ ap Jor. ap Ednyved Vychan
p. Llyfr Mr. Edd. Herbert o Drefaldwyn."

It would appear from a letter in the *Archæologia Cambrensis*
No. XXI, third series, page 62, quoting an original record in
the Imperial Library of France, that the names of Sir Ievan
of Wales were " Ivain agruffin," doubtless Ievan ap Griffith.
—W.

Owen Gwynedd was Prince after his father.[1]

He married to his first wife Gwladys, daughter to Lowarch ap Trahayarn, Lord of Divet, by whom he had only Yerwerth [2] Drwndwn or Edward *with the broken nose*,[3] and by his second wife called Christian, daughter of Gronow ap Owen ap Edwyn Lord of Englefield, being his cosen, he had David who after him was Prince; he had also Rodri Lord of Anglesey,[4] and Cadwallon who was Abbot of Bardsey, and Angharad wife of Griffith Maelor.[5] He had besides these by diverse women Conan, Llewellin, Meredith, Edwal,[6] Rûn, Howel, Cadelh, Madoc, Eneon, Cynwric, Philip, and Riryd Lord of Clochran in Ireland. (v. Powel's

qd. ego Griff. filius Conani concessi dedi et confirmavi deo et Ecclesiæ Sti Johanis Evang. de Hagemon & Canonicis ibidem deo servientibus ad Ecclesiam eorum de Nevyn tres acres in Nevyn et Abraham Filium Aldredi Sutoris et duos filios Serence. Co. W. et Jo. in perpetuam Eleemosynam libere & quiete ad Ecclesiam S. Mariæ de Nevyn & prædictis Canon. de Hagemon jure perpetuo pertineat. . . . . Omnibus Sta dei Eccles. filiis tam præsentibus quam futuris David rex filius Owini Salutem. Notum sit vobis me concessise Abbati & Canonicis de Hagemon illam terram quam T. D. habuit in villa de Nevyn ab omnibus terrenis consuetudinibus immunem concedoque similiter prædict' Canonicis decimationem molendini mei de Nevyn ad perpetuam Eleemosynam. T. Jo. de Burcheto Rado de lega. Einion seys &c.

David filius Oweni Principis North-Walliæ Universis xti fidelibus Francis & Anglis Salutem in Domino Sempiternam. Sciatis me assensu Emmæ uxoris meæ et Oweni hæredis mei &c. His Test. Remö Epo. Rado de lega, Domina Emma soror. Hen: Regis ux. Davidis fil. Oweni Princip. Northwall. &c. &c. Sciatis me assensu Davidis mariti mei et Oweni hæredis mei &c.

T. Einion Seys, Rado de lega.—L.

In the *Brogyntyn* MS. the words "and are extant" follow "Bishop of Bangor." [See p. 12, [3]].

[1] Owen Gwynedd died in 1169.

[2] This account differs very materially from that given by Dr. Powel in his *History of Cambria*, p. 226. It should seem however that the author made use of some materials in compiling this

short chronicle of the Princes of Wales, which Dr. Powel had no opportunity of consulting; and he hath already mentioned a life of Griffith ap Conan written by a *most ancient Friar or Monk of Wales*. Dr. Powel's *History* was published in 1584, and as the author refers to it in this page, it proves that this part of the MS. was written after that year.—B. Evan Evans informed Mr. Barrington of a Latin History of Wales, by one Davydd Maelor, which Dr. Powel wrote some notes upon; he likewise told him that the Chronicle of Thomas Williams is in the Hengwrt Library. J. Ll.—L.

[3] "Yerworth Drwyndon near to Brute." Out of a charte of the Genealogie of the Dukes of Yorke inserted in Leland's *Collect*. vol. II. p. 616. 2d edit.—B.

[4] There is a poem addressed to Rodri, by Gwalchmai, in the *Myvyrian Archæology*, ed. 1870, p. 146. The tomb of Rodri was found upon the reparation of the choir of Holyhead church, in 1713, and on it a small brass shell, curiously wrought with net work *(Camb. Reg.* vol. III. p. 215.)

[5] Gryffith Maelor Lord of Bromfield, who died in 1191. [See Anderson's *Royal Genealogies*.] He was brother of Maryed, mentioned hereafter.—P.

[6] Edwal, or Idwal, was murdered at Llyn Idwal, by Dunawt, son of Nefydd Hardd, one of the Fifteen Tribes of North Wales, to whom Owen had entrusted the youth to be fostered. (See Pennant's *Tours*, vol. 2, p. 162. quarto ed. 1784.)

Chron.) This Prince Owen with his brother Cadwalader (as the Welsh Chronicle maketh mention) in his father's time made many victorious voyages into South Wales against the Normans that incroached mightilie on that country, and in a pitched field slew 3000 men, and put the rest to flight. Being prince after his father's death, he overthrew the Earle of Chester and a number of March Lords, and (as Giraldus Cambrensis hath it in his History, intituled Itinerarium Cambriæ) repulsed K. Henry II. who made three voyages royall against Wales with all the Power of England, Normandy, and Aquitane, together with the succours of Flanders and Britayne. In one of the voyages at Counsyllt wood the whole army of the King was put to flight, as the French Chronicle[1] sayth, the King's person endangered, and the great standard of England overthrowne and forsaken[2], which was the cause that Robert Mountfort, a noble baron, impeached Henry of Essex the standard bearer, (who held that office by inheritance), for beginning the flight, of treason, which being tried by combate, the standard-bearer was overthrowne, his office, lands, and goods, confiscate, and himselfe shaven a monke in the Abbey of Reading. After that this Prince had reigned most victoriously thirty-two years, he died. It is written of him, that he was soe fortunate, as that he never attempted that enterprise which he atchieved not.

Cadwalader, brother to prince Owen[3], was married to Alice, daughter to Richard earl of Clare, and was lord of Ceredigiawn or Cardiganshire.

---

[1] As there are several French Chronicles which occasionally treat of what happened in England, it is difficult to ascertain what History the author alludes to. He also does not explain in any instance what Welsh Chronicle he so often refers to, whether that of Caradoc of Lancarvan, that before mentioned to have been written by a Friar of Conway, or perhaps some other compilation of the same sort. The author also cites the copy of a Welsh Chronicle in the possession of his relation, Sir Thomas Williams of Trefriw. (See afterwards).—B.

[2] See Gulielmus Neubrigensis's account of the action, l. 2, c. 5. which agrees with the author's in most particulars.—B.

[3] Cadwalader *frater Owini magni* salutem in Domino; Notum sit universitati vestræ quod ego Cadwalader pro salute animæ meæ & omnium antecessorum & heredum meorum dedi & concessi Deo & Ecclie S. Joannis Evan' de Hageman & Canonicis ibidem Deo servientibus in puram & p'petuam Eleemosynam Ecclesiæ de Nevin. T. Alic' de Clara uxore mea, Ranulpho comite

Though this record is attested[1] by Cadwalader king of Wales[2] because he had kingly authority in this countrey, yet he was no more than a subject to his brother, by whom he was banished, and lost his lands, till by composition the same was restored. The Welsh Chronicle calleth him Prince of Wales : he dwelled most at the castle of Aberystwythe. He was murthered by the English souldiers which the King sent to conduct him to his countrey.

After the death of Owen, Yerwerth (or Edward), his sonne, being thought unfitt to governe by reason of the deformity of his face, David his brother became Prince in his father's roome.

I find that Yerwerth Drwndwn, or Edward *with the broken nose*, being put from the government of the principality, had assigned him for his part of his father's inheritance, the hundreds of Nanconwy and Ardydwy.[3] He dwelled at the castle of Dolwyddelan,[4] where it is thought credible his son Llewelyn the Great, or prince Llewelyn[5], was borne, whose mother was *Maryed* the daughter of Madog ap Meredydd prince of Powys.

Conan ap Owen Gwynedd his son had for his part the country of Merioneth.[6]

David married[7] Emma sister to King Henry the II. and had by her a sonne called Owen ; upon confidence of that match he banished his base brethren, and imprisoned his brother Roderike, because he desired the portion of inheritance. But Rodericke,

---

Cestriæ, &c. Precipio quod Abbas Salop & Conventus habeant totam tenuram suam inter Ryblam & Mersam [Two rivers in Lancashire] T. R. comite de Clara & *Cadwaladro ap Gr. ap Cynan rege Walliarum*, & Roberto Basset & Gaufrid apud Cestriam.—B.

[1] See note [2] page 14.

[2] For "is attested by" the Bala MS. has it "calleth this."—L.

[3] Nantconway is a hundred of Carnarvonshire, through which the river Conway runs; Ardydwy is a hundred in the N.W. part of Merionethshire. —B.

[4] This castle is situated in the South Eastern parts of Carnarvonshire, and in perhaps the least frequented part of the mountains. The remains at present are very insignificant.—B.

[5] It is therefore always stiled by Giraldus Cambrensis, *Terra filiorum Conani.*—B.

[6] A charter of Llewelyn, the son of Griffith, Prince of Wales and Lord of Snaudon, is dated at Dolwyddelan, the next Thursday before the Festival of S. Lawrence 1281. (*Record of Caernarvon*, p. 211).

[7] "What! in loud reply Madoc exclaimed, Hath he forgotten all!
David, King Owen's son . . my father's son .
He wed the Saxon . . the Plantagenet!"
(Southey's *Madoc.*, First part, p. 7, 8vo. edit., 1807).

(Quere, Where his possessions were ? and who are come of him ?)
Howell ap Gruff' ap Conan was buried at Conway.

I find not, during Prince Llewelyn ap Jerwerth's raigne, any
mencion made of any thing done by the posterity of Rodri ap Owen
Gwynedd: a man may easily guesse the reason, for this Prince
held them under, and suspected lest they should aspire to the
princely dignity, which their ancestors sometime had held.

In the raigne of David, sonne to the said Prince Llewelyn by
Joane King John's daughter, who began to raigne anno 1240,
Eignan and Gruff' ap Cariadog tooke parte with their sister's
sonne, Llewelyn ap Gruff', the last Prince of Wales of that line,
afterwards slayne at Buellt.

We receave it by tradition from father to sonne in Evioneth,
that David ap Llewelyn being Prince by the ayde of his uncle,
the King came to the towne of Pwllhely in Llûn to parle with
the bretheren Eingan and Gruff'; whom the bretheren met with
such a force on the day of truce, that the Prince told them they
were too strong to be subjects; whereto they answered, that
he was rather too weake to be Prince, and soe parted without
any conclusion or agreement. In the end they were forced by
long warrs to forgoe that countrey, and to lose their land there,
and to joyne themselves to their nephew Llewelyn ap Griffith,
who then had his court at Maesmynan in Flintshire. He also
held, as is before mentioned, the cantreds of Englefield, Dyffryn
Clwyd, Ros, and Rovoniawg, against his uncle David; haveing
warre on the one side with the King, on the other side with his
uncle, who gave them greate possessions (as some thinke) as afore
is remembered about Denbigh Castle.

Llewelyn, the sonne of Gruffith, their nephew, after the death
of his uncle David, attayning the government of Wales, restored
to his uncles their lands and possessions in the county of Carnarvon. I find noe record of any thing done by them in the time
of the same Prince.

Eingan ap Cariadog [1] had a sonne, of whom mention shall be made hereafter, called Tudur Lord of Penychen [2], Penyberth, and Baladeulyn, and whether he had any more sonnes is to me uncertain.

Gruff' ap Cariadog maried Leuki, daughter of Llowarch Vaughan ap Llowarch Goch ap Llowarch Holbwrch, and had but one sonne to my knowledge, called David ap Gruffith [3], which David maried Eva the sole heiress of Gruffith Vaughan ap Gruffith ap Mereithig of Penyfed in Evioneth, by whome he had three sonnes; viz. David, Meredith, and Howell. This appeares by the record of the extent made of Denbigh land, in the time of Edward the first, by Henry Lacy [4] Earle of Lincolne, to whome the King gave that land upon the conquest of Wales : for Henry Lacy minding to make a princely seat of the castle of Denbigh, per force compassed [5] the children of the said David ap Gruff' to exchange their possessions about Denbigh Castle (which were great) with him for other lands of lesse value in the said lordship, in the furthest part from him : the words of the record follow thus [6].

How they left the lordship of Friwlwyd, and other their lands in the County of Carnarvon, I can find no record of, but only have it by tradition, that it was taken from them by the King's officers, for to this day it is parte of the principalitie [7] of

[1] Eingan ap Caradoc Arglwyd Penychen yr hwn sydd a mur ei Lys etto iw weled ym mhennychen. (A note in a more modern hand in *Hengwrt MSS.* 324).

[2] This is a township near the sea, in the Parish of Abererch in Carnarvonshire, and situated between the towns of Crekeith and Pullhely.—B. See note on page 19.

[3] He had also a daughter, Guerfil (or Gwerville) married to Inon ap Einion, according to Collins's account of the Wynne family. (Baronetage, vol. I.) But perhaps this may be a mistake, for Gwerville daughter of Eignan ap Cariadock mentioned hereafter.—P.

" Rex concessit David, filio Griffini, quod ipse & heredes sui habeant et teneant de se & heredibus suis totam terram de Diffrencloyt, & de Rewinnock, cum pertinentiis in Nor-Wallia." Rotulus Wallie de anno 6 Regis Edw. I. Sir Joseph Aylofie's *Calendars of Ancient Charters.* Query, was the grantee in this charter this David, or David brother of Prince Llewelyn? I believe it was the latter, who is styled " Lord of Denbigh." See also Pennant's *Wales*, vol. 2, p. 37.—W.

[4] The cantreds of Ros and Revoniawg, and the Comote of Dynmael, were confirmed to him by charter dated 16 Oct: 10 Edw. I. Judging from the dates, it was probably David ap Griffith, and not his children who made this exchange with Lacy. See the MS. dates Tables 1 and 2. The Earl of Lincoln died in 1311.

[5] "Compelled " in *Denbigh MS.*—L.

[6] By some mistake however the record is omitted in the MS.—B.

[7] *Principality* here means lands held under the Princes of Wales, eldest sons of the Kings of England.—B.

E

Wales; which is not unlike, considering what befell to the other cozens, the heirs of Penychen, Penyberth, and Baladeulyn, whereof there is a very good record and certaine, remayning in the prince's treasury in Carnarvon.

Eingan ap Cariadog had one sonne called Tudur ap Eingan, and one daughter called Gwervile,[1] whereof the record ensueing after maketh mention. You are to understand, that after the conqueste of Wales, the countrey in generall, as well as in particular, found themselves aggrieved for the wronges offered by the English officers, and soe sent certaine men with their generall and private grieffes to the prince lying at Kennington[2] neare London, in the time of the parliament in anno 33d of Edward[3] the First, among the which these are mentioned.[4]

It is necessary, for the understanding of this record, and the sense thereof, that you first understand, that after the death of

[1] See MS. additions Table I. There was another daughter.

[2] This place in Domesday is stiled *Chenintuns*, but now *Kennington*. It is situated in the parish of West Lambeth, and was formerly a royal palace. See Maitland's *London*, vol. II. p. 1387. —B. i.e. Kyningstune or Kingstown.

[3] In *Brogyntyn MS.*, 29 Edw. I., but in the abstracts from the petitions, in the same MS., as underneath, 33. There is a copy of these petitions in the Hengwrt Library. 33 Edw. I. is correct. *Hengwrt MS.* 118.

[4] Petitiones de Kennington factæ apud Kennington p'homines North-Walliæ p'Comitatibus p' sing'lares personas exhibitæ D'no principi filio Regis Edwardi conquestoris Walliæ & concilio suo apud Kennington extra London tempore Parliamenti p'dict' regis habiti apud Westmesterium 1ᵐᵃ Dominica quadragesimæ an'o regni Regis p'dict' Edwardi 33°, & Responsiones ad easdem Petitiones factæ & liberatæ Justic' North-Walliæ sub privato sigillo dicti D'ni Prineipis ad executionem responsionum p'dict' faciend' & eas firmiter observandum in p'tib' North-Walliæ.

Ad petitionem Leolini & Gruffini filioru' Oweni ap Llewelyn de eo q'd Tudur ap Eingan avunculus erat D'nus de Baladeulyn, Penechyn, &

Penyberth in Com' Carnarvon & seisitus post pacem p'clamat' fere p' unum annum, post cujus decessum tenementa p'dict' ad Gwervillam sororem dict' Tudur' descendisse debuerunt, sed domina Regina mater Principis affectavit tenementa illa & ea a D'no obtinuit, quæ quidem tenementa nunc sunt in manu principis & ad eos jure hereditatis spectant ; unde petunt remedium. Responsum est, q'd Justic' informet se sup' content' in p'dicta petitione, & quo tempore dictus Tudur obiit, & si forisfecit necne, & omnibus circumstanciis, & certificet inde dominum ad petitionem eorum dicti Llewelyn & Gruffini q'd dominus velit concedere eis aliquas ballivas in Com' Carnarvon p' debita firma inde reddenda quosq' discussum sit quid de eorum hæreditate fuerit faciendum. Responsum est quod p'tinet ad Justic' ordinare de ballivis p'ut utilitati domini melius viderit expedire.

There are very fine transcripts of these Petitions presented to the King at Kennington, in Nᵒ· 4776 of the Harleian MSS. which is a large Folio, containing chiefly a most complete extent or survey of the counties of Anglesey, Merioneth,[a] and Carnarvon, made in the 26th year of Edward the Third. The date agrees except in the difference of 32d year of Edward the Third instead of the 33d.—B.

[a] The survey of Merioneth was taken in 7 Hen. V.

Prince Llewelyn in Buellt, the King made a proclamation of peace to all the inhabitants of Wales, receiving them all that would come in and yeald themselves to him into his protection; graunting the use and fruition of their lands, liberties, and privileges they held before in their countrey under the Princes of Wales. This is the peace specified in the record: after which Tudur ap Eingan had held his lands almost one yeare. To whom or to what family this Gwervill was married I cannot as yet learne. This land soe taken is part of the possessions of the principalitie of Wales to this day. It is to be noted here, that all the selfe same time, in the raigne of Edward the First, the Queene his wife tooke perforce the land of Eingan ap Cariadog's offspring in the county of Carnarvon, and Henry Lacie exchanged perforce, with Gruff ap Cariadog's offspring in Denbigh land, and that the cozens stood in equall degree of kindred one to another, viz., cozen germans removed; which hard dealing must needs pull downe a kindred. It cannot be otherwise alsoe, but that Friwlwyd was by the same Queene, or by the Justice Will' Sutton or others, who dealt hardly with the gentrie of these parts in those days, taken from the posterity of Gruff', for it is parte of the principalitie to these daies, although the record proving this happened not to fall into my hands.

But to recurre to the offspring of Gruff' ap Cariadog, and their succession, with the estate and condition they lived in from time to time unto this day; it being my purpose to treat thereof. Out of the three brethren, David, Meredith, and Howell, who exchanged, as above is remembred, with the Earle of Lincolne, the posterity onely of Howell doth remaine in credite and shew in their countrey, the posterity of the other two being by division and subdivision of gavelkind (the destruction of Wales) brought to the estate of meane freeholders, and soe haveing forgotten their descents and pedigree, are become as they never had been. If you ask the question why the succession of Howell sped better

than the posterity of the other two brethren, I can yeald no other
reason, but GOD's mercy and goodness towards the one more than
the other, as GOD sayd in the booke of Moses, " I will have mercy
" on whome I will have mercy," for they lived in the same commonwealth, and under the same storme of oppression, soe as if
GOD had not left us a seed, we had beene like Sodom, or compared to Gomorrha.   Nevertheless by the goodness of GOD we
are and continue in the reputation of gentlemen from time to
time sithence unto this day, as shall appeare by the discourse
following.   The offspring of David ap Meredith hold the land
exchanged by the Earle of Lincolne with their ancestors, viz., the
towneship of Yscorebryll in Eglwys vach[1] and halfe Maethebroyd
in Llanrwst,[2] and are reputed to be descended from Gruffith ap
Conan in the quarter where they dwell, but yet are not able to
lay downe the certayntie of their pedigree.

David ap Gruff' ap Cariadog (as before mentioned) maried Eva
the daughter and heiress of Gruff' Vaughan ap Gruff' ap Morythig, and by her had that land which in the extent of North
Wales is called Gwely Griffry in Penyved in Evioneth in the
county of Carnarvon; the quit rent of the Prince out of this
Gwely[3] is £. 3. 19s.   Which Morithig the grandfather of this
woman was, I am uncertaine, for there were two of that name;
one in North Wales, who is descended from Sandde Hard O Vor-
tyn, from whome the chiefe men in *Yale* and *Maelor*[4] derive
their descent;   and another in South Wales, called Morithyg
Warwyn, of whome are come all the Vaughans.   It did not
appear by the Welsh pedegrees, that this Griffry was descended
of Morythig, till I found the record in the Exchequer of Carnar-

---

[1] Eglwys vach is a parish in the S.W. part of
Denbighshire.—B. Eglwys vach signifies the church
in the vale, from the obsolete word Bâch, which
bears that import.—Evan Evans. Others say that
this church is so called, from Bach ab Carwed, a
chieftain in the seventh century. See Owen's Biography. W.D.—L.

[2] The town of Llanrwst is also in Denbighshire,
not far distant from the parish of Eglwys vach.—B.

[3] This word hath been before explained.—B.

[4] Extensive Lordships in Denbighshire.—B.

TABLE No. 11.

TABLE II.

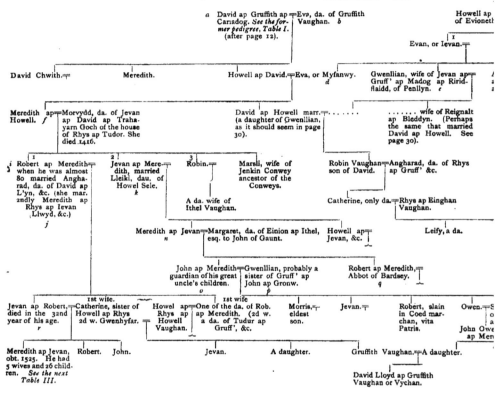

a David ap Gruffith ap ᵭEva, da. of Gruffith   Howell ap
Canadog. *See the for-* | Vaughan. *b*   of Evioneth
mer pedigree, Table I.
(after page 12).

          | I
          Evan, or Ievan.ᵭ

David Chwith.ᵭ   Meredith.   Howell ap David.ᵭEva, or Myfanwy.   Gwenllian, wife of Jevan apᵭ
                          d   Gruff' ap Madog ap Ririd-
                                          flaidd, of Penllyn. *e*

Meredith apᵭMorvydd, da. of Jevan   David ap Howell marr.ᵭ......   ...... wife of Reignalt
Howell. *f* | ap David ap Traha-   (a daughter of Gwenllian,   ap Bleddyn. (Perhaps
      | yarn Goch of the house   as it should seem in page   the same that married
      | of Rhys ap Tudor. She   30).   David ap Howell. See
      | died 1416.   page 30).

| I   2 | 3 |
i Robert ap Meredithᵭ Jevan ap Mere-ᵭ Robin.ᵭ   Marsli, wife of   Robin VaughanᵭAngharad, da. of Rhys
j when he was almost dith, married   Jenkin Conwey   son of David. | ap Gruff' &c.
  80 married Angha- Lleiki, dau. of   ancestor of the
  rad, da. of David ap Howel Sele.   Conweys.
  L'yn, &c. (she mar.   *k*   Catherine, only da.ᵭRhys ap Einghan
  2ndly Meredith ap   A da. wife of | Vaughan.
  Rhys ap Ievan   Ithel Vaughan.
  Llwyd, &c.)

           Meredith ap JevanᵭMargaret, da. of Einion ap Ithel, Howell apᵭ   Leify, a da.
                 n   esq. to John of Gaunt.   Jevan, &c. |

           John ap MeredithᵭGwenllian, probably a   Robert ap Meredith,ᵭ
           guardian of his great | sister of Gruff' ap   Abbot of Bardsey. |
           uncle's children. | John ap Gronw.   *q*
                o   *p*

    1st wife.   1st wife
Jevan ap Robert,ᵭCatherine, sister of Howel apᵭOne of the da. of Rob. Morris,ᵭ Jevan.ᵭ   Robert, slain   Owen.ᵭS
died in the 32nd Howell ap Rhys Rhys ap | ap Meredith. (2d w. eldest   in Coed mar- | o
year of his age. 2d w. Gwenhyfar. ᵭ Howell | a da. of Tudur ap son.   chan, vita | a
   r   Vaughan. | Gruff', &c.   Patris.   John Owe
                                                       ap Men

Meredith ap Jevan, Robert. John.   Jevan.   A daughter.   Gruffith Vaughan.ᵭA daughter.
obt. 1525. He had
5 wives and 26 child-
ren. *See the next*
 Table III.   David Lloyd ap Gruffith
                                           Vaughan or Vychan.

Ieredith ⚭

2
Gruffith. ⚭
c

Ilswn, a third da. marr. Howell ⚭ p Gronw ap Jevan ap Gronw p Howel of Maelor.

Einion ap Gruff ' ⚭

Gwervil, wife of Tudur ap Hob-y-dili.

Alician van, wife of John ab Madog Puleston: from whom are descended the Pulestons of Emeral and l Havod-y wern m

Ievan, ancestor of many families in Carnarvonshire. g

Sir Howel of the Battle-ax, knighted at Poictiers, h

Gwenhwyfar, married Robert, 4th son of Thomas Salisbury, of Leweny, esq.

Another da. wife of Gruffith ap Madog Vaughan. ⚭

Owen ap Griffith ap Madog.

Bonet da. Howell Rhys. ap John edith s

Gruffith. ⚭

a See page 25.

b Eva, the daughter of Griffith Vaughan, wife of David ap Griffith, bore the arms of Moriddic Warwyn. She was heiress of Kesailgyfarch, and the possess᷈ᴺˢ called Gwely Griffry, in Evioneth.

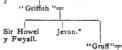

c "Griffith" ⚭

Sir Howel y Fwyall.

Jevan.*

"Gruff" ⚭

* *Hengwrt MS.* 113. Autograph of Gutyn Owen, fol. 41. Jevan ap Gr. ap Howel was living 19 Edw. III. See *Rymer* edit. 1825, pt. 1, p. 68.

d Eva, daughter of Jevan ap Howel, wife of Howel ap David, bore the arms of Collwyn. By her the houses called y Llys in Kevn y Van, burned by Owen Glyn Dwr, & Ystymkegid, and other great possessions in Evioneth, came to Howel ap David.

e His tomb is in Llanuwchllyn Church.

f Living 26 Edw. III.

g   "Shire"

Howel Vychan.

*
Madoc, party to a deed 8 Hen. V., 1416.

Rees.

Grono.

* "Madoc ap Jevan ap Einion" is a feoffee to the settlement (referred to) dated 10 Oct., 34, Hen. VI., to which Howel ap Grono is feoffor. Perhaps this is the person, as he and Howel were third cousins.

h See pages 30 and 79. He was brother not son to Einion.

i Living the 9 Hen. IV.

j See pages 34 and 64.

k Jevan was living in 2 Hen. IV., (1401) See *Ministers' Accounts* for period ending at May in that year.

l " Emeral and " crossed out in MS. note.

m The pedigree opposite is wrong, as the following extract

[TURN OVER.

from the emblazoned Salisbury Manuscript at Wynnstay, proved in a great degree by copies of deeds, &c., in that Vol., will shew :—

*Howel ap Grono ap Jevan ap=Agnes, dau. of Jevan ap
Grono ap *Hwfa* ap Jorwerth, | Madoc, of Maelor; wife
of Hafod-y-wern, party to a | of Howel on 24 Dec., 7
conveyance 24 Dec., 7 Hen. | Hen VI., living upon 10
VI., and to another on 10 Oct. | Oct., 34 Hen. VI.
34 Hen VI.

Alswn only child=Howel ap Jevan
living 10 Oct., 34 | ap Griffith of Bersham.
Hen. VI.

Alswn Vychan, settlement=John Puleston,
upon her and her heirs by | died 1461.
John Puleston her husband,
made in court of the ville
of Wrexham† 10 Oct., 34
Hen. VI.

Alicia, dau. of=John Puleston, mar-
Thomas Salis- | riage settlement
bury, sen. | made in a Court of
the Ville of Wrex-
ham 12 July, 15
Edw. IV.

* It was Grono ap *Hwfa* ap Jorwerth who married a daughter of Jevan ap Howel (see above). The wife of Hwfa, and Grono's mother is stated to have been Margaret, daughter to Llewelyn ap Ynyr of Yale.

† That is, Licence was granted therein to make the feoffment or settlement.

n Living 26 Hen. VI.

o Living 20 July, 2 Edw. IV.

p Read " Gwenever daughter of Gronw ap Jevan ap Einion."

q See page 34.

r Living 6 Edw. IV.

s This pedigree shows that Rees ap Jevan was cousin german to his wife's grandmother, but the dates, taken from contemporary Records, exhibit the possibility of it. There must have been about 35 years between the ages of my mother and one of her first cousins, my mother being the younger. There was not quite ten years difference in the ages of my mother and the grandson of her first cousin, she being born in July, 1780, and the late Sir Richard Puleston, Bt., in June, 1789.—W.

Einion ap Griffith,
10 Rich. II. say 1387.

Jevan ap Einion,   A dau.=Howel Sele,
1427.   murdered
                                   about 1401.

=Meurice Vychan   A dau.=Jevan ap Mere-
1464. See Char-   dith, 1401, died
ter of Confraternity   during Glyn-
of that date, from   dwr's wars.
the Abbot, below.

David ap Meuric   Meredith ap Jevan,   Howel Vychan
Vychan. Will   20 Hen. VI., say
1494-5.   1442.

John ap Meredith   Robert, Abbot
1485. Marriage   of Bardsey
settlement of his   1464, probably
son Owen 2 Rich.   then a young
III.   man.

David   Rees ap=Gwenhwyfar, heiress.
1461-8.   Jevan
            31 Hen. VI.

Jevan ap Rhys
1513.

von. If a man list to be curious which of both Morythigs this was, let him find whether of them lived nearest this time, and that sure was he.

Howell ap David maried Eva[1] the daughter and heire[2] of Jevan ap Howell[3] ap Meredith of Evioneth (by some cards[4] of pedigree she is called Myfanwy[5]) and had with her large possessions in Evioneth, which to this day remaine in the posterity of the said Howell, yet mangled with division and subdivision of gavelkinde.'

Memorandum, That Evan ap Howell ap Meredith had another daughter and coheiress, maried to one of Penllyn of the stocke of Riridflaidd of Penllyn, her name was Gwenllian, and she maried Jevan ap Gruff' ap Madog[6] ap Riridflaidd of Penllyn.[7] The said Jevan ap Howell ap Meredith had a third daughter and coparcener that maried Howell ap Gronw ap Jevan ap Gronw ap Howell of Maelor, and by him she had two daughters, viz. Gwervile, maried to Tudur ap Hob-y-dili,[8] the other was Alician, who maried Puleston, and brought Hafod y werne to that family. Evan ap Howell ap Meredith, father to this Eva, was brother to Gruff' ap Howell ap Meredith, who was father to Einion ap Gruff', father to Jevan ap Einion[9] and Howell. This Howell was knighted at the field of Poyctiers, and by our countrymen is reported to have taken the French King; but howsoever it was, he did such service there, that the Prince bestowed a messe of meate to be served up dayly

[1] The descendants of David and Eva have always borne the arms of Morythig Warwyn. She was heiress of Cesailgyfarch, and of the possessions called Gwely Griffry, in Evioneth.

[2] Rather Co-heir.—P.

[3] Jevan ap Howel ap Meredith appears as Ringild for the Comote of Evioneth, in a Roll of Ministers' Accounts, Co. Carn : from Michaelmas 23rd Rich. II. to 1 Hen. IV., and so on to the month of May, 2 Hen. IV.

[4] This is used for charts.—B.

[5] See an ode to Myfannwy Fechan amongst Evans's Specimens of Welsh Poetry. Meufaniw i.s. my woman or my dear.—E.

[6] The ancestor of John Owen of Kefn in Evioneth, living 1683.—History of the Gwydir Family, in Hengwrt MS., 350, fol. 15.

[7] Penllyn is a hundred in Merionethshire.—B.

[8] Tudur ap Hob-y-dilli and others enter into a recognizance for £60 to Rich. Boule " parson " of the church of Mold, 21 July, 1386.—36th Report of the Deputy Keeper of Public Records, p. 347.

[9] In the Brogyntyn MS. this sentence has a comma at " Einion." This Howel was certainly brother to Einion ap Gruff, who was appointed Sheriff of Carnarvonshire, for 3 years, 1 Oct. 25 Edw. III.; though it would seem from the sentence in the text, that he was son. He was in receipt of an annuity from the Crown at Michaelmas 2 Rich. II. of £20 a year.—Account of Chamberlain of North Wales for that year, at Michaelmas.

during his life before his battle-axe, which after was bestowed on the poore, whereof he was called Sir Howell y *fwyall*.[1] He was alsoe Constable of Chester and Criketh Castles,[2] and had the mills to farme, and other many great office, and places of profit. Of Jevan ap Eingan his brother are descended very many gentlemen of principall account in the county of Carnarvon. Howell[3] begate Meredith and David; Meredith ap Howell[4] dwelled in Evioneth at his houses Keffin y fan, and Keselgiffarch, and David ap Howell in Llanrwst in Denbigh land, at his house called Henblas in Maethebroyd. Meredith ap Howell maried Morvydd the daughter of Jevan ap David ap Trahayarn goch of Llûn, who was descended of the house of Rys ap Teudwr. In the extent of North Wales, made in the 26th of Edward the Third, you shall find that Meredith ap Howell[5] and others are the heires of Gwely. Griff' David ap Howell his brother maried[6]

viz. Jevan ap Howell ap Meredith, the daughter of Gwenllian,

---

[1] Fwyall signifies an axe.—B. Howel was also "Raglot" of Aberglaslyn, and died between Michaelmas 2 Rich. II, and the same time 6 Rich. II.—*Ministers' Accounts;* and *Account of Chamberlain of North Wales.* (See *Peniarth MS.* 45, No. 2, pp. 7 and 28.)

[2] Some small remains of this Castle still continue. It is on the sea-coast of Carnarvonshire.—B.

[3] Not Howel of the Battle-axe, but Howell ap David ap Gruffith ap Cariadog, &c. According to Collins, Howell ap David had five sons by Eva daughter of Jevan ap Howell ap Meredith; viz. Meredith, Robert, Tudor, Gruffith, and David.—P.

[4] It appears in a Roll of *Ministers' Accounts* from Michaelmas 5 to do. 6 Rich. II, that at that time Meredith ap Howel held in farm from the Crown the Lordship of Gest.

[5] Davydd ab Howell, brother to Mredd. ab Howell, married the grand-daughter of Iefan ab Howel ab Mredd., being the daughter of Gwenllian. Denbigh MS.—L.

[6] There is some mistake here undoubtedly in the pedigree, probably occasioned by the chasm in the MS.—B. Miss Llwyd fills up this blank as follows :—" his brother married the grand-daughter

of Jevan ap Howell, &c.," but Mr. Wynne thinks Miss Llwyd has not cleared the matter up. The late Mr. Joseph Morris of Shrewsbury, suggested the following :—

Ieuan ap Griffith ⚯ Gwenllian dau. of
ap Madoc, of   Ieuan ap Howel
Nantffreur to   ap Meredith, of
Ririd Flaidd.   Evionydd.

Gwenllian dau. ⚯ David ap Howel, &c.
of Ieuan.   to Owen Gwynedd.

Robin Vychan ⚯ Angharad, dau. of
               Madoc ap Rys* to
               Ednyved Vychan.

Catherine dau. of ⚯ Rys ap Einion
Robin.   Vychan, to
                   Penwyn

Gwenhwyfar, f.h. wife   Lleiki, f.h. wife of
of Robt. Salusbury   Griffith ap Madoc
of Llanrwst.   Vychan, to Jarddwr.

(From a letter of the late Mr. Joseph Morris). This partially clears up the imperfect passage above, but not that part of it relating to Reignall ap Bleddyn.

* Madoc ap Rys ap David ap Rys Van ap Rys

and Jevan ap Griff' ap Madog ap Jerweth was wife to[1] Reginall ap
Bleddyn, and had by her issue Robin Vaughan ap David ap
Howell, who maried Angharad the daughter of Rys ap 'Gruff' ap
Rys ap Ednyfed Vaughan, and had no issue male,[2] but one daughter called Cattrin vch Robin Vaughan, who maried Rys ap Eingan Vaughan of Llanrwst, a gentleman of the house of Penwyn
in Nanconwy and Denbigh Land ;[3] who having noe issue male by
her, but daughters, the greatest parte of the possessions of that
house, which were now worth a thousand markes a yeare, came
to the Salisburies. For Robert Salisbury the elder, fourth sonne
of Tho. Salisbury of Lleweny, in the county of Denbigh, Esq.
maried Gwenhwyfar, the daughter of Rys ap Eingan and Cathe-
rin the daughter of Robin Vaughan ap David ap Howell. Rys

ap Edneved Vychan. (Robert Vaughan of Hengwrt, *Hengwrt MS.* 96, p. 853, quoting Griffith
Hiraethog.)

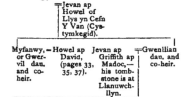

Other issue   a daughter – Howel Pickhill*
Hengwrt MS. 436 (quoting Gutyn Owen,) folio 41,
and folio 118, and *Hengwrt MS.* 96, pages 743, 853,
and 889.

*Jevan ap Howel Pickhill held lands in Holt,
30 Sept. 1397. (See 36th Report of Deputy Keeper
of Public Records, page 242.)

The following is the text of the passage as it
stands in the *Brogyntyn MS.* of The Gwydir
Family:—"In the Extent of North wales made
in the 26 of Edward the 3d you shall find that
Meredith ap Howell and others are the heires of
Gwely Griffri [David ap Howell his brother
maried verch Jenn (Jevan) ap Howell ap Meredith]
the daughter of Gwenllian, and Jevan ap Gruffith
ap Madoc ap Jerwerth, was wife to Reignall ap

Bleddyn (sic) and had by her issue Robin Vaughan
ap David ap Howell who married Angharad the
daughter of Rys ap Gruffith ap Rys ap Ednyfed
vaughan, and had noe issue male but one daughter called Cattrin vz Robin vaughan who married
Rys ap Eingan vaughan of llanrwst, a gentleman
of the house of Penwyn of Nanconwy and Den-
bighland who haveing no issue male by her but
daughters." It is stated in the *Brogyntyn MS.*
that the words bracketed were a note in the margin of the original MS.

[1] If the words "was wife to Reignall ap Bleddyn" were left out, the page would be sense, and
would agree with the pedigree.—W.

[2] Should not the word "and" in this line be
struck out ?—W.

[3] In all the printed copies of the *History of the
Gwydir Family*, and in all the manuscripts of it
which I have examined, the passage from the
words " David ap Howell " down to "Denbigh
Land" inclusive is very obscure. There can
be no doubt that here the original manuscript
has been carelessly written, or the transcripts inac-
curately made. In the Brogyntyn manuscript a line
is drawn round the words from " David ap Howell"
down to and including " Howel ap Meredith," and
in the margin occurs this note—" This is a note in
the margin." The late Mr. Joseph Morris, of Shrewsbury, in a pedigree which we insert at page 30,
attempts to clear up this difficulty, but not success-
fully, nor does Miss Llwyd, in a note at page 39

ap Eingan had one other daughter by her, called Lleify,[1] to whom he gave faire possessions ; but nothing comparable to the other, that was married to Gruff ap Madog Vaughan in Abergeley.[2]   All the inheritance of this Robin Vaughan ap David ap Howell, held after the Welsh tenure, within the lordship of Denbigh, was, by the custome of the countrey,[3] to descend to his heire male, and so descended to Jevan, the sonne of Rob't ap Meredith his cosen, as hereafter shall be laid downe in the life of the said Jevan. I have in my house the probate of the testament of Morvydd, the wife of Meredith ap Howell, as faire to behold as at the first day, bearing date anno 1416.   The probate of the will is dated at Krikieth, before one Rob't Swaython, official of the Archdeacon of Merioneth. (Meredith ap Howell had by her two sonnes, Rob't and Jevan, and a daugher, called Marsli,[4] married to Jenkin Conwey of Ruddlan, mother to Hen Sion acer[5] y Conwey, of whome all the Conweys, of Ruddlan and Bodriddan, and Lords of Prestatyn, are descended.   She was the first Welshwoman that was maried into that house, as John Conwey, Esq. my cosen, (now Lord thereof) told me.   John Tudur,[6] one of our Welsh heraulds, sayth, that there was a third brother, called Robin, whose daughter and heire Ithel Vaughan maried, and there. fore those descended from him doe quarter Owen Gwynedd's egletts.[7]

---

of her edition; but if the word " and," in line 7 of that page, and the words from " was wife " down to and including " Bleddyn" were struck out, the passage would be sense, and agree with all the pedigrees.—W.

[1] Leuci who married Owen ab Gryffydd.—L. Lleiki in *Brogyntyn MS.*

[2] Abergeley is a town in the western part of Denbighshire near the sea.—B.

[3] Whether by this custom is meant y[e] of gavel. kinde. (Note to the *Brogyntyn MS.*)

[4] According to the Great Book of Pedigrees, by the antiquary of Hengwrt, Robert Vaughan (*Hengwrt MSS.* 96), this Marsli was the grandmother of John Hen aer y Conwey.   In the 36th and 37th Reports of the Deputy Keeper of the *Public Records*, where there are such voluminous references to the landowners of Flintshire, there

appears no *Jenkin* Conwey, but Jenkin and John are the same name, and there appear to have been several in successive generations bearing the name of John ; so that it is very difficult to identify each as they occur in the pedigrees.   It is certain, however, that *Sion Hen aer y Conwey* died on the next Saturday after the feast of St. Mary the Virgin, 1487.

[5] There is no word in Dr. Davies's Dictionary nearer to this than *achor*, which he supposes to signify *little*.—B. Aer, i.e. the heir of Conwy.—L. The word is aer in the *Brogyntyn MS.*

[7] John Tudur of Wigfair, in Rhôs, Denbighshire, was John Conwy's domestic Bard.   He was a skilful Herald : and satirized the vices of the age very freely.—L. He died in 1602.

[6] These are mentioned in the Preface, to have been the arms of Owen Gwynedd.—B.

I find an obligacion, bearing date 20 July, 2° Edward IV.
wherein John ap Meredith standeth bound to Jevan ap Robert
Meredith to stand to the award of Gruff' ap Robin ap Gruff',
and Lewis ap Howell ap Llewelyn, arbitrators elect for the said
John ap Meredith, and Meredyth ap Rys, and Jevan ap Howell
ap Rys ap Eingan, arbitrators elect for the said Jevan ap Robert,
to parte certaine tenements betweene them in Evioneth : and in
case they could not agree, then was Howell ap Eingan ap Howell
Coetmore[1] named umpire.

Memorandum, That during Robert ap Mered' his time, the
inheritance descended to him and his brother was not parted after
the custome of the countrey, as being gavelkind ; but Jevan
being maried enjoyed both their houses, viz. Keven y vann[2] and
Keselgyfarch : and for that Jevan, then Constable of Criketh,
clave fast to the King, Owen Glyndwr burned them both to
cold ashes.[3]   Neither was the inheritance betwene their posterity
divided, untill such time as Jevan the sonne of this Robert was
maried and had many children, as may appeare by the indentures
of partition betweene Jevan the sonne of this Robert, and John
ap Meredith ap Jevan, grandchild to the other brother Jevan,
the one parte of which indentures I have. Those that made partition betweene them were these, Thomas ap Robin [4] of Kych-
willan, that maried Gwenhwyfar, and Jevan ap Meredith. This
Thomas ap Robin was after beheaded neare the castle of Conwey
by the Lord Herbert, for that he was a follower of the house of
Lancaster :[5] and his wife is reported to have carried away his head
in her apron. Some affirme Jevan ap Meredith to be the elder
brother, and soe doth all the race that are of him contend : my-

---

[1] Howell Coytmor, in consequence of his heroic
behaviour in the French wars, got new armorial
bearings, azure a chevron between three spears'
heads argt. embrued gules.—L.

[2] Now called Ystymcegid. This place passed by
the marriage of Catherine daughter of Robert Owen,
Esq., with Robert Wynne of Glynn, into that
family, and from them through the Owens of Porkington to the late Mrs. Ormsby Gore.

[3] A similar expression of *cold coals* is used afterwards in this History.—B.

[4] Thomas ab Robin assisted in conveying the
Earl of Richmond to France.—L.

[5] In 1466.

F

self, and those that are come of Robert, have this reason to think him to be the elder. Robert had issue Jevan, Jevan his brother had issue Meredith, Meredith had issue John, John being of man's estate had the tuition of his uncle Jevan ap Robert,[1] my ancestor, and yet Robin Vaughan ap David ap Howell's land in Denbigh land, being cozen to them both, descended to Jevan ap Robert, my ancestor, and not to John ap Meredith; which I hold for an invincible argument that Jevan is descended from the elder. Alsoe I have the King's Writte, directed to Robert Meredith, Meredith ap Jevan ap Meredith, and to the principall gentlemen of Evioneth, for the apprehension of Jevan ap Robin Herwr, a notable rebell outlaw, and others of his qualitie; which writt doth place Robert ap Meredith first before his nephew, which alsoe may fortifie the opinion of them who hold him to be the elder[2] brother to Jevan ap Meredith. The wordes of the writ doe follow, in hæc verba.[3]

[1] Observe yᵗ though Robin Vaⁿ his lands descended as is alledged to Evan ap Robert, yet this descent was not according to yᵉ comen law of England but according to the Welsh custom & laws then in effect, if soe then yᵉ Author's argument is but weak to conclude yᵗ Robert was yᵉ elder brother of Evan ap Mredith, for if yᵉ Welsh law was yᵗ yᵉ land should descend to yᵉ next heyre male of . . . . . . ᴇ blood, then though Evan and Robert ap Mredith by yᵉ Gavel . . . . ap Robert was next of kinne to Robin Vaug . . . . by one descent as is apparent by the Pedigrees in this booke and otherwise and soe as next of kinne, he also might be next heyre male to Robin Vaⁿ. (A note in the *Brogyntyn MS.*)

[2] This is of noe weight for it is everie dayes observac'on & experience yt not only in yᵉ Commissions of yᵉ peace &c. but alsoe in Acts of Parliam't younger brothers are named before their elder brothers & meane p'sons before Bronetts Kᵗˢ. and gents of ye best ranke and quality being of farre better estates and of better descents. (A note in the *Brogyntyn MS.*)

[3] HENRICUS Dei gratia Rex Angliæ & Franciæ & D'nus Hiberniæ, dilectis sibi Roberto ap Meredith, Meredith ap Jevan ap Meredith, Rys ap⁻ Tudur, Howell ap Madog ap Jevan, John ap Gronw,

& Howell ap Jevan Vaughn, Salutem.* Quia p' certo sumus informati, q'd Jevan ap Robin & alii diversi notorii utlegati & incogniti de die in diem vi & armis cum diversis felon' in comitiva sua, ut dicitur, faciunt ambulationes sup' diversos fidelium nostrorum infra comitatum n'rum de Carnarvon & diversos de eisd' fidelib' spoliaverunt, & male tractaverunt in destructionem & depaup'ationem ligeorum nostrorum manifestam, ac contra formam statutorum progenitorum nostrorum in hac p'te p'visorum. Assignavimus vos & unumquemq' vestrum conjunctim & divisim ad arrestandum & capiendum p'dict' Jevan ap Robin† & alios in comitiva sua existent' p' corpora ubicumq' inventi fuerint infra co'motum de Evioneth & eos salvos & securos usq' castrum n'rum de Carnarvon indilate duci faciatis constabulario n'ro ibid' liberandos & in eodem castro moraturos quousq' de eorum deliberatione aliter duxerim' ordinandum; & ideo vobis mandamus q'd circa p'missa diligenter intendatis & ea faciatis cum effectu sicut inde coram nobis respondere valueritis. Damus autem univ'sis & singulis fidelibus n'ris tenore p'sentium firmiter in mandatis quod vobis & cuilibet vestrum in omnib' quæ ad arrestationem & captionem p'dicti Jevani ap Robin & aliorum p'tinent intendentes sint, auxiliantes, fortificantes,

But howsoever it be, the gavelkind and custume of the country not yealding to the elder any prerogative or superiority more than to the younger, it is not a matter to be stood upon. Indeed Jevan ap Meredith maried in his youth Llenau[1] the daughter of Howell Sele ap Mereicke, of the house of Nannau in Merioneth-shire,[2] and begat by her Meredith ap Jevan ; whome in his youth he matched with Margaret the daughter of Einion ap Ithel of Rhiwedog[3] in Penllyn in the county of Merioneth Esq. of the tribe of Ririd flaidd, and Howell ap Jevan ap Meredith.

Quere. If any males descended of this Howell be living now? Owen Holland of Berw, and Rytherch ap Richard of Myfyrion in Anglesey are descended by females from him, as Richard Gruffith ap Hugh affirmith ? Alsoe it should be knowne how this land is gone from his posteritie.

This Einion ap Ithel was Esquire to John of Gaunt Duke of Lancaster, to whome for his service, as well in the time of warre

---

& p' omnia respondentes. In cujus rei testimonium has litteras nostras fieri fecimus patentes. T. meipso apud Carnarvon 28 die Augusti anno regni n'ri vicesimo.—B. [1442]

* [See p. 34, note 3] I suspect that "Howell ap Jevan Vaughan" above is the same person as occurs at page 35, the brother of Meredith ap Jevan ap Meredith. He is called in nearly all our Pedigrees "Howel Vychan ap Jevan" and was owner of Fronoleu, between Tremadoc and Pont Aberglaslyn, now (1878) the property of Lord Harlech.—W. †Quere, whether this Iefan ap Robin was not Iefan ap Robin bâch of Trerudd, in the parish of Towyn, whose pardon was procured and obtained by means of Siencin Vychan of Caethle, Squier of the body to H. 7.— L. This note occurs in the *Brogyntyn MS.*

[1] Lleiki, in edit. of 1770.

[2] *Nannau* is a very ancient family-seat about three miles N. of Dolgelley in Merionethshire. It stands perhaps on higher ground from the valley beneath, than any *Gentleman's* house in Great Britain. In Saxton's maps it is spelt *Nanna*, as it continues to be commonly pronounced. There are some traditional anecdotes about Howell Sele, or Selif, which is the same with Solomon, in the neighbourhood of Nanney. Howel Sele of Nanney stood out for Hen. IV. against Owen Glendower.— MS. Life, penes the Rev. Mr. Price, Librarian of

the Bodleian Library.—Howel was attacked by David Gam of Brecknock. Ibid.—B. Copper ba'lers, a spit, and two silver spoons were found at Nannau by the late William Vaughan, Esq.—L. Sir Walter Scott refers to the tradition of the death of Sele in *Marmion*, and gives as a note the Rev. G. Warrington's graphic ballad on the subject.

[3] Rhiwedog is also a very ancient family-seat in Merionethshire, about a mile S. E. from Bala. In Saxton's maps it is spelt Ruedok. The name is said to signify the *bloody-bank*, and by tradition a great battle was fought near this spot—B.

Llywarch Hên addresses his son Cynddelw in the words following in a poem still extant,

Cynddelw, cadw dithau y rhiw
Ar a ddel yma heddiw
Cudeb am un mab nid gwiw.

"Cynddelw, defend thou the steep pass of the hill against all that assault us to day, it is in vain to be fond of the only son which is remaining."

Llywarch Hên in the *field at Rhiwedog*, after he had lost all his children but Cynddelw.—E. As we feel sure Mr. Evans never spelt some of the words in this quotation from the "Lament," as given by Mr. Barrington, we have ventured to correct it.

as peace, he gave a pension of twenty markes per annum, issuing out of his manor of Halton:[1] The charter I have seene being in French, with the Duke's seale and armes, and it remaineth in the custody of John Owen of Ystymcegid,[2] Esq. the heire of Owen ap John ap Meredith.

Meredith ap Jevan[3] ap Meredith begat by the daughter of Ei-

[1] There are many Haltons in England. See Spelman's *Index Villaris*.

[2] Ystymcegid was formerly one of the seats of the Owens of Cleneney, and is in the parish of Dolbenmaen in Carnarvonshire. The mansion-house of this family is now at Porkinton in Shropshire; and it may be perhaps said that there is stronger proof of the same spot having been the capital mansion of the Owens for a longer time, than probably can be produced by any other family in Europe. The following order of Henry III., transcribed from Rymer, proves that Porkinton belonged to the Owens nearly 650 years ago. " Rex Lewelino Principi Sal. Sciatis quod—& Bledh filius *Oeni de Porkinton* venerunt ad fidem & servitium nostrum." See Rymer, vol. I. par. i. p. 79. A.D. 1218. and 2 Hen. III.—B.

[3] Kowydd Mredydd ap Ifan amrhedydd
o ystymkegid.

Pa wrol ion pur i wledd
prav blaenio pobl wynedd
Mredydd o fionydd faenawr
mab Ifan ail gogfran gawr
sy lowydd teg, sylwedd twr
syth gwŷnn ymlaen saith gannwr
a ffennaeth hoff i anian
fry a gae lwk efrog lan
ag er yn fab gwiwran fodd
hap ras orfod prysurfodd
i bob gwaith i bob gwthiaw
i bob aer drom bybyr draw
diwarth rym, i doe wrth raid
derwen y penaduriaid
ag nid oes walch glanfalch gledd
nenn fynys yn un fonedd
wyr fredydd irfrau ydiw
ap howel gwych hepil gwiw
gwaed dafydd ap gruffudd gryf
gwych gynnes ag iach gennyf
Ymwel ai lys aml i wledd
Mark hynod ymrig gwynedd
ystum wenn blas da yma i waith
Kegid nid hendy koegwaith

Neuadd fawr newydd furwen
uwch ael ffordd uchel i ffen
lle kair gida am llew kowrain
lliosog hir bob lles kain
arian a gwin urien ged
ag aur ai law'n egored
o ddwys bur dda syberwyd
a rhoi'n ddi ball, rhinwedd byd
Ifor yw fo fawr i fudd
a fraisg fynn frisg ifionydd
llew ag awch ffwg lliwgoch ffonn
llawen gorf, llyn ag arfonn
da reolwr dewr eilwaith
holl benllyn hyd ferwyn faith
ag yno rhwydd i gwna rhawg
evro a dail riwedawg
efo i wraig wenn fry a gaid
o bur iawn ryw barwniaid
Marged lawhyged yw hon
Mawr i chynyrch merch einion
wyr ithel lan, araith lwys
yw bwrdd gwin, beirdd a gynwys
ir liosog roi lusen .
eurgain hil wrgenau hen
da loer yw honn, deuliw 'r haf
dirion siriol, dwrn saraf
a da wyneb di anoeth
i fionydd, fu'r ddydd i doeth
at fredydd arf derydd dân
dur bafais dewr ab ifan
gwr y sydd mewn gras heddyw
glew union farn, glana'n fyw
eb yr un pur, barwn parch
ail kyfflyba kaiff loewbarch
draw hyd yn hynn, drud ion hael
dawn ofeg duw'n i afael
kafas air byd, bryd, breuder
a chlod gann weiniaid a chler
ag efo, pan ddel gofyn
aur naf teg, gwr, nowfed dyn
i gadw rhwysg y gwaed yrhawg
o brint ais bronn y tywyssawg
Mal Owain wych ymlaen nod
gwynedd hen gynnydd hynod

nion [1] ap Ithel, John ap Meredith, [2] (who maried and was at man's estate afore his grandfather's brother, Robert ap Meredith, my ancestor, ever maried;) and Robert ap Meredith, Abbot of Bardsey. This may be accounted for, as we have it by certaine tradition, that Robert was almost eighty years old before he ever married, and then in his dotage fancied and married Angarad the daughter of David ap Ll'yn ap David of Kefn-melgoed in the county of Cardigan, whose wife was the daughter of Rytherch ap Jevan Llwyd of that countrey; by her he had issue Jevan ap Robert and several daughters. From this Robert the Abbot [3] are descended my three *Pencenedle*, [4] because they are descended of church nobilitie, viz. Gruffith ap Richard of Madryn issa, Robert ap Richard [5] of Llocheiddor, and Owen ap John [6] ap Jevan ap Robert of Bron y foel, and Kefn Kyfanedd in Evioneth.

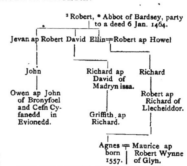

diwid fryd doed i fredudd
dalaith aur hen, dilyth rhudd
a gardys amlwg eurdeg
Rolant ail ar i lin teg
yrllynedd mowredd mirain
o bru'n y cwrt barwn kain
Harri goel ierll, hir i gledd
bumed ag ni bu omedd
Aroes iraidd res arian
ar i warr glew, eryr glân
rhoed eto er llwyddo lles
aur fynwer ar i fonwes
a graddied hwnn gwreiddiad hedd
baun y gwin yn benn gwynedd.
          I. llowdden ai kant.

Brogyntyn MS. No. 13. Cowydd 11.

Ievan Llawdden was an eminent poet of the vale of Llychwr in Caermarthenshire, who flourished from about A.D. 1430 to 1470. He spent a great part of his life as minister of the church of Machynlleth, but in his old age he retired to the place of his nativity, where he died.—*Cambrian Biography*, page 203.

[1] This Einion, after the death of Walter Lord Mauney (who was by patent sheriff of Merionethshire for life) succeeded him in that office, being in great favour with Henry the Fourth, in the beginning of whose reign he died.—E., citing a MS. of Mr. Robert Vaughan of Hengwrt.—B.

[2] John ap Meredith, party to a deed on the 12th Jan., 2 Rich. 3, (1485).

[3] Robert, * Abbot of Bardsey, party to a deed 6 Jan. 1464.

* "Yr hwn a briodod ar ol troi i ffyd." From a MS. in the handwriting of Simwnt Vychan, formerly in the possession of Mr. Vaughan of Shrewsbury.

Pedigree above from *Hengwrt MS.* 360, adding the name of "Griffith ap Richard" from Sir John Wynn.

[4] *Pencenedle* signifies *head of a family*.—B.

[5] Robert ap Richard was living in 1590.

[6] He is party to a deed at Brogyntyn of 19 Nov. 27 Eliz. (1584). In the *Brogyntyn MS.* the passage runs thus:—"Of Kefn Kyfanedd, in Evioneth," "Bronyfoel" being erased and "Kefn Kyfanedd" substituted for it, in a much more modern hand.

The case why this Robert ap Meredith was soe long unmaried may appeare partly by record, and partly by tradition; it is certaine, that as in the time of Henry the Fourth, Jevan ap Meredith had matched his sonne (as is aforesaid) to Einion [1] ap Ithele's daughter, who belonged to the house of Lancaster: soe he clave fast to that house in the time that Owen Glyndwr rebelled in Wales. Soe that in the time of that warre he and Meredith ap Hwlkyn Llwyd of Glynllifon, [2] had the charge of the town of Carnarvon, and an English captain was over the castle; in revenge whereof, Owen burned his two houses, Keven y van and Keselgyfarch in Evioneth. In the processe of continuance of this warre Jevan died at Carnarvon, and was brought by sea (for the passages by land were shut up by Owen's forces) to Penmorfa, [3] his parish church, to be buried.   Robert his brother, taking a clean contrary course, was out with Owen Glyndwr, as may be gathered by a pardon granted him in the ninth yeare of Henry the Fifth, [4] then Prince of Wales, which I have to shew, whereof the true copie ensueth. [5]

[1] Einion ab Ithel of Rhiwaedog covenanted with John Duke of Lancaster, to attend him for one year in his expedition to Cuienne, with one man at arms and one archer: this indenture is still extant at Rhiwaedog. " Cest endenture faite entre le tres haut & puissant jo: Duc de Cuyen & Lancestre d'un parte et Eignon ab Ithel dautre parte, &c., &c."—L.

[2] This place lies about Six miles S. of Carnarvon. —B.

[3] *Penmorva* signifies *at the end or head of the marsh.* This village is situated at the entrance of the Traethmawr sands, which divide Merioneth and Carnarvonshire.—B.

[4] 9th of Henry IV. Amongst the Records of the late Welsh Audit Office is a licence for him to build a mill upon his lands in the ville of Dynlley, dated 20 May 22 of King Henry—doubtless Henry the VI.—W.

[5] HENRICUS illustris Regis Angliæ & Franciæ primogenitus, Princeps Angliæ, Dux Aquitaniæ, Lancastriæ & Cornubiæ, & Comes Cestriæ, locum tenens metuendissimi d'ni n'ri regis & patris in p'tib' South Walliæ & North Walliæ o'ibus & singulis p'sentes literas n'ras inspecturis, Salutem. Sciatis quod nos authoritate & potestate nobis p' ipsum metuendissimum d'num n'rum regem & patrem com'- issis, ac etiam pro quadam fine nobis p' Rob'tum ap Meredith- ap Howell nuper rebellem dicti d'ni n'ri regis & patris in partib' Walliæ, ad opus ejusd' d'ni n'ri regis & patris soluta; recepimus & admisimus dictum Robertum ad gratiam p'dicti d'ni n'ri regis & patris, & ei pardonamus no'ie ejusd' d'ni regis & patris sectam pacis suæ quæ ad ipsum d'num n'rum regem & patrem p'tinet p' omnimodis p'ditionib', rebellionibus, incendiis, feloniis, adhæsio- nib', transgressionibus, misprisionib' & malefactis quibuscumq' p' p'dictum Robertum in p'tibus & marchiis Walliæ ante hæc tempora factis sive p'pe- tratis, unde indictatus, *vetatus*, rectatus, vel appel- latus existit, ac etiam utlegariis, si qua in ipsum his occasionib' fuerint p'mulgata, & firmam pacem p'dicti d'ni regis & patris inde concedimus, ac ea bona & catalla sua quæcumq' dicto d'ino n'ro regi & patri occasionibus premissis forisfacta no'ie & authoritate p'dictis concedimus p' 'psentes: ita tamen q'd stet rectus in curia p'dicti d'ni regis & patris &

Rys Goch[1] of Eryri, a bard of that time, made him a song, shewing what notable qualities he had, and yet durst not name him therein, for that as it seemeth he was an outlaw at that time when the song was made, but sheweth in the song his descent from Gruff' ap Conan[2], and that he was the hope of that stocke.

The Song that Rys Goch made to Robert ap Meredith beginneth thus :—

> HIR y bu Ruffudd ruddbar
> Waywdan fab Cynan ein car
> Ar goesgeirch hir gwayw ysgwyd
> Yn gorwedd Llew Flamgledd Llwyd
> A'i dalaith Llwybr goddaith Llaw
> Fynnodd gynt yn kelffeiniaw
> Tann oerfab bid tan arfoll
> Na chryn ddyn ni chrynodd oll

n'ra, si quis versus eum loqui voluerit de p'missis vel aliquo p'missorum ; in cujus rei testimonium has litteras n'ras fieri fecimus patentes. Dat' London xx die Septembris anno dicti metuendissimi n'ri regis & patris Henrici quarti post conquestum ix°. Irrotulatur ad sessionem tentam apud Carnarvon die Lunæ proximo post festum assumptionis beatæ Mariæ Virginis an'o principatus dn'i H. principis Walliæ, undecimo.—B.

* [See p. 38, note 5] This word properly signifies to *injoin* or *forbid;* it is corruptly used for *vetitus.* See du Cange, in articulo. Rectatus from *rectum* signifies prosecuted. –B.

[1] Rys Goch flourished about the year 1400. See Lluyd's *Arch.* He liv'd at Havod Garregog near Beddcelhert. The late heiress [Jane, daughter of Morys Wyn, married Zacheus Hughes, A. B. of Trefan. She died in 1764.—L.] of this place (who married Mr. Hughes of Trevan) was descended from him in a direct line.—E. "This Rys Goch o Erryrri descended paternally from Collwyn, one of the 15 tribes, he being the son of Davydd ab Iorwerth ab Iefan Llwyd ab Birid ab Carwed ab Gwyn ab Ednowen, &c., and lived upon his own lands at Havod-garegog in Nanmor, in the Parish of Bedd Gelert, and Mawris Williams Nanmor is his heyre, and enioieth that house and lands at this day, being

the sonne of William ab Hugh ab Lewys ab Morys Gethin, the sonne of Margaret the dau : and heyre of Rhys goch o Ryri. The sayde Mauris Williams of Nanmor is alsoe paternallye descended from Tydyr Hob y dili, (mentioned in a former page), and Gwerfil his wife the dau : of Howell ab Gronw by his wife the daughter of Iefan ab Howell ab Meredydd, as being the sonne of William ab Huw ab Lewys ab Morys Gethin ab Iefan ab Rhys ab Tydyr ab Hob y dili, whose right name was Robert ab Tudor ab Einghan ab Cynric ab Llowarch ab Heylin ab Tyfid ab Tangno ab Ysbrwyth ab Marchwystl ab Marchweithian. · Also the wife of Morys Gethin was Gweryl verch Gryffydd ab Davydd ab Iefan ab Mredydd ab Gronw ab Iefan ab Llowarch ab Davydd goch ab Davydd ab Gryffydd, who was the sonne of Llewelyn the great, and father of the last Prince Llewelyn ab Gryffydd. This Gryff. ab Ll'nn is mentioned in page 16 of this Book because these ancestors of mine are mentioned in this Book, and I copieng the same, I thought good to lay downe my descent from them in a different character, that it may appeare I am descended from many others mentioned in this Booke." The above note was transcribed out of an old MS. copy apparently of the time of Syr John Wynn, and now in the possession of Mrs. Dd. Jones, of Ruthyn.—L.

[2] *i.e.* Gruffith ap Conan Prince of Wales.—P.

Mae arno gaink llathrfaink Llv
Etifedd propr yn tyfv
Yn dwyn ystod fragod frig
Garw ben hydd gwr boneheddig
O bryd a Llafn hyfryd hedd
Ag ysgythr brwydr ag osgedd
O gampau anwydav naid
Frytanawl hen frytaniaid
Om Gofyn emyn ymwal
Dyn anosbarthys ei dal
Pwy i henw nim difenwir
Bedydd ar dv gwerydd dir
Y gwr a elwir yn gainc
Dylwyth-fawr ar dalaith-fainc
Alexander niferoedd
A mvr a phen mawr hoff oedd
Trystan ddoethran addeithryw
Dvlath avr ei dalaith yw
Bonedd ond odid benoeth
Y cwysg yn hen farwn coeth
Rhwng Hafren hoywddwr gloywglan
Llu gwrth a lli a garthan
Ni ad gwawd pechawd heb pwyll
O gandaith genfigendwyll
Son am y cymro os iach
Pwyllog doeth a fo pellach
Pe megid evrid araith
Cenav o neb Cynan iaith
Hir ddewr lan hardd eryr lid
Henw mygr o hwn y megid
Ymgroesed gwawd dafawd hen
Ymgais ni wn i amgen.

> Rys Goch or Eryri ai kant.

"Long did our friend [or kinsman] Gryfudd ap Conan, with his bloody spear, fiery lance, shield, and flaming sword, lye dormant like a greyheaded lion, whilst his country was all in a blaze by the hands of the enemy, who heaped together dry wood to kindle [welcome] the fire. Tremble not at the relation, he did not tremble. From him there grows a beautiful branch eminent in battle and master of the British Games.[1] If my *disordered head*[2] is asked the Christian name of him who is called a descendant of the great family on the throne of the province, it is Alexander, the beloved chief of the multitude with the golden crown of *Trystan the Wise*.[3] I prophecy, he will deserve the high title of a wise baron, and withstand an army between the famous water of the Severn and the clear stream of Garthen. Dark envy and detraction will not suffer his praise to be celebrated. If it is his desert, timid caution avaunt. If any strait, beautiful, and brave offspring of Cynan's lineage[4] was ever bred, this must be he. Beware the scoff of those who have before detracted; if I speak of him it must be to his honour."

Composed by Rees Goch (or Rhys the Red) of Eryri[5].

---

[1] These were the four and twenty games *(Y Pedair Camp ar Hugain)* which every British youth aspired to excel at. See Jones's *Musical and Poetical Relics*, 1794.

[2] This is a common expression in the Welsh language: when anything dangerous was spoken, they feigned madness.—This explanatory note was added by the learned gentleman who made the version of this poem.—B.

[3] Trystan was the son of a King of Cornwall, who was educated under Merlin, and became a most famous Knight errant of Arthur's Round Table.— See the adventures of this Knight, printed at Venice, 1552, 2 vol. 4to. From his having been instructed under such a tutor, and many of his atchievements having been performed in Cornwall, Wales, and Ireland, it is not extraordinary that he should be celebrated by the Welsh Bards. As for the epithet of *wise*, he merited this title probably from the instructions of Merlin, and the ancient Knight Errant was supposed commonly to have every other virtue, as well as that of valour. Hence *les neuf Preux* most

probably signifies the *nine Worthies*, though they are at the same time *Champions*. Thus a MS. in the French King's library is entitled, "Les nobles faits du tres *preux* & bon Chevalier Messire Tristan."— See the *Bibliotheque des Romans*, p. 252. Dean Percy hath a very fair MS. in old French, of the adventures of the same Knight amongst his curious and valuable collection: it is supposed to be of the 13th or 14th century, and is thus entitled, "La Grande Istoire de Monseigneur Tristan."

Vidi Paris, *Tristano* & piu di mille

Ombre Mostrommi, & nominoll' a dito

Ch'amor di nostra vite dipartille.

Dante, *Inferno*, c. 5.—B.

[4] The expression *iaith* in the original signifies properly *tongue*: thus *lingua Walensium* in some old records signifies the *Welsh nation*. For more ample satisfaction, however, on this head, the reader is referred to Hurd's learned and ingenious *Dialogues*, vol. ii. p, 17. where he instances the use of the word *laga*, which signifies both a law and a country.—B.

[5] This Bard is placed by Llwyd in his *Archæologia*

G

This is the most ancient song I can find extant which is addressed to any of my ancestors since the raigne of Edward the
First, who caused our bards all to be hanged by martial law[1] as
stirrers of the people to sedition, whose example being followed by
the governours of Wales, until Henry the Fourth his time, was
the utter destruction of that sort of men.[2] Sithence, this kind of
people were at some further libertie to sing and to keep pedegrees,
as in ancient time they were wont; since which we have some
light of antiquitie by their songes and writings.[3]   From the
reigne of Edward the First to Henry the Fourth, there is therefore noe certainty, or very little, of things done, other than
what is to be found in the Princes records, which now, [4] by tos-
singe the same from the Exchequer at Carnarvon to the Tower,

in the 15th century, about 1420. He stiles him
Rys Goch o Eryri, or *of the Snowdon mountains.*
It should seem that the inhabitants of this country
have long been much addicted to poetry, as a rock
is shewn by the shepherds, pretty near the summit,
under which, if two persons sleep on a midsummer's
eve, the one will wake out of his senses, and the other
a poet.—B.   A similar tradition is told of Cader Idris,
which Mrs. Hemans has recorded in a short poem.

[1] Edward the First hath also been accused of having destroyed all the ancient records and writings
in Scotland, after his conquest of that kingdom.
See this however very ably refuted by Sir David
Dalrymple, in his *Examination into the supposed
antiquity of the Regiam Majestatem.* Edinburgh,
1769, 4to.—B. And by William Owen in the preface
to the 1st vol. of *Archæology of Wales.*

[2] " This paragraph is full of mistakes. The poem
of Rhys Goch is stated to be the most ancient after
the time of Llewelyn; and yet I shall presently in-
troduce the reader to several " . . . .
"this order of men could not therefore have been
destroyed. The statement that Edward caused all
the bards to be hanged does not appear to be sup-
ported by a single contemporary historian; and it is
probable that the worthy Baronet was led to form
this conclusion from knowing that Edward had
issued an edict against the bards. Aware of this
fact and not having met with many poems belonging to that period, he ranged the two facts as cause
and effect. . . . . The facts that all the poets

were not hanged, that the poems are not so scarce
as he fancied, and that the law issued by Edward
ordains no such punishment, go very far to in-
validate this conclusion." . . . . . . "The
various laws passed by Edward I., Henry IV., Henry
VIII., and Elizabeth were passed not to injure the
orderly bards but to protect them from the excesses
of the wandering vagabonds who plundered the
people by their demands for ' Cymmortha.' . . . . .
Mr. Price has an acute discussion of this matter
(*Hanes Cymru*, pp. 753-4) in his history, and con-
cludes that if any were hanged, they must have
been the *Clerwyr.* I am not convinced that any
were executed; on the contrary, as the sole authority
bases his conclusion on a premiss known to be false,
we may safely conclude that there were none."
" There are other mis-statements in this paragraph.
The government of Edward was not as oppressive
as is assumed, and instead of being ' followed in
cruelty by the governors of Wales,' those very
governors were objects of regard." "I cannot
therefore trust either the logic or the history of the
patriotic Baronet as regards this statement which
Carte has repeated, upon which Warrington has
moralised, and which has inspired one of Gray's
finest odes."—Stephens's *Literature of the Kymry,*
pp. 343-5 Ed. 1849.

[3] See a commission, in the time of Q. Elizabeth,
to settle who were real bards or otherwise, prefixed
to Evans's *Specimens of Welsh Poetry.*—B.

[4] It should seem, from this, that these records

and to the offices in the Exchequer at London, as alsoe by ill keeping and ordering of late dayes, are become a chaos and confusion from a total neglect of method and order, as would be needful for him who would be ascertained of the truth of things done from time to time. I have, to my chardge done what I could, but for my travell have reaped little or nothing, as you see.[1]

You shall finde in the ministers accompt, in Henry the Fourth his time, Robert ap Meredith,[2] farmour of Dolbenman,[3] the King's weare of Aberglaslyn,[4] the mill of Dwyfor, and of other the King's thinges about his dwelling.

Jevan the sonne of Robert ap Meredith being a child of tender age, on the death of his father, was in the tuition of his cosen german's sonne, John ap Meredith ap Jevan, his next kinsman, who crosse maried him and his sister with Howell ap Rhys[5] ap Howell Vaughan of the house of Bron y foel in Evioneth. This family, in those dayes was of greate possessions and abilitie, and was then accounted the chief house descended from Collwyn, whereof there be many of great account in that countrie.

The widdow of Robert ap Meredith married Meredd' ap Rhys ap Jevan Llwyd of Vchaf without the consent of her allie John ap Meredith, and soe was faigne to flie the day she was married

---

were removed from Carnarvon near the time when the author wrote.—B.

[1] Mr. Stephens quotes the above paragraph in support of his argument against the "supposition that many Welsh MSS. were sent to the Tower of London for the use of the Cambrian Princes there imprisoned, and there destroyed by one Scolan."— *Lit. of the K.*, p. 351, Ed. 1849.

[2] Ievan the son of Robert ap Meredith held in Lease the ville of Navyskyn in Evioneth, at Michs. 12 Edw IV. *(Ministers' Accounts.)*

[3] Dolbenman is a village in Carnarvonshire, not far from Penmorva, the situation of which hath

been before described.—B.

[4] There is a famous salmon-leap at Aberglaslyn in Carnarvonshire, about a mile from the mouth of the river of that name, which divides Merionethshire from that county.—B. The fishery of Aberglaslyn, and some cottages near the bridge, were sold about the year 1800, by Wm. Wynne of Peniarth, Esq., my father, to T. P. Jones Parry, Esq., of Madryn. I know not how they got into the possession of my family.—W.

[5] Howell ap Rhys is witness, and his father, Rhys ap Howell Vaughan, party to a deed dated on the next Thursday after the festival of All Saints 20 Hen. VI. (2nd Nov., 1441).

to her husband's house before she dined, foure and twentie miles
off, and that of rough way.

At this time, or near about it, fell a dislike and variance betweene Will' Gruffith, Esq. Chamberlaine of North Wales, and
John ap Meredith, who at that time bare chief rule and credit
in the quarters where he dwelled: the one by reason of his au-
thoritie (which in those dayes was greate to them who held that
roqme [1]) expecting that all should reverence and obey him, the
other in regard of his descent kindred and abilitie in his countrey, acknowledgeing none but his Prince his superior.   Here-
hence grew the debate,

— nec Cæsar ferre majorem, [2]
Pompeiusve parem, ——

which continued long.   To John ap Meredith his kindred and
friends clave like burres, soe that then it began to be a pro-
verbe, or a phrase, to call the septe [3] and family of Owen Gwynedd, *Tylwyth Sion ap Meredith;* which Englished is "the kindred of John ap Meredith." [4]   This beginning of division how-

---

[1] *Roome* is here used in the same sense with
place or *office.* Thus we find in Rymer, vol. vi. p.
iv. p. 69. a grant of Q. Elizabeth, anno 1559, of the
office or *Rooms* of reading the Civile Lectures in the
university of Oxford. As also ibid, p. 154, anno
1559, of the *Rooms* or office of Chief Master of our
games, pastimes, and sports, ibid p. 155. See likewise afterwards a grant to Roger Askam of the
Room or office of Yeoman of our bears. Ibid.—B.

[2] This is printed as it stands in the MS., though
it may shew the author was not very accurate in his
Latin prosody.—B.

[3] This word is frequently applied by Spenser, and
Sir John Davis, to the Irish families and clans.—B.

[4] Kowydd moliant i Sion amrhedydd
o fionydd
O dair i rifo dewrion
Pumil o swm pwy mal sion
Syth gorff a fwriai seith gawr
Sion sy ar fodd sain sior fawr
Mae erioed fab Mredydd
y gair i hwn a gwayw rhydd
Aeth dra dig wrth dorri dydd
yw o fynwes y fionydd

ef a lifodd fal ifan
lafn dur fel afon ne dân
ffrolo wrth gyffroi alon
ffrwyth tywysowglwyth yw sion
O uchel waed o iach lan
Owain gwynedd neu gynan
fo ar gamp o fwrw gwyr
eb law dyn oblaid ynyr
onnen hir wyr einion hael
a saethodd megis ithael
gwnai dann fron bren gwydn yn frau
gwr a gwyneb gwrgenau
wyr farchudd arfau erchyll
I ddifa kaith fal oddf kyll
Mawr yw ar draed mor wyr dro
mwyar wasgwyn ym rosgo
deth fu saith o'r doethion
enwaf o saith un yw sion
Tai fal ysbytai Ifan
teg ywr llys to gwydr y llan
gwledd hu gadarn ef barnwn
mwy yw kost y makwy hwn
gweled gan deg i goler
gild Sion fal goleuad ser

ever bred in the posteritie of the two houses a conceit of dislike
which continued long after in the kindred, the one towards the
other, but with matches and continuance of time it is worne
out.

This John ap Meredith was cosen to Owen Tudur, and went
with a hundred gentlemen of North Wales his kinsmen to visit
the said Owen, being in trouble at Rwsg castle, called *Brynbyga*. [1]
In his returne being beset with enemies, favourers of the house
of Yorke, he made an oration to comfort his people, willing
them to remember at that time the support of the honour and
credit of their ancestors, and concluding, that it should never in
time to come be reported, that there was the place where a hundred North Wales gentlemen fled, but that the place should carry
the name and memory, that there a hundred North Wales gentlemen were slayne.   Because also• some of his kinsmen had
brought· with them all their sonnes, and some others had but one
sonne to succeed in their name and inheritance, (as Howell ap.

Ifor oedd ym i fardd wyf
yn wedig i nai ydwyf
mae arnaf chwant y mor nest
a gwyr Ieirll a gwayw orest
nid Kystal rhag Kofalon
i phwys o aur a ffais Sion
bron angel medd ai gweles
brigawn dur mal wybr gan des
ym ni chaid i ymwan chwyrn
gloch hwy o gylche heurn
tonau dur towyniad ia
toniau fal pen ty anna
trwst a wnan trowstau unud
teils dur oll fal tân y serud
Erchi yrwy fi oryw fan
wisg aur ffyrf ysgraff arian
ysgyrion neu hinon haf
y sydd fal o sau addaf
o wyr ond teg oryn twr
aroes hudol ar sawdiwr
mwy yw ao gwn a maen gan
ag a mil o gymalau
llafnau krymanau llyfnion
llwyth o ia ar frig llethr y fron
pils dur palis a drig
pysg ir pais gei o warwig

a thailiwr a wnaeth hoelion
aur ym hwys i rwymo hon
Kyfliw maes ydiw'r kofl mau
Kan kwyllion y kyn kwyllau
Kwyr oridens krair ydynt
Kawod o gnav coed ganwynt
Kad gamlan friwdan frwyd
Kenllysg ywch y park kwnllwyd
Kassel gadfan am danaf
i chau a gwagav a gaf
torchau galawnt a erchais
twr Sion i anturiaw sais
aed yngofal om kalon
os a fy mendith i Sion.
                    RHOBIN DDU ai kant.
Brogyntyn MS. 13.   Cowydd 19.

[1] In Sir John Price's description of Wales prefixed to Wynne's *History*, p. 20, Usk in South
Wales is said to be called likewise *Brynbyga*
Rwsg Castle therefore should perhaps be written
Yr Usg or *Wsg*, when it would signify the *Castle
upon the Usk*. As this place lies at such a distance
from Gwedir, and the inhabitants of the two
divisions of the Principality have so little connexion
with each other even to this day, such a mistake is
by no means improbable.—B.

Llewelyn ap Howell, and others,) he placed all these in the rearward, out of the fury of the fight, whilst all his sonnes were in the vanward, which himself led, where he was sore wounded in his face, whereof he was called Squier *y graith*[1] to his dying day: but GOD gave his enemies the overthrow, he opening the passage with his sword.

Queen Catherine, being a French woman borne, knew noe difference between the English and Welsh nation, untill her marriage being published, Owen Tudur's kindred and countrey were objected to disgrace him, as most vile and barbarous ; which made her desirous to see some of his kinsmen.   Whereupon he brought to her presence John ap Meredith and Howell ap Llewelyn ap Howell his neare cosens, men of goodly stature and personage, but wholey destitute of bringing up and nurture, for when the Queene had spoken to them in diverse languages, and they were not able to answer her, she said, *they were the goodliest dumbe creatures that ever she saw.*

This being not impertinent to the matter I treat of, and preserved by tradition, I thought fit to insert here.

John ap Meredith had by his wife five sonnes, viz. Morris,[2] Jevan, Robert, Owen, and Gruff', whereof Robert in his father's time was slayne without issue neare Ruthyn in the following manner. [The rest survived their father, and have many descended from them]:

The Thelwals of Ruthyn[3] being ancient gentlemen of that countrey, who came into it with the Lord Grey, on whome King Edward the First bestowed the countrey of Duffryn Clwyd,[4] were at contention with a septe or kindred of that countrey called the family of Gruff' Goch.   These being more in number than the Thelwals (although the Thelwals carried the whole offices of

---

[1] Squier y graith signifies Esquire with a scar.—B.

[2] Morris was Arbitrator in a dispute between Gruffith Lloyd ap Ellis and Gruffith ap Einion, and Hoel ap David ap Meredith, 16th July, 15 Hen. VII.

[3] Thelwal, who published the *Digest of Writs*, was of this family, and dates his work from his *poor house* near Ruthyn. It is about a mile from that town, on the road to *Mold* in Flintshire.—B.

[4] Or the *vale* of Clwyd, *Dyffryn* bearing that signification in Welsh.—B.

the countrey, under the Lord thereof, the Lord of Kent,[1] then treasurer of England) drave the Thelwals to take to the castle of Ruthyn for their defence, where they besieged them, untill the siedge was raysed by John ap Meredith, his sonnes, and kindred, to whome the Thelwals sent for ayde. In that exploite Robert the sonne of John ap Meredith[2] was slayne with an arrow in a wood, within the view of the castle of Ruthyn called *Coed marchan*[3] ; in revenge whereof many of the other side were slayne, both at that time and afterwards. Some affirme John ap Meredith to have beene at a field in Penyal[4] for Tho' Gruff, which field was fought betweene Tho' Gruff' ap Nicolas and Henry ap Gwillim, and the Earle of Pembroke's captaines, where Tho' Gruff' got the field, but received there his death's wound.

Henry VII. minding on his entry into England to clayme the crown against the tyrant Richard the Third, wrote this letter, which is still extant, to John ap Meredith in hæc verba :[5]

---

[1] The Earl of Kent was Treasurer of England in 1464 and 1465.

[2] Sciant p'sentes & futuri q'd Ego John ap M'ed ap Ieuan ap M'ed Armig' libten' dn'i Regis ville de Pennant Comot' de Evion' in Com' Caern' dedi concessi & hac p'senti Carta mea confirmaui Oweyn ap John ap M'ed' filio meo om'ia mesuagia terr' tenement' molend' toft' prat' pasc' pastur' mor' maresc' turbar' silu' bosc' subbosc' reddit' & s'uicia cu' suis p'tin' una cu' Nativis villanis & eor' sequel' que h'eo in villis de Penna't Berkyn' Trefdrevan Trefverthir & Treflys in p'dict' Comot' de Evion' in Com' Caern'. H'end & tenend omni'a p'dict' Mes' err' tenement' Molend' toft' prat' pasc' mor' maresc' turbar' silu' bosc' subbosc' reddit' & s'uicia cu' suis p'tin' vna cu' Nativis Villan' & eor' sequel' p'fato Oweyn ap John ap M'ed' filio meo & hered' suis de corpore suo int' ipm' Oweyn & Elenam filiam hugonis lewys legittime p'creat' De Capit'lib' dn'is feod' ill' p' s'vicia inde debit' & de iure consuet' imp'petuu'. Et ego v'o p'dict' Joh'n ap M'ed' & hered' mei omi'a p'dict' mesuagia terr' tenement' molend' toft' prat' pasc' pastur' mor' maresc' turbar' silu' bosc' subbosc' reddit' & s'uicia cu' suis p'tin' vna cu' Nat' villan' & eor' sequel' p'fat' Oweyn ap John ap M'ed' filio meo & hered' suis int' ipm' Oweyn & p'fat' Elenam filiam p'd'ci hugonis lewys legittime p'creat' cont' ome's gentes Warrantizabim' & im-

p'petuu' defendemus. In cuius rei testimoniu' huic p'senti Carte mee sigillum meu' apposui. hiis testib', William ap Gruff' ap Robyn, henrico Balfront, Res ap ll'e' ap hulkyn, Ken' ap d'd' ap Ithel, & Ric'o ffoxwist, & multis aliis. dat' apud Penna't duodecimo die Januarii Anno regni Regis Ric'i t'cii post conquestum Anglie Secundo. (L.S.) [From the original at Brogyntyn.]

[3] *Coed* in Welsh signifies a wood.—B.

[4] Pennal, the place where Tho' Gruff' ap Nicholas was wounded, is knowne by tradition ; and lieth in Wttra Bennal, in the parish of Towin, over against Llidiart y parke crache, and in the midst of the way ; being a little round pavement, and almost covered with grass.—This note was added by some person who had perused the MS. with attention.—B. Between the words " Pennal " and " the place " (in note) the word " for " is inserted in the *Brogyntyn MS.*

[5] Henry the Seventh, when he claimed the crown of England against Richard the Third, landed at Milford Haven, and marched from thence through South and North Wales into Leicestershire, where the battle of Bosworth was fought. He had probably been informed at Milford that John ap Meredith had considerable influence in N. Wales. [He might also know it from his family, as they were nearly related.]—P.

By the King.

Right trusty and well beloved, wee greete you well: and
whereas it is soe, that, through the helpe of Almighty God, the
assistance of our loveing and true subjects, and the greate confidence that wee have to the nobles and commons of this our principalitie of Wales, we be entred into the same, purposing by
the helpe above rehearsed, in all haste possible, to descend into
our realme of England, not only for the adoption of the crowne,
unto us of right appertaining, but alsoe for the oppression of the
odious tyrant Richard late Duke of Glocester, usurper of our
said right; and moreover to reduce as well our said realme of
England into its ancient estate, honour, and property, and pros-
peritie, as this our said' principalitie of Wales, and the people of
the same to their dear*est*[1] liberties, delivering them of such mise-
rable servitude as they have piteously long stood in. We desire
and pray you, and upon your allegiance strictly charge and command you, that immediately upon the sight hereof with all such
power, as ye may make, defencibly arrayed for the warre, ye
addresse you towards us, without any tarrying upon the way,
untill such time as ye be with us, wheresoever we shall be, to our
aide, for the effect above rehearsed, wherein ye shall cause us in
time to come to be your singular good Lord, and that ye faile
not hereof as ye will avoyd our grievous displeasure, and answere
it unto your perill.   Given under our signet at our,[2] &c.

To our trustie and well-beloved John ap Meredith ap Jevan
ap Meredith.[3]

Jevan ap Robert ap Meredith,[4] my ancestor, haveing, as afore
is remembred, crosse maried with the house of Bron y foel in

<hr>

[1] *erst*, liberties, in all the copies which I have examined.—E.

[2] The date and place from which this order issued are omitted in the MS.—B.

[3] "I have seen ye original of this letter and perused it at Gwedir 1690. H. Bangor." (From a note in the autograph of Bishop Humphreys, in a MS. of the "History of the Gwydir Family," at Wynnstay.)

[4] By the *Ministers' Accounts* for the year ending Michs. 12, Edw. IV., in the Augmentation Office, London, it is shewn that at that time Jevan ap Robert ap Meredith held in lease for a term of four years, the ville of "Navyskyn" in Evioneth, the present year being the first of the term.

TABLE No. III.

TABLE III.

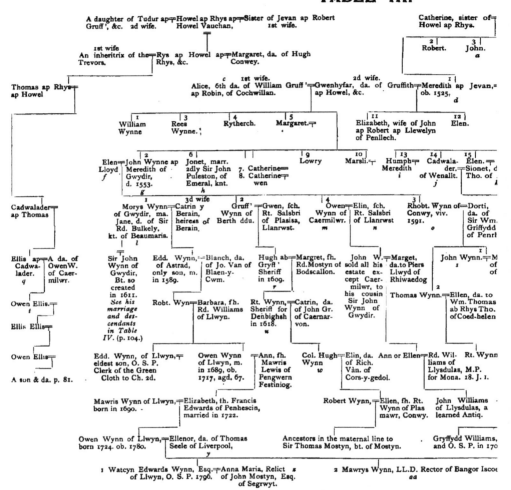

A daughter of Tudur ap⹀Howel ap Rhys ap⹀Sister of Jevan ap Robert
Gruff', &c. 2d wife.   Howel Vauchan,   1st wife.

Catherine, sister of⹀
Howel ap Rhys.

2 | 3 |
Robert. | John.
a

1st wife
An inheritrix of the⹀Rys ap Howel ap⹀Margaret, da. of Hugh
Trevors,   Rhys, &c.   Conwey.

Thomas ap Rhys⹀
ap Howel

c 1st wife.
Alice, 6th da. of William Gruff'⹀Gwenhyfar, da. of Gruffith⹀Meredith ap Jevan,⹀
ap Robin, of Cochwillan. ap Howel, &c. 2d wife. ob. 1525,
d

1 Meredith ap Jevan,

1 | 3 | 4 | 5 |
William | Rees | Rytherch. | Margaret.
Wynne | Wynne.

11 | 12 |
Elizabeth, wife of John | Elen.
ap Robert ap Llewelyn
of Penllech.

2 | 6 | | | 9 | 10 | 13 | 14 | 15 |
Elen⹀John Wynne ap | Jonet, marr. | | Lowry | Marsli. | Humph⹀ | Cadwala- | Elen. ⹀
Lloyd | Meredith of | 2dly Sir John | 7. Catherine⹀ | | | Meredith | der.⹀Sionet, d
f | Gwydir, | Puleston, of | 8. Catherine⹀ | | | i | of Wenallt. | Tho. of
d. 1553. | Emeral, knt. | wen | | | | | j | k
g | h

3d wife | 2 | 4 | 3 |
Morys Wynn⹀Catrin y | Gruff'⹀Gwen, fch. | Owen⹀Elin, fch. | Rhobt. Wynn of⹀Dorti,
of Gwydir, ma. | Berain, | Wynn of | Wynn of | Rt. Salsbri | Wynn of | Rt. Salsbri | Conwy, viv. | da. of
Jane, d. of Sir | heiress of | Berth ddu. | of Plasisa, | Caermilwr. | of Llanrwst | 1591. | Sir Wm.
Rd. Bulkely, | Berain. | | Llanrwst. | m | n | o | Griffydd
kt. of Beaumaris. | | | | | | of Penrh
l

Cadwalader⹀
ap Thomas

Sir John | Edd. Wynn,⹀Blanch, da. | Hugh ab⹀Margret, fh. | John W.⹀Marget, | John Wynn.⹀M
Wynn of | of Astrad, | of Jo. Van of | Gryff' | Rd.Mostyn of | sold all his | da.to Piers | s | of
Gwydir, | only son, m. | Blaen-y- | Sheriff | Bodscallon. | estate ex- | Llwyd of | of
Bt. so | in 1589. | Cwm. | in 1609. | | cept Caer- | Rhiwaedog
created | | | r | | milwr, to
in 1611. | | | | | his cousin
See his | Robt. Wyn⹀Barbara, fh. | Rt. Wynn,⹀Catrin, da. | Sir John | Thomas Wynn.⹀Ellen, da. to
marriage | Rd. Williams | Sheriff for | of John Gr. | Wynn of | Wm. Thomas
and des- | of Llwyn. | Denbighsh | of Caernar- | Gwydir. | ab Rhys Tho.
cendants | | in 1618. | von. | | of Coed-helen
in Table | | u
IV. (p. 104.)

Ellis ap⹀A da. of
Cadwa- | Owen W.
lader. | of Caer-
q | milwr.

Owen Ellis.⹀
t

Ellis Ellis⹀

Owen Ellis

A son & da. p. 81.

Edd. Wynn, of Llwyn,⹀ | Owen Wynn⹀Ann, fh. | Col. Hugh⹀Elin, da. | Ann or Ellen⹀Rd. Wil- | Rt. Wynn
eldest son, O. S. P. | of Llwyn, m. | Mawris | Wynn | of Rich. | liams of
Clerk of the Green | in 1689, ob. | Lewis of | w | Vàn. of | Llysdulas, M.P.
Cloth to Ch. 2d. | 1717, agd. 67. | Pengwern | | Cors-y-gedol. | for Mona. 18. J. 1.
| | Festiniog.

Mawris Wynn of Llwyn,⹀Elizabeth, th. Francis | Robert Wynn,⹀Ellien, fh. Rt. | John Williams
born in 1690. | Edwards of Penhescin, | Wynn of Plas | of Llysdulas, a
| married in 1722. | mawr, Conwy. | learned Antiq.

Owen Wynn of Llwyn,⹀Ellenor, da. of Thomas | Ancestors in the maternal line to | Gryffydd Williams,
born 1724. ob. 1780. | Seele of Liverpool. | Sir Thomas Mostyn, bt. of Mostyn. | and O. S. P. in 170
y

1 Watcyn Edwards Wynn, Esq.⹀Anna Maria, Relict   z
of Llwyn, O. S. P. 1796. of John Mostyn, Esq.
of Segrwyt.

2 Mawrys Wynn, LL.D. Rector of Bangor Iscoe
aa

p Robert.=Gwenhwyfar.
ble II.
28.)

uffith Vaughan= | Jevan= | A daughter.
| *b* |

rd wife | 4th wife *e* | 5th wife.
et, da. of=Jonet, da. of=A da. of Jevan
ap John | Jenkyn Gruffith | ap John ap Heilin.
edith. | Vaughan.

| 24 | 23 | 25 | 26
rt, Catha- | John | Hugh | Jevan.
est rine. | Coetmor=

17 | 18 | 19 | 20 | 21
Agnes, | Alice= | Gwen= | Mar-= | Eiliw.=
wife of | | | garet.
Robert
Salisbury

mas=Lowri, da. of John | William.=
Wynn, of Ben-
dd : narth.

la. | Cadwalader=Jane, da. | John Williams,=
van ab Thomas | of Thomas | a goldsmith in
gedol. of | Madryn, of | London. See
Wenallt. | Madryn. | page 87.

aghan=Winifred | Sir John Wil- | Sir Edmund | Sir Morris
d. of Da- | liams, Bt. of | Williams, bt. | Williams,
vy dd Lld | the Isle of | of Marnehall | Physician
of Trall- | Thanet. | Dorsetshire. | to the Qu.
wyn. | | created bart. | page 87.
| | in 1642.

et, da. of | Cadwalader Ván, A. M.=
ey Pry- | Rector of Osgarthorpe
, of | Leicestershire.
rian. | *x*

, da. Ellen, fh=Robert Wynn ab | Col. A son who sold
ger | Wynn of Berth ddu. | Glasfryn to William
es of | | Lloyd of Trallwyn
Coch |

s Estates

Ellenor=P. Ll. Fletcher, Esq. of Gwern Haelyd.

Notes to Table III.

a Party to a deed 30 June 22 Hen. 8.

b "Vaughan= | Jevan= | A daughter."

David Lloyd
Griffith Vy-
chan (see pp.
63 and 77).

c Before " 1st wife " put " reputed " and strike out " 6th "
after Alice.

d " 1525," aged about 65.

e " 4th wife " and " 5th wife " should be struck out, and
the down lines below the = connecting Margaret with Jonet,
and Jonet with Jevan (as well as the connecting mark itself)
should be a " wavy " line to show that the descent is not
legitimate.

f " Elen Lloyd," referee in an award in Nov. 1563, died
1572. A " Marwnad " on her death in *Hengwrt MS.* No. 309.

g " 1553 " should be 1559.

h " Puleston of Emeral, Knt." strike out " of Emeral." He
died in 1550.

i Living 4th June 1578.

j Living 5th Nov. 1563. Dead before 4th June 1578.

k Of the age of 60 years in Dec. 34 Eliz : as appears by
some depositions in a law suit upon the 29 of that month and
year.

l And ob : 10 Aug. 1580.

m Party to a deed on 1 Jan. 9 Eliz : died 1590.

n Died in 1578.

o He was living Nov. 30, 1598. There was another son,
Jevan " a doctor " dead in 1574.

p He appears to have had a brother named John, who in
the above-mentioned depositions is stated to have been of
the age of 30 upon 29 Dec., 30 Eliz.

q Ob : 1597.

r And another son, Ellis.—*Brogyntyn MS.*

s Died 14 Nov. 1637. He was brother-in-law to John Owen,
Bishop of St. Asaph.—*Piers Roberts's Journal*, in the possession of Mr. Breese.

t Ob : 1622.

u Died in Feb. 1640-1.

v He was of Glasfryn; died 5 Nov. 1664, and was buried at
Llanarmon, co. Carnarvon.

w Ode on his birth in *Hengwrt MS.* 362a p. 68.

x Probably graduated A.M. at Oxford 5 July 1671.

[TURN OVER.

y   1st wife

Ellenor daughter of = Owen Wynne = Susannah 2nd dr. of Broughton
Thomas Seele, Esq.,   of Llwyn born   Whitehall Esq. of Broughton.
of Liverpool, Mer-   1724 died 1780.   2nd wife—Relict of John Lloyd,
chant.   Esq. of Hafodunos.

Watkin Edwards—Anna Maria dr. of	Owen Molyneux	MauriceWynne Ll.D.	Ellenor marrd. to
Wynne, Esq., of Meyric Meredith,	Wynne, born 11	born 18 Dec. 1759,	P. Lloyd Fletcher,
Llwyn and Pen- Esq. of Pengwern	Aug. 1757, marrd. his	Rector of Bangor,	Esq. of Gwern-
gwern, born 13 April Co: Carn: relict	cousin, Miss Seel	Co. Flint, and Vicar	hayled Co: Flint,
1754, died s. p. 1796, of John Mostyn of	and died s.p.	of Wenlock, Co:	and left issue.
at Dover, bur. at Segrwyt, Esq.		Salop: possessor of	
Llanrhaiadr in Cein-		Pengwern, Co. Mer-	
merch, Co. Denbigh.		ioneth & Llwyn,	
		Co. Denbigh. Sup-	
		posed to be the last	
		descendant in the	
		male line of the	
		Wynn's of Gwydir *	
		(ob: s.p.) Dr. Wynne	
		died in 1835.	

* Since the above was written, I have seen reason to believe that I am wrong here. Dr. Rice Wynne
now (1840) of Shrewsbury is descended from the Wynne's of Maesmochnant, and through them
lineally from the house of Gwydir.—W.

z   *
      Relict   2 Owen Molyneux Wynne marrd.   "2 Mawrys"
                to his cousin Miss Seele and
                died s. p.
aa Maurice not "Mawrys." Living 1834, died s. p.

Md. the ixth day of July ao rra Ed. sexti qui't' that I John Wyn ap Md. of Gwedyr in the com of Caern.
Esquyer have received of Elys ap Mores Esquyer the sum of xxll sterlyng due vnto me the said John by the
sc'pte obligacorne of the said Elissa of the wiche sum of xxllI the said John do Knowledge my self to be
paid and the said Elissa his execut' & assign' thereof discharged & acquieted by this p'sent bill written
wt my one hande & subsc'bed wt my name the day & yere above written.

                                            P' me Joh'em Wyn ap M'ed.

(From the original at Brogyntyn.)

The children of Maurice Wynn, of Gwydir, are not all given in Tables III and IV. They are here all
inserted.

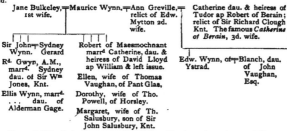

Jane Bulkeley,=Maurice Wynn.=Ann Greville,=	Catherine dau. & heiress of
1st wife.	relict of Edw.	Tudor ap Robert of Berain;
	Mytton 2d.	relict of Sir Richard Clough
	wife.	Knt. The famous *Catherine*
		of Berain, 3d. wife.

Sir John=Sydney	Robert of Maesmochnant		
Wynn. Gerard	marrd. Catherine, dau. &		
Rd. Gwyn, A.M.,	heiress of David Lloyd	Edw. Wynn, of=Blanch, dau.	Jane, wife of
marrd. Sydney	ap William & left issue.	Ystrad. of John	Simon Thel-
dau. of Sir Wm	Ellen, wife of Thomas	Vaughan,	wall of Plas
Jones, Knt.	Vaughan, of Pant Glas.	Esq.	y-ward, Esq.
Ellis Wynn, marrd.	Dorothy, wife of Tho.		
... dau. of	Powell, of Horsley.		
Alderman Gage.	Margaret, wife of Th.		
	Salusbury, son of Sir		
	John Salusbury, Knt.		

From *Hengwrt MS.* 96, in the autograph of Robert Vaughan, the antiquary of Hengwrt, page 862.

"Sep. 29, 1623. Mr. Ellis Winne (was buried) on the south side of the long aisle (in Westminster Abbey);
third son of Maurice Wynn of Gwydir, Esq., by his first wife, Jane, dau: of Sir Rich. Bulkeley, of Beaumaris, Knight. He was one of the clerks of the Petty Bag in the High Court of Chancery. His will dated
25 Sept., proved 16 Oct., 1623. His wife, dau: of Alderman Gage, survived him, but he evidently left no
issue." (*Westminster Abbey Records*, 8vo., London, 1876, p. 121).

Evioneth, had by his wife, called Catherine, three sonnes, Meredith, Robert,[1] and John. After her death he maried Gwenhwyfar, daughter of Madog Vaughan, of the house of Llwyn Dyrus,
descended of Sir Gruff' Lloyd, by whome he had two sonnes,
Gruff' Vaughan and Jevan, and a daughter. Jevan died[2] being
but one and thirtie yeares of age, of the plague, at Keselgyfarch
his house.

In the warrs betweene the houses of Yorke and Lancaster, he
(as all his) were Lancastrians, and he was one of the captaines
who laid waste the Duke of Yorke's estate in Denbigh land; in
revenge whereof, the King sent Will' Herbert, Earle of Penbroke,
in Edward the Fourth's time, who came with a greate army to
recover the Castle of Harddlech,[3] held by David ap Jevan ap
Einion for Jasper Earle of Penbroke, then beyond the seas. He
also wasted with fire and sword all Nanconway, and the whole
countrey lying betweene Conway and Dovi. He graunted at the
same time a protection or safe conduct to Jevan ap Robert ap
Meredith, and to his followers to come to parle with him, which
I have to shew, under his seale of armes in hæc verba.[4]

---

[1] Robert had issue Jevan who dyed without issue and Catherine married to Griffith ap Evan of Gwyddgwion descended of Gwaithvoed P. of Cardigan. (From a note to the *Brogyntyn MS.*—which note, I am certain,'is in the handwriting of Wm. Vaughan, of Caethley, Esq., who was buried at Towyn, 7th Sept., 1677. W.)

> John ap Ievan ap
> Robert ap Meredith
> of Treflys, Co :
> Carn ; demisee of
> Garth Morthin in
> Gest, in the same
> Co. ; by deed dated
> 30 June 22 Hen.
> viii. (1538)

| Ievan ap John | Owen John ap Ievan ap Robert devisee in the will of Ievan ap John, & his heir—living 7. Nov. 1607. | Griffith ap John, · sole executor to the above John |

[2] i. e. Jevan ap Robert, the father. See before.—P.

[3] When this town is thus spelt, it is said to signify *the beautiful or high rock* [see Llwyd's *Archæolog*. page 276. article *fair*] ; when in the common way [*Harlech*], it may be rendered *the town upon the rock*. As, unfortunately, the lately published Memoirs of Lord Cherbury are become excessively scarce, it may not perhaps be improper to insert from thence an anecdote relative to this siege of Harlech. The governor being summoned to surrender, sent an answer to the following effect : " That he had held out a castle in France " till all the old women in Wales talked of him ; " and that he would defend his Welsh castle till all " the old women in France should hear of it."—B.

[4] OMNIB', &c. fidelibus ad quos p'sens scriptum p'venerit, Guilielm' Comes Penbrochiæ Justic' d'ni regis in p'tibus suis North Walliæ, salutem. Sciatis nos dedisse & p' p'sentes concessisse Jevan ap Rob't de Com'oto Evioneth in Comitatu Carnarvon salvum & securum conductum intrandi, veniendi, ambu-

H

He was a most goodly man of personage, of greate stature,[1] (as may appeare by the Welsh songes made unto him), and most valiant withall.   Besides the turmoyles abroad, he sustayned deadly feud (as the northerne man termeth) at home in his *doore*,[2] a warre more dangerous than the other.

His sister, having been married to Howell ap Rys,[3] died within few years after the marriage, leaveing noe issue male : and Howell ap Rys maried Tudur ap Gruff'[4] ap Einion's daughter of Ardydwy, a courageous stirring woman, who never gave over to make de- bate betweene her husband and his next neighbour and brother- in-law, my ancestor.   Many bickerings passed betweene them, either makeing as many friends as he could, and many men were slayne, but commonly the losse fell on Howell ap Rys his side.

David ap Jenkin being a neare kinsman to Howell ap Rhys, and then an outlaw, a man of greate valour, came to aide his cosen against my ancestor, but prevailed not, though they came upon the suddaine on my ancestor's house, and whilst he was from home.   Thereupon (as we have it by credible tradition) David ap Jenkin wished his cosen to keepe friendship with his brother- in-law, for, said he, I will not come with thee to invade this man's house when he is at home, since I finde such hot resistance in his absence.

This woman[5] caused the parson of Llanwrothen[6] to be mur- thered, because he had fostered[7] to my ancestor; but GOD so

---

landi, expectandi, com'orandi ac salvo eund' & redeundi p' & infra Comitatum de Carnarvon & Merioneth p' se' bonis, & catallis, sine arestatione, molestatione, impechimento, damno, violentia, manucaptione, p'turbatione, seu gravamine aliquo tam ad sectam d'ni regis, quam ad sectam partis alterius, p'sonæ cujuscumq' a die confectionis p'sentium quosq' p' nos habuerit p'monitionem sex dierum. Datum sub sigillo nostro quarto die mensis Novembris anno regni regis Edwardi 4ti post Con- questum octavo.—B.

[1] i. e. Jevan ap Robert. See before.—P.

[2] A mode of expression which seems to explain itself.—B.

[3] Howel ap Rys, and Rys ap Howel Vychan, his father, are, the former witness, and the latter party, to an original deed at Brogyntyn, dated at Pen- nyved the next Thursday after the Festival of all Saints 20 Hen. VI (2 Nov. 1441).

[4] Ellis brother of this Tudur ap Griff. ap Enion died in 1489. (See a note in *Hengwrt MS.* No. 5.)

[5] The second wife of Howell ap Rhys, before mentioned.—P.

[6] Llanvrothen is a parish in Merionethshire, which borders upon Traethmawr sands.—B.

[7] The strong connexion and affection between the Foster-father and son seems to be now much dropped in Wales ; it continues however in full force

wrought that the murtherers, being three brethren, were all slayne afterwards by my ancestor, in revenge of the parson's unworthy death.

I have a number of obligations wherein Howell ap Rys standdeth bounden for the observation of the peace, and awards touching that controversie; but the plague taking away my ancestor, ended the strife betweene them, which was likely (if he had lived) to have ended with the death of one of them or both. Soe bloody and irefull were quarells in those dayes, and the revenge of the sword at such libertie, as almost nothing was punished by law, whatsoever happened.

The cause of this mortal hatred betweene them grew (as it is credibly reported) in this sorte: John ap Meredith and Howell ap Rys were ever highly at variance; my ancestor having had bringing up with his cosen John ap Meredith, affected him best, though allied nearly to the other, which was taken so heinously by Howell ap Rhys, that he converted the summe of his rancor upon his brother-in-law and next neighbour. This quarell, my ancestor being dead, never ended till, in assaulting the house of the said Howell, by the sonnes of John ap Meredith with their cosen Gruffith ap John ap Gronw (a gentleman of great account, who had been captaine, as is reported, of a company of launsiers in Aquitaine): the said Gruffith ap John ap Gronw was slayne, being shot into the beaver with an arrow out of the house, whereupon the said Howell was faigne to leave the country to avoyd the furie of the revengment of blood.

In the partition of the inheritance of Jevan ap Robert ap Meredith betweene his five sonnes, according to the custome of Wales; Henblas in Maethbrood and all the land in Llanrwst in Denbigh land descending unto him,[1] (as afore is mentioned as cosen and next heire to Robin Vaughan ap David[2] ap Howell ap

---

in the uncivilised parts of Ireland. In a letter from Mr. Wynne [penes P. Panton, Esq.] to his father, and dated in 1623, he desires that the widow of an Evan Thomas may be *bestowed* on his *foster-*

brother who worked in the garden at Gwedir.—B.

[1] " Descended unto him " in *Brogyntyn MS.*

[2] See pages 31, 34.

Gruff'), fell to be the parte and portion of Gruff' Vaughan, his sonne, who maried the daughter[1] of Gruff' ap Madog Vaughan, who was grandchild to Rees ap Einion Vaughan, viz., his daughter's daughter. You are to understand that though Robin Vaughan, did not defeat his cosen and next heire Jevan ap Robert ap Meredith of the land held in the Welsh tenure, yet minding the preferment of his daughter, as much as law would suffer him, he charged the land with a mortgage of £. 12. to Rys ap Einion Vaughan his sonne-in-lawe, which the said Rys ap Einion Vaughan did release to Gruff' ap Jevan ap Robert in parte of his mariage goods with his cosen, the daughter of Owen ap Gruff' ap Madog: the very release I have in my custody.[2]

GOD hath shewed such mercy to our kind, that ever since the time of Rodericke the sonne of Owen Gwynedd, Lord of Anglesey, our common ancestors, there lived in the commonwealth in eminent sorte one or other of our name, and many together at times. I have in my minde, in the perusal of the whole course of the history of our name and kindred, compared or likened GOD's worke, in that to a man striking fire into a tinder-box, by the beating of the flint upon the steele there are a number of sparkles of fire raysed, whereof but one or two takes fire, the rest vanishing away. As for example, in Einion ap Cariadog, Gruff' ap Cariadog, and Sir Will' Cariadog alias Willcocke[3] Cari-

---

[1] She is called soon after this the daughter of Owen ap Gruff' ap Madog. It is here given more contracted.—P.

[2] The copy thereof ensueth—Omnibus Christi fidelibus ad quos p'sens scriptum p'venerit Rhys ap Einion salutem in d'm'no sempiternam. Sciatis me p' fatum Rys remisisse duodecim libras de prido quæ habeo sup' terram Robin Vaughan ap d'd ap Howel cum p' tin' iacent' et existent' in Comoto de vvchdulas in dominio de denbigh Griffino ap Jevan ap Robert heredibus et assignatis suis, in p'petuum. Ita viz. quod nec ego p'dictus Rys nec hæredes mei, neq' executores mei neq' aliquis alius per nos pro nobis, seu nomine n'ro aliquid ius, statum, titulum, clameum, interesse, sive demand' de vel in p'dictis duodecim libris neque in p'dicta terra et tenement' cum p'tinent' vt p'dicitur iacentes et existentes in Comoto predicto, nec de vel in aliqua inde parcella de cœtero exigere clamare vel vindicare sive demandare poterimus, neq' poterit in futurum quovismodo, sed ab omni actione, iure, statu, titulo, clameo, interesse, et demand' inde in posterum exinde sumus penitus exclusi in p'petuum per presentes; In cuius rei testimoniu' huic presenti scripto meo sigillum meum apposui coram his testibus Mrydd' ap d'd ap Eingan d'd ap Mrydd' ap d'd llwyd, S' Robert Cowsyth cler'c', Tho: Cowseth et Ievan ap d'd ap ll'yn cum multis aliis. dat 20 die mensis Octobris anno regni regis Henrici septimo vndecimo.—(From the *Brogyntyn MS.*)

[3] Will Gôch, or red Will.—L.

adog, brethren ; Einion ap Cariadog as should seeme the elder brother, was Lord of Penychen, Penyberth, and Baladevlyn. His sonne, Tudur ap Einion, died without issue of his body, and his lands were begged by the Queene, King Edward the First his wife, as appeareth in this history.   Gruffith, the second brother, was Lord of Friwlwyd, Ystrad, and Eskibion ; he had issue David, which David had three sonnes ; David Chwith ap David, Meredith, and Howell ; which are mentioned before to have exchanged their estate at Denbigh with Henry Lacie, earle of Lincolne. Will' alias Wilcocke Craidog, the third brother, maried an inheretrix in Penbrokeshire, where his posteritie have remained ever since, haveing, from the house called Newton, named themselves Newton Craidog,[1] both in Pembrokeshire and Somersetshire.   Some of the Newtons claim their lineal descent from Howell ap Gronw, Lord of Ystradtowin, an'o D'ni 1100, descended from Rytherch ap Jestin, Prince of Wales. Note, among these three brethren, the posteritie of the one remaines; of the other two, the one is vanished, and the other gone out of the countrey.   Of Gruffith[2] his grand-children, only the posteritie of Howell are extant, who was before stated to be the youngest of the three sons of Gruffith Lord of Friwlwyd. Lastly, in Jevan ap Robert ap Meredith his children, which were five,[3] only the posteritie[4] of Meredith are extant, and of account. Whereupon comparing things past with things to come, I presage God's mercy to the kindred hereafter, as heretofore.

Now after this large digression, to returne to the course of this former historie, Rys ap Einion Vaughan haveing had warning, as aforesaid, that Henblas[5] should be redeemed, hasted to

---

[1] Some of the Newtons claime ther lineal descent from Howel ap Grono Lord of Ystrad A.D. 1100. desc: from Ryderch ap Jestin Prince of W . . . (A note to the *Brogyntyn MS.* in a more modern hand than the other notes.)

[2] I.e., Gruffith ap Cariadog's grand-children.—P.

[3] "Meredith his children, which were five."— *Brogyntyn MS.* has it "being five."

[4] This is not true, vide ye page 56 and ye note to ye Brogyntyn MS.—[In the hand of Wm. Vaughan, of Caethley, Esq.]

[5] *Henblas*, as well as Brynsullity, is afterwards described, as being in the Lordship of Denbigh. It is supposed that *Henblas* is the same with *Plashên*, or *The old mansion.*—B. It is curious that this word Hên is generally prefixed and the word Newydd

build Brynsullty, before that Michaelmas appointed. I have seene
an old man in my time called Jevan ap John ap David Vaughan,
at least of ninety years old; this man's mother served Rys ap
Eingan Vaughan at that time, and she was wont to reporte,
that corne[1] fayling them to *build*[2] the house, they reaped the
corne that grew in the *raine*[3] to serve that turne, as the corne in
the ridge was not readie.

The warrs of Lancaster and Yorke beginning this summer,
made Jevan ap Robert ap Meredith forgetfull of his promise to
redeeme the lands; for in the time of that civill warre land was
not ought worth, neither was it redeemed during his life. In
those warrs Jevan ap Robert ap Meredith, even in the sixth of
Edward the Fourth, with David ap Jenkin and other captaines
of the Lancastrian faction, wasted with fire and sword the suburbs
of the town of Denbigh. In revenge of this, Edward the Fourth
sent William Earl of Penbroke with a great army to waste the
mountaine countreys of Carnarvon and Merioneth shires, and
take the castle of Hardlech (held then by David ap Jevan[4] ap
Einion, for the two Earles Henry Earle of Richmond,[5] and Jasper
Earle of Pembroke) which Earle did execute his chardges to the
full, as witnesseth this Welsh rime.

> Hardlech a Dinbech pob dor
>   Yn Cunnev,
> Nanconway yn farwor
> Mil a phedwarcant mae Jor
> A thrugain ag wyth rhagor.[6]

added, thus: Hêngwrt,Cwrt newydd, Henbont, Pont
newydd, Hên gastell, Castell newydd, Hênblas.
Plas newydd, Hêndre, Trev newydd, &c. It is
certainly not the same place as Talhenbont or Plas
hên in Evionedd, which is near Criccieth.

[1] i. e. to be used as straw.—P.

[2] i. e. to thatch it.—B.

[3] *Rains*, in some parts of England is used for
furrow, or the lower part of the ridge. Wormius
derives the word *Rans* (from whence the Runic
character) from either *ryn*, a furrow; or *ryn*, a gutter

or channel. See lett. *Run*, p. 2. 1636, cited in the
New Translation of Mallet's Denmark, vol. I.
p. 363.—B.

[4] Iefan ab Einion of Cryniarth, in Llandrillo,
Edernion, and Maesyneuadd near Harddlech.—L.

[5] Edmund dyed A.D. 1456. (*Brogyntyn MS.*) So
in the original MS.; but "Edmund" is underlined
and "Henry" written above, in the more modern
hand referred to in a note on page 53.

[6] "At Harddlech and Denbigh every house was
in flames, and Nantconway in cinders; 1400 from our

In that expedition Jevan ap Robert lay one night at the house of Rhys ap Einion at Henblas, who was maried to his cosen Catherine daughter of Robin Vaughan; and setting forth very early before day unwittingly carried upon his finger the wrest [1] of his cosen's harpe, whereon (as it seemeth) he had played over night, as the manner was in those days, to bring himselfe asleepe. [2] This he returned by a messenger unto his cosen, with this message with all, that he came not into Denbigh land to take from his cosen as much as the wrest of her harpe : whereby it appeareth, that by his means neither her house, nor any of her goods were burnt, wasted, hurt or spoyled. Thus both her houses, Henblas and Brinsyllty, escaped the Earle Herberte's desolation, though the same consumed the whole burrough of Llanrwst, and all the vale of Conway besides, to *cold coals*, [3] whereof the print is yet extant, the very stones of the ruines of manie habitations, in and along my demaynes, carrying yet the colour of the fire. John ap Meredith being cosen german's sonne to Jevan ap Robert ap Meredith, notwithstanding he was soe much elder than he, (as the one was in man's estate, and the other but a youth), had the government of his uncle, [4] and of his *livings* [5] : during which time of his nonage, Robin Vaughan ap David ap Howell dying, as aforesaid, John ap Meredith came over with his uncle to Llanrwst and the Lordship of Denbigh, to

---

LORD, and sixty and eight more." This translation was made by a learned Divine, well known in the literary world for several publications. He was also so obliging as to add the following metrical version in the stile of Sternhold and Hopkins :

" In Harddlech and Dinbech ev'ry house
  Was basely set on fire,
But poor Nantconway suffer'd more,
  For there the flames burnt higher :
'Twas in the year of our LORD
  Fourteen hundred sixty-eight,
That these unhappy towns of Wales,
  Met with such wretchèd fate."—B.

[1] The wrest of a harp is the hollow iron with which the strings are tuned ; this term is still used by the harpsicord tuners for an instrument which they use for the same purpose.—B.

[2] The oldest Welsh tunes are very plaintive.—B. " Some of the Welsh Harpers, in the memory of man, were able to play from the character used for the old Welsh musical notes : and there are many such MS. notes in the Hengwrt Library." E. Evans.—L.

[3] i. e. To cinders : the author hath before used *cold ashes* in the same sense.—B.

[4] i. e. His Welch Uncle, for Jevan was cousin-german to John's father.—P.

[5] *Livings* hath before been used by the author in the same sense with *estate*.—B.

take possession of the inheritance lately befallen him, called the Henblas in Maethbrood, where Rys ap Einion Vaughan and Catherine daughter of Robin Vaughan then dwelled. Haveing surveyed the land, they gave Rys ap Einion Vaughan then warn-ing that he should avoyd the land at Michaelmas, for then he should have the twelve pounds mortgage-money payed him. On this he requested to be tenant, and was answered by Jevan ap Robert ap Meredith, that he should lie there at times himselfe, and therefore would not sett it. Whereupon Rys ap Einion Vaughan built Brynsullty house, upon parte of that land which Henry Lacie, Earle of Lincolne, Lord of Denbigh, exchanged with our ancestors, and which he had bought of some of our kinsmen that had the same by gavel-kind. Their name, how-ever, is forgotten, as is the pedegree of two other freeholders in Maethebrood besides, which held land in my time in that towne, lineallie from that grant and exchange. The one was called Rys ap Llewelyn ap David, whose posteritie doth yet inherite parte of this land : the other the wife of one Lancelott a weaver whose inheritance my uncle, Gruff' Wynne, [1] bought, being but a matter of three pounds a-yeare. Into soe little partes did the gavelkind by many descents chop our inheritance, being at first large. Conferring oft with the freeholders of the parish of Llanrwst, my neighbours, how they held their lands, and from what common ancestor they were descended; most of them are said to be descended lineallie from Ednyfed Vaughan, in the township of 'Tybrith and Garthgarmon. Inquireing also of them whence the freeholders of Maethebrood (Rys Llevelyn ap David, and Lancellott's wife) were descended, they said they were fo-reigners, and came from the castle of Denbigh, as though the castle of Denbigh did procreate men : which sheweth that the tradition is not yet forgotten, from whence they came. The most parte of that towne of Maethebrood is in our blood, blessed be GOD !

[1] Of Berth-ddu. See the pedigree at the end of the MS.—P. Berth-ddu is in Llanrwst parish.—B.

This Prosp.ᵒᶠ of Towⁿ Gwid's & yᵉ Hund.ᵈ of Uwchdulas
is humbly Dedicated to yᵉ Noble Lᵈ Marquis of Lynd

Robin Jachwr, the greatest antiquarie of our countrey, being at Gwedir with my grandfather, and going one day to a *chwarevfa gampav*,[1] where the countrey was assembled at a place called Gardd y felin in the parish of Llanrwst, asked whether he would command him any service thither.   Nothing, said my grandfather, having a nosegay in his hand by chance, but deliver this nosegay to the best gentleman thou seest in the company, upon the credit of thy skill; who delivered the same with protestation of his charge in the presence of all the company to Llyn ap David, Rys Llyn ap David's father.   I cannot however get his pedigree, nor Lancellot's wife's pedigree in any certaintie, to joyne them to ours: the reason is, that poverty soone forgets whence it be descended, for it is an ancient received saying, that there is noe poverty but is descended of nobilitie, nor noe nobilitie but is descended of beggerie.

> When Adam delv'd and Eve span,
> Who was then a gentleman?
> Then came the churle and gathered good,
> And thence arose the gentle blood.[2]

Yet a great temporall blessing it is, and a greate heart's ease to a man to find that he is well descended, and a great griefe it is for upstarts and gentlemen of the first head[3] to looke backe into their descents being base, in such sort, as I have known many such hate gentlemen in their hearts, for noe other cause, but that they were gentlemen.   The conditional promise by GOD to David was, "that if his children would keepe his laws, he should not want a man of his loynes to sit on his seat for evermore."   Whereby he had two things promised him, propagation of his seed, and eminence of continuance in the world.   The Recabites, for their

---

[1] *Chwarevfa gampau.* Country games or exercises.—B.

[2] "Now bething the, gentilman,
    How Adam dalf and Eve span."--

(From a MS. of the 15th century in the Brit. Mus. *Songs and Carols.*)

[3] A metaphor from deer, a young buck of the second year is called a buck of the first head.—P.

I

obedience to their father's commandment, not to drinke wine, have the like promise of God.[1]

During the time the Earle of Pembroke's armie lay in Snowdon, Jevan ap Robert was faigne to leave his owne house, and lodge at night in the rocke called Ogo filen, standing at Meillionen, in the parish of Beddcelert, and continued all the next day with the Lancastrians. His friends and followers skirted the armie, and skirmished with them in the strait and rough passage of Nantwhynen,[2] untill at last he was sent for by the Earle under his protection and received into grace, as may appeare by the Earle's deed under his hand and seale; the like he did not graunt to any in North Wales, as farre as I can heare.

The begining of the quarell and unkindness between Jevan ap Robert and Howell ap Rys ap Howell Vaughan grew in this sort. Jevan ap Robert, after his sister's death, upon some mislike, left the company of Howel ap Rys, and accompanied John ap Meredith his nephew, and his children, who were at continuall bate with Howell ap Rys. The fashion was, in those days, that the gentlemen and their retainers met commonly every day to shoote matches and masteries: there was noe gentleman of worth in the countrey, but had a wine cellar of his owne, which wine was sold to his profit; thither came his friends to meete him, and there spent the day in shooting, wrestling, throwing the sledge, and other actes of activitie, and drinkeing very moderately withall, not according to the *healthing*,[3] and gluttonous manner of our dayes.

Howell ap Rys ap Howell *did draw a draught*[4] upon Jevan ap Robert ap Meredith, and send a brother of his to lodge over night at Keselgyfarch, to understand which way Jevan ap Robert ap Meredith meant to goe the next day, who was determined to

---

[1] See Jeremiah, ch. xxxv.—B.

[2] *Nantwhynen* lies within a small distance of Bedd-celert. The rough and strait passage, mentioned by the author, soon opens into a most picturesque valley.—B.

[3] i. e. *Drinking of healths.*—B.

[4] This is a phrase frequently used by the author, and imports *drawing a plan* or *settling a scheme.*—B.

shoote a match with John ap Meredith's children at Llanvihangel
y Pennant, [1] not farre from John ap Meredith's house.   This
being understood, the spie, Howell ap Rees, his brother, slips
away the night to his brother, and lets him know where he
should lay for him. Now had Howell ap Rys provided a
butcher for the purpose, that should have murthered him ; for
he had direction by Howell to keepe himselfe free, and not to
undertake any of the company untill he saw them in a medley,
and every man fighting.   Then was his charge to come behinde
the tallest man in the company (for otherwise he knew him not,
being a stranger), and to knocke him down ; for Howell ap Rys
sayd; " Thou shalt soone discerne him from the rest by his stature,
and he will make way before him.   There is a foster-brother
of his, one Robin ap Inko, a little fellow, that useth to match
him behind : take heed of him ; for, be the encountre never
soe hot, his eye is ever on his foster-brother."   Jevan ap Robert, according as he was appointed, went that morning with
his ordinary company towards Llanvihangel to meete John ap
Meredith.   You are to understand, that in those dayes, and in
that wild worlde, every man stood upon his guard, and went
not abroad but in sort and soe armed, as if he went to the field to
encountre with his enemies.   Howell ap Rys ap Howell Vaughan's
sister being Jevan ap Robert's wife, went a mile, or thereabout,
with her husband and the company, talking with them, and soe
parted with them ;   and in her way homewards she met her
brother a horseback, with a great company of people armed, ride-
ing after her husband, as fast as they could.   On this she cried
out upon her brother, and desired him, for the love of GOD, not
to harme her husband, that meant him noe harme ; and withal
steps to his horse, meaning to have caught him by the bridle,

---

[1] This parish is very near to Beddcelert. All this part of the country is very mountainous,
and therefore very proper for ambuscades. —B.

which he seeing, turned his horse about.   She then caught the
horse by the tail, hanging upon him soe long, and crying upon
her brother, that, in the end, he drew out his short-sword, and
struck at her arme.   Which she perceiving, was faine to lett
slippe her hold, and running before him to a narrow passage,
whereby he must pass through a brooke, where there was a foot-
bridge near the ford; she then steps to the foot-bridge, and takes
away the *canllaw*,[1] or handstay of the bridge, and with the
same letts flie at her brother, and, if he had not avoyded the
blowe, she had strucke him down from his horse.

        —*Furor arma ministrat.*

Howell ap Rys and his company, within a while, overtooke Jevan
ap Robert and his followers, who turned head upon him though
greatlie overmatched.   The bickering grew very hott, and many
were knocked downe of either side.   In the end, when that
should be performed which they came for, the murthering butcher
haveing not strucke one stroake all day, but watching opportunity, and finding the company more scattered than at first
from Jevan ap Robert, thrust himselfe among Jevan ap Robert's
people behind, and, makeing a blow at him, was prevented by
Robin ap Inko his foster-brother, and knocked downe ; GOD
bringing upon his head the destruction that he meant for another:
which Howell ap Rys perceiving, cryed to his people, "Let us
away and be gone, for I had given chardge that Robin ap
Inko should have been better looked unto:" and soe that bickering brake with the hurt of many, and the death of that one
man.

It fortuned anon after, that the parson of Llanvrothen [2] tooke
a child of Jevan ap Robert's to foster, which sore grieved Howell

---

[1] Richards in his Dictionary, renders this word
accordingly a long rail used as a side fence to a
bridge. It also signifies a *counsellor* or *attorney*.
—B. From the literal meaning of the words *can*

" with," and *llaw* the " hand."

[2] Llanvrothen is a small village in Merionethshire
situated near Traethmawr sands.—B.

Vaughan's wife, her husband haveing then more land in that parish than Jevan ap Robert had; in revenge whereof she plotted the death of the said parson in this manner. She sent a woman to aske lodgeing of the parson, who used not to deny any. The woman being in bed, after midnight began to strike and to rave; whereupon the parson, thinking that she had been distracted, awakeing out of his sleepe, and wondering at soe suddaine a crie in the night, made towards her and his household also; then she said that he would have ravished her, and soe got out of doores, threatening revenge to the parson. This woman had her bretheren three notable rogues of the damn'd crew fit for any mischiefe, being followers of Howell ap Rys. In a morning. these bretheren watched the parson, as he went to looke to his cattle, in a place in that parish called Gogo yr Llechwin,[1] being now a tenement of mine, and there murthered him; and two of them fled to Chirkeland in Denbighshire,' to some of the Trevor's who were friends,[2] or of a kinne to Howell ap Rys, or his wife. It was the manner in those dayes, that the murtherer onely, and he that gave the death's wound should flye, which was called in Welsh a *llawrudd*, which is *a red hand*, because he had blouded his hand: the accessaries and abetters to the murtherers were never harkened after.

In those dayes, in Chirkeland and Oswaldstreland,[2] two sects or kindred contended for the soveraignty of the countrie, and were at continuall strife one with another: the Kyffins and Trevors. They had their alliance, partisans, and friends in all the countreys round thereabouts, to whome, as the manner of the time was, they sent such of their followers as committed murther or manslaughter, which were safely kept as very precious jewells; and they received the like from their friends   These

---

[1] Gogo y Llechwin, " the cave of the white rock", a cave of crystal spar on a farm called Hirynys, close to Llanvrothen, belongs to Castell Deudraeth estate.—(Ex inf. Edward Breese, Esq.)

[3] " Some of the Trevor's friends, or of a kinne to

Howell," in edition of 1770.

[2] Now called *Oswestry* : it adjoins to Chirkeland, where the Trevors continue still to be a very considerable family.—B.

kind of people were stowed in the day time in chambers in
theire houses, and in the night they went to the next wine-house
that belonged to the gentleman, or to his tenants houses not
farre off, to make merrie and to wench.   Meredith ap Howell ap
Moris, in those days chief and leader of the sect of the Kyffins,
was a kinne to Jevan ap Robert and in league with him, to
whome he sent to desire him, to draw him a draught to catch
those murtherers; who sent him word, that he should come privately into Chirkeland only accompanied but with six, and he
made noe doubt to deliver the murtherers into his hands.   As
Jevan ap Robert was in his way going thither, passing by Ty yn
Rhos,[1] being a winehouse, standing in Penrhyn Deydraeth,
Howell ap Rys ap Howell Vychan's wife, being in the house,
said to the people that were with her, Yonder goeth Jevan ap
Robert, *Hwyr y dial ef ei dadmaeth*, which is as much as to say,
" that he would not in haste be revenged of the wronge done to
his foster."   Being come to Chirkeland, he abode there many
dayes in secret and unseene, sleeping in the day, and watching all
night.   In the end, with the helpe of his friends, he caught the
two murtherers, whom he had no sooner in hand, but the crie
did rise, *The Trevors to their friends, and the Kyffins to their
leaders*.   To the latter of these cries Meredith ap Howell ap Moris
resorted, who told Jevan ap Robert that it was impossible for
him to carry them out of the country to any place to have judi-
ciall proceeding against them, by reason that the faction of the
Trevors would lay the way and narrow passages of the countrie;
and if they were brought to Chirke castle gate to receive the triall
of the countrie lawes, it was lawfull for the offender's friends,
whosoever they were, to bring £. 5. for every man for a fine to
the Lord, and to acquit them, soe it were not in cases of treason.

---

[1] *Ty yn Rhos*, signifies the house in the rough
common.—B. " Tynyrhos is a very old cottage at
Minffordd, which was a public house up to 40 years
ago. It is just under the Castell Deudraeth drive and
close to Plasnewydd. Before the embankment was
made, the ford across the Glaslyn was near it."
It is upon the Castell Deudraeth estate.—(From a
letter of Edw. Breese, Esq., dated 14 March, 1875.)

A damnable custome used in those dayes in the lordships marches, which was used alsoe in Mowddwy,[1] untill the new Ordinance of Wales, made in the seven and twentieth yeare of Henry VIII. Hereupon Jevan ap Robert ap Meredith commanded one of his men to strike off their heads, which the fellow doeing faintely the offender told him, that if he had his necke under his sword, he would make his sword take better edge than he did: soe resolute were they in those days, and in contempt of death; whereupon Jevan ap Robert in a rage stepping to them, strucke off their heads.

David Llwyd ap Gruffith Vychan, grandchild to Jevan ap Robert ap Meredith, in his youth waited upon Hugh, sonne to Mr. Robert ap Rys at Cambridge, elected Abbot of Conway by his father's procurement in his minoritie. He being at Plas Jolyn,[2] at the house of Mr. Robert ap Rys, an old woman that dwelt there in Rys ap Meredith's time, told him that she had seene his grandfather Jevan ap Robert at that house, both in goeing and comeing from his voyage into Chirkeland, and that he was the tallest and goodliest man that ever she had seene; for, sitting at the fire, upon the spûr,[3] the hinder parte of his head was to

[1] Mowddwy is by that statute of Henry the Eighth now annexed to Merionethshire, whereas it was before part of Montgomeryshire.—B.

[2] Plas Jolyn is in Denbighshire, not far from Gelar and Voelas: it now belongs to Mr. Myddelton of Chirk Castle.—B.

[3] Spûr (or, as it should seem to have been pronounced by the author, Spere) means that seat near a kitchen or hall fire, which generally goes by the name of a Settle. It is not very obvious however whence such a seat should have obtained the name of Spûr or Spere. I find the following passage in the Saxon Chronicle, which shews the word Spûr to be originally a term in that language "nomen Saxon:" which Bishop Gibson renders scabellum. See the Chron. A.D. 1070. It appears from the context to have been the stool on which an image of CHRIST was represented to place his foot on.—B. "Rhowch y spâr ar ben y spûr" is an adage, which seems to imply that the spûr was a kind of a shelf used as a Safe to place a dish of spare meat upon, until further secured. The Spûr jutted out of the palis or wooden wall behind the table in alto relievo. Few men standing could be as high as a Spûr. W. Davies.—L. At Glanhavon fawr in the big kitchen may be seen a unique fixture, part of an ancient piece of furniture, which is called the "y-sbùr." The word is pronounced nearly like "sbeere;" and is a pure Welsh word, denoting a short post or pillar to set things upon. It consists of a massive Gothic carved oak pillar, surmounted by three ornaments, and having attached thereto a piece of oak pannelling within a broad and deep-moulded frame. The lowest ornament on the pillar represents a wooden butter-box with its lid, similar to what is used by country people when going on a journey; the next figures, similar to each other, differing only in size, are wedge-shaped pieces cut from a sphere, representing

be seene over the spûr, which she never saw to any other man. She alsoe said that in his returne from Chirkeland she saw Lowry, daughter of Howell, Rys ap Meredith's wife, his kinswoman wash his eyes with white wine, being bloudshot by long watching.[1]

Jevan ap Robert in his returne from Chirkeland, riding home to his house by Gallt y Morfa-hir by moonshine (the tide in Traeth mawr[2] giveing him noe sooner passage) talking with his men carelesly, and out of danger, as he imagined, suddenly lighted an arrow shot amongst them from the hill side, which was then full of wood. On this they made a stand, and shot wholly all seven towards the place from whence the other arrow came, with one of which arrowes of theires shot soe at randome they killed him that shot at them, being the third brother of the murtherers; GOD revenged that wicked murther by the death of every one of the three bretheren. Howell ap Rys ap Howell Vaughan, and especially his wife, boyling in revenge, drew another draught against Jevan ap Robert, in this manner. Jevan ap Robert's mother was of the house of Kefnmelgoed, in the countie of Cardigan, whose mother was sister to Rytherch[3] ap Jevan Llwyd, then and yet the greatest family in that countie. It hath before been mentioned to have been customary in Chirkelande and other

---

perhaps the quarterings of a round (Dutch-like) cheese, attached to each other. Its present position is near the fire-place; originally it was near the door in the kitchen of the old house. Tradition states that its uses were to support a sideboard, whereon was placed provisions of bread-and-cheese, &c., for any poor and wayfaring man who might choose to call.—*Montgomeryshire Collections* of the Powysland Club, Vol. 6, p. 324. (1873.)

[1] It appears before that that Jevan had been obliged to watch for some time in Chirkland, sleeping in the day, and watching in the night, for the murtherers, &c.—P.

[2] Traeth mawr, signifies the *greater* tract of sand, to distinguish it from the *less*, which is the road from Penmorva in Carnarvonshire to Harlech in Merionethshire. These sands are not commonly passable till the tide hath ebbed nearly three hours.—B.

[3] In the 25th Report of the Keeper of the Public Records, Appendix No. 1, page 4, I find as follows:— "Cardigan S. Wales. 34 Hen. 9 (8) Jenkyn ap Ievan ap Lewes, of Abbermayt, in the Comote of Meveneth (lease to him of) one tenement with the appts. called Keven Melwyd in the parish of Llanvuncharon, in the Comote of Mevenith Cardigan. Late of the possessions of Rethor ap Ievan Lloid, gent., lately outlawed for murder."

There must be something wrong here, for Rytherch ap Jevan Lloyd could not then have been *lately* outlawed for murder; for in an original roll of *Ministers' Accounts* for the County of Cardigan in the Public Record Office, for the year ending at Michs. 22, Rich. II. I find as follows: [Roll of debts] "de anno xxi. Rich. II. Roth ap Jeun lloit nup' bedell' de_ Mabwynn de plur' debit' suis att'iat Jankyn ap Roth' & quatuor fratribus suis coher' suis eiusdem Roth' p' Will'm Asshe cam'ar Southwa'll" &c., &c.; so

parts of Wales, for the *Llawrudds*[1] to resort to the most power-full of the gentry, where they were kept very choisely. Howell ap Rys understanding that Jevan ap Robert and his people had occasion to goe to Carnarvon to the assises, thought it fit time by force to enter on his house; and to apprehend all those, and to bring them to Carnarvon to be hanged ; for there was none of them but was outlawed of murther. To this end, to strengthen himselfe in this purpose, he sent for his trustiest friends about him, and among the rest procured David ap Jenkin his cosen german, then a famous outlaw in the rocke of Carreg y Walch,[2] with his crew and followers to assist him, and suddenly came in a morning to the hall of Jevan ap Robert's house, where they were in outhouses about, and stowed in upper chambers in the lower end of the hall, and none to be seene. These people of Jevan ap Robert's that were in the hall raysed a crie, and betooke themselves to their weapons ; whereupon the outlawes awaked, and betooke themselves to their weapons, and bestirred themselves handsomely. It happened the same time that Jevan ap Robert's wife stood at the fire side, lookeing on her mayd boyling of worte to make metheglyn, which seething worte was bestowed liberally among the assailants, and did helpe the defen-dants to thrust backe them that were entered, and afterwards to defend the house. The house was assalted with all force, and pierced in diverse places, and was well defended by those that were within ; for having made diverse breaches, they durst not enter, a few resolute men being able to make a breach good against many. Upon this the crie of the countrie did rise, and Jevan

It would appear that Rytherch ap Jevan Lloyd was *then* dead. He appears to have owed £179 2s. 10d. then a very large sum.—W.

[1] The signification of the word *llawrudd* hath before been explained by the author, and to import a *red* or *bloody hand*, or the murderer who had given the blow.—B.

[2] There is a rock on the road from Shrewsbury to Oswestry, which is to this day called *Kynaston's*

Cave, from its having been a receptacle to some robbers of that name. - B. It is said to have been the fortress of " Cynast Wyllt," or " Humphrey Cynaston the wild," ancestor to Sir Edward Kynaston, Bart. of Hardwick, Salop. Tales of this Cynaston are as numerous as those of Robin Hood or Rob Roy : his [grand] mother was Antigony, [natural] dau : of Humffrey the great [or good] Duke of Gloucester.—L.

ap Robert's tenants and friends assembled in greate numbers, (whereof Robin ap Inko was captaine), who fought with the besiegers, and in the end with their arrows did drive the besiegers from the one side of the house, who continually assaulted the other side. After they had continued all that day and all that night in that manner, the next morning, seeing they could prevaile little to enter the house, they came to a parley with Robin ap Inko, who advised them to be gone in time: "For," said he, "as soon as the water of Traeth mawr will give leave, Jevan Krach, my master's kinsman, will be here with Ardydwy men, and then you shall be all slaine." (This Jevan Krach was a man of greate account in those dayes, in Ardydwy,[1] and dwelt at Kelli lydan, in the parish of Maentwrog.) Whereupon they gave over their enterprise, and returned to Bron y foel, to Howell ap Rys ap Howell Vaughan his house, where David ap Jenkin advised his cosen Howell ap Rys to take Jevan ap Robert for his brother-in-law, neighbour, and friend: "For," said he, "I will not be one with you to assault his house when he is at home, seeing I find such hot resistance in his absence."

Dayly bickerings, too long to be written, passed betweene soe neare and hateful neighbours. In the end the plague, which commonly followeth warre and desolation, after the Earle of Pembroke's expedition, tooke away Jevan ap Robert, at his house in Keselgyfarch in the flowere[2] of his age, being thirty-one years of age; whose death ended the strife of those houses; for his three eldest sonnes were sister's sonnes to Howell ap Rys ap Howell Vaughan.[3]

Enmitie did continue betweene Howell ap Rys ap Howell Vaughan, and the sonnes of John ap Meredith. After the death

---

[1] Ardudwy is a district in the north-western part of Merionethshire. Maentwrog is also a parish of the same county, not far distant from Ardudwy; it adjoins to Llanvrothen, the parson of which the author hath before had occasion to mention.—B. Maentwrog is in the commot of Ardydwy.

[2] "Flowers" in Miss Llwyd's edition. This would be a literal translation of the Welsh expression "yn mlodeu ei oes."

[3] He held in lease the ville of Bodewyn and fishing of Stymllyn at Michs. 12 Edw. IV. (*Ministers' Accounts* in Public Record Office.)

of Jevan ap Robert, Gruffith ap John ap Gronw, (cozen german
to John ap Meredith's sonnes of Gwynfryn,) who had long served
in France, and had charge there, comeing home to live in the
countrey, it happened that a servant of his comeing to fish in
Stymllyn,[1] his fish was taken away, and the fellow beaten by
Howell ap Rys his servants, and by his commandment. Gruffith
ap John ap Gronw tooke the matter in such dudgeon, that he
challenged Howell ap Rys to the field; which he refusing, and
assembling his cosens John ap Meredith's sonnes and his friends
together, assaulted Howell in his owne house, after the manner
he had seene in the French warres, and consumed with fire his
barnes and his out-houses. Whilst he was afterwards assaulting
the hall, which Howell ap Rys and many other people kept,
being a very strong house, he was shot out of a crevise of the
house, through the sight of his beaver, into the head, and slayne
out-right, being otherwise armed at all points.   Notwithstanding his death, the assault of the house was continued with great
vehemence, the doores fired with great burthens of straw; besides this, the smoake of the out-houses and barnes not farre
distant, annoyed greatly the defendants, soe that most of them lay
under boordes and benches upon the floore in the hall, the better
to avoyd the smoake. During this scene of confusion, onely the
old man Howell ap Rys never stooped, but stood valiantly in the
middest of the floore, armed with a *gleve*[2] in his hand, and called
unto them, and bid them " arise like men, for shame, for he
had knowne there as greate a smoake in that hall upon a Christ-
mas even." In the end seeing the house could noe longer defend them, being overlayed with a multitude, upon parley betweene them, Howell ap Rys was content to yeald himselfe
prisoner to Morris ap John ap Meredith, John ap Meredith's
eldest sonne, soe as he would sweare unto him to bring him safe j

[1] Stymllyn is on the Carnarvonshire coast, not far
from Crekeith. There is a pretty large pool of
water near the sea, where there are some good
trouts, and in which this fishing probably happened.—B.

[2] *Gleve* signifies a sword, from the French *Glaive*
—B. And probably the Welsh *Cleddyv*.

to Carnarvon castle, to abide the triall of the law, for the death
of Gruff' ap John ap Gronw, who was cosen german removed, to
the said Howell ap Rys and ot the very same house he was of.
Which Morris ap John ap Meredith undertakeing, did put a guard
about the said Howell. of his trustiest friends and servants, who
kept and defended him from the rage of the kindred, and especially of[1] Owen ap John ap Meredith his brother, who was very
eager against him. They passed by leisure thence, *like a camp*[2]
to Carnarvon; the whole countrie being assembled, Howell's
friends posted a horse-backe from one place or other by the way,
who brought word that he was come thither safe, for they were
in great fear lest he should be murthered, and that Morris ap
John ap Meredith could not be able to defend him, neither durst
any of Howell's friends be there for feare of the kindred. In the
end, being delivered by Morris ap John ap Meredith to the constable of Carnarvon-castle, and there kept safely in ward untill
the assises; it fell out by law, that the burning of Howell's houses
and assaulting him in his owne house, was a more haynous offence
in Morris ap John ap Meredith and the rest, than the death of
Gruff' ap John ap Gronw in Howell ap Rys, who did it in his
owne defence; whereupon Morris ap John ap Meredith, with
thirty-five 'more, were indicted of felonie, as appeareth by the
copie of the indictment, which I had from the records.

Howell, delivered out of prison, never durst come to his owne
house in Evioneth, but came to Penmachno,[3] to his mother's
kindred, Rys Gethin's[4] sonnes, and there died. It is a note worthy
observation that the house by little and little decayed ever since,
neither hath any of his posterity beene buried in his owne sepul-
chre, being four descents besides himselfe.

Rys ap Howell ap Rys his sonne, cosen german to my greate

---

[1] "From." *Ruthyn* MS.—L.

[2] i.e. Like an army, which makes regular en-
campments during their march.—B.

[3] Penmachno is a small village in Carnarvonshire,
on the road between Llanrwst and Festiniog.—B.

[4] Rhys Gethin, a great warrior, sided with Owain
Glyndwr.—L.

grandfather Meredith ap Jevan ap Robert, maried to his first wife, an inheretrix of the Trevors, by whome he had greate possessions in Hopesland.[1] He afterwards, by the procurement of my great-grandfather, maried Margaret, daughter to Hugh Conwey, the elder, Reinalt ap Meiricke's widdow, his next neighbour in Gwedir, and was overseer of his workes when he built Gwedir-house, as William David ap Ellis Eytyn[2] his cosen, who lived with him in those dayes, told me. He was buried on the right side in the chancel in Llanrwst; and was taken up at the burying of Cadwalader ap Robert Wynne of Havod y maidd,[3] as my uncle Owen Wynne guessed by the greatness of the same.

Thomas ap Rys ap Howell sold all his mother's lands and *living* in Hopesland, and a great part of his owne, and was buried in Hopesdale.

Cadwalader ap Thomas, his son and heire, lying at Chester, died there.

Ellis ap Cadwalader,[4] (who had maried my cosen german,[5] my uncle Owen Wynne's daughter), my kind cosen and friend, a man endued with many good parts, being sicke of an impostume, went to one Dr. Davies,[6] neare Brecknock, and there died.[7] This man's name I am bound to make an honourable mention of, for diverse kindnesses he shewed unto me, and especially for the wise advice and counsell he was wont to give me. Among many, one especially is by me and my posterity to be remembered, which I doe thinke worthy to be recorded in writeing. Unkindness and variance befalling betweene myselfe and my uncle Owen Wynne being neighbours, for wayes crosse my ground for the carrying of

---

[1] Hopesland is a part of Flintshire, situated in the hundred of Rhew.—B.

[2] Dd. ab Elis Eytyn of Watstay, now called Wynn-stay.—L.

[3] Havod y maidd is a farm in Denbighshire, not far from Caerydrydion, it signifies the *whey* farm.—B.

[4] Amongst the records at Brogyntyn' is a letter from the great Lord Burleigh, addressed to Mr.

Wm. Maurice of Clenenney (afterwards Sir William Maurice), and this Ellis ap Cadwalader, on 19th July, 1586.

[5] She died in 1638.

[6] Evan Evans told me that the Dr. Davies here mentioned was no other than the famous Sion Dafydd Rhys. J. Ll. See page vi.—L.

[7] In 1597. His will at Doctors' Commons.

his hay from the King's meadow in Trefriw to his house at Caermelwr, I grew to a great heat, and said that he should not passe
that way without the losse of men's lives. Whereupon, he being
present, and wishing well unto us both, reproved me sharpely,
wishing me to follow the course of my ancestors, who with wis-
dome, unanimity, and temperance, from time to time, had raised
their fortunes, assureing me his ancestors might be an example
unto me of the contrary, who with headiness and rashness did
diminish and impaire theire estates from time to time. Which
counsel of his tooke deepe roote in me ever after, and, to my
great good, I bridled my choller, whereunto I was much subject.

Owen Ellis, the sonne of Ellis Cadwalader, died by a fall from
his horse goeing home from Crikeith in the night, haveing beene
there all the day drinking.[1]

Ellis Ellis, his sonne, fell mad, and continued soe a long time,
and at length *in that case*[2] died.[3]

Owen Ellis, his sonne, being a young man, newly maried,
going home in the night betweene Nanhoren and Vaerdre, in
Llûn,[4] where his wife lived, haveing by her one daughter, and
leaveing her greate with child, (which after proved to be a sonne),
by a fall from his horse, upon the way, died.

These three were buried in their own sepulchres in the church
of St. Katherine's in Crikeith, after this booke was by the author
written.[5]

It may be a question here, and a doubt to the reader, wherefore

---

[1] In 1622.

[2] This is a singular method of expressing himself,
which the author frequently uses.—B.

[3] In 1631.

[4] Llûn is the S. Western peninsula of Carnarvonshire.—B.

[5] In the *Brogyntyn MS.* a line is drawn round the
four paragraphs commencing "Owen Ellis," and
ending, "by the author written." These Ellises
were of Ystymllyn. The old house there, still remains as a farm-house, but externally is much
modernized. The hall, however, with the exception
of the windows, remains much as it was. It has a
very good roof, with very solid chamfered beam,
and chamfered rafters. Upon the chimney-piece
are, carved in oak, the arms of Collwyn ap Tangno,
and Prince Owen Gwynedd. On the west wall
hangs an heraldic painting; quarterly, the bearing
of Collwyn ap Tangno, and Montague. There are
some old portraits upon the walls.—W. (1872.)

the land of Robert Vaughan ap David ap Howell should descend to
Jevan ap Robert ap Meredith, his cosen and next heire, he
haveing a daughter and heire of his owne body lawfully begot-
ten? To answere this question you are to understand that Henry
Lacie, Earle of Lincolne, upon the conquest of Wales, haveing
received of Edward the First his gift the countries of Ros and
Royoniog; now Denbigh land, and planted the same with diverse Englishmen, who held their lands, as well as their posteritie, by the English tenure; the rest of the Welshmen, loaded
with many bad customes, held their lands in the Welsh tenure.
One condition thereof was, that the inheritance should not descend to daughters, but should goe to the heire male of the house,
if there were any[1] such within *their*[2] degrees to the dead man, and
if not, that it should escheate to the Lord of the soyle; yet in respect of the possibilitie of issue male, which the owner of the
land might have while he was alive, the custome of the countrie
did permit him to mortgage the land to serve his need, without
the Lord's leave. You see hereby that Robin Vaughan did what
he could, according to the custome of the countrie, towards the
preferment of his daughter,[3] and the reason why Jevan ap
Meredith his next kinsman and heire, had the lands. Which
proveth alsoe that Robert ap Meredith was eldest brother to Jevan
ap Meredith, John ap Meredith's grand father, which his
posteritie greatly gainsaid;[4] for if Jevan ap Meredith had been

[1] It is uncertain in the *Brogyntyn MS.* whether this is ane (one) or any, the MS. being mended here.

[2] *Three*, perhaps.—B. " Three " in *Bala MS.*—L. Also in *Brogyntyn* and *Hengwrt MSS.*

[3] But q. why should not these lands descend to them both according to yᵉ custom of gavelkinde: and whether this is not a weake argument, &c.:° v'e Cooke Litt : 140. Sect. 210. Soe it is more pro-bable yᵗ Joⁿ ap Mredith gave this share or Pᵗ of these . . . . ds to ye other . . . . Robert in regard of the before . . . . being this happened before yᵉ new ordinance (as is evident by this booke) or

that John ap Mredith had an allowance of other lands in Evioneth where he had a far greater estate then Evan ap Robt. had; as is conceived sed inde q.—(From the words " or that " to " q. " appears in a different hand trom the rest of the note, but I am by no means sure that it was not written by the same person.—W.)

° So far of this note to the *Brogyntyn MS.* seems to be in the autograph of William Vaughan, Esq. if not the whole of it, down to the words "or that."—W.

[4] This is a repetition of what hath been mentioned before.—B.

elder brother, then John ap Meredith should have inherited this land, and not Jevan ap Robert his father's cosen.

Meredith, sonne to Jevan ap Robert[1] his eldest sonne, in the time of his father, was taken to nurse by an honest freeholder in the hundred of Yscorum Isgurvai,[2] who was owner of[3] the Creigiaw[4] in Llanvaire, and the best man in the parish, and haveing noe children of his owne, gave his inheritance[5] to his fosterchild.[6] Creige[7] standeth some sixteen miles from Keselgyfarch, whereby it may appeare how desirous men were in those dayes to have a patron that could defend them from wrong, though they sought him never soe far off. Creige standeth betweene Carnarvon and Bangor, two miles off from Carnarvon. In those days Carnarvon flourished as well by trade of merchandise as alsoe for that the King's exchequer, chauncery, and common law courts for all North Wales were there continually residing, whilst the way to London and the marches was little frequented. By this, civility and learning flourished in that towne, soe as they were called, *the lawyers of Carnarvon, the merchands of Beawmares, and the gentlemen of Conway.* I heard diverse of judgement, and learned in the lawes, to report that the records of the King's Courtes, kept in Carnarvon in those dayes, were as orderly and formally kept as those in Westminster. Thither did his foster father send my greate grandfather to school, where he learned the English tongue, to read, to write, and to understand Latine, a matter of great moment in those dayes. For his other brethren loseing their father young, and nursed in Evioneth, neare their father's house, wanted all this; soe as to the honest man, his

---

[1] "Jevan ap Robert, his eldest sonne." In the *Brogyntyn MS.* there is a comma after Robert.

[2] In Carnarvonshire.—B. In the *Brogyntyn MS,* "Isgurvai" is above the line in the more modern hand previously referred to.

[3] Evan had more lands in Evioneth: vid: postscript—note to the *Brogyntyn MS.* by the said Wm. Vaughan.

[4] Creige in edition of 1770, and in *Brogyntyn MS.*

[5] Q. how he could by the lawes of Wales either give or sell his lands (a note in the *Brogyntyn MS.*)

[6] This should seeme to be after the new ordinance, otherwise it could not be soe granted. q. contrary to the said first recited custome. . . This guift was before ye new ordinance as may appere. (A note in the *Brogyntyn MS.,* all of it in the autograph of the said Wm. Vaughan.)

[7] Crfig, in Llanfair parish.—L.

THE EAST VIEW OF DOLWYDDELAN CASTLE, IN THE COUNTY OF CAERNARVON.

foster and second father, (for he gave him with breeding alsoe his inheritance) may ꙮbe attributed his good fortune (GOD's providence always excepted) which sometimes worketh by secondary meanes, whereof this man was the instrument. Haveing lived there till the age of twenty yeares, or thereabouts, his foster-father being dead, he fell in liking with a young woman in that towne, who was daughter-in-law to one Spicer, the reputed daughter of William Gruffith ap Robin, sheriffe of the county of Carnarvon. This Spicer was a landed man of £50 per annum, which descended to him from his ancestors, yet had an office in the Ex. chequer,[1] and dealt with trade of merchandise alsoe, that he became a great and wealthy man. His sonne, John Spicer,[2] was a justice of the peace in the first commissions after the new ordinance of Wales, and was brother by the mother to Alice[3] William, the wife of Meredith ap Jevan ap Robert. Their mother is said to be of the Bangors, whome I have knowne often to have claymed kindred of me by that woman. At Creig he began the worlde with his wife, and begate there by her two daughters, Jonett, the first, maried to Edmund Griffith, and afterwards to Sir John Puleston; and another called Catherine, maried to Rowland Gruffith of Plas Newydd.[4] After this, finding he was likely to have more children, and that the place would prove narrow and straight for him, he was minded to have returned to his inheritance in Evioneth, where there was nothing but killing and fighting, whereupon he did purchase a lease of the castle and frithes[5] of Dolwyddelan, of the executors of Sir Ralph Berkinnet.

[1] The author means the Exchequer for the Principality, then kept at Carnarvon.—B.

[2] "John Spicer, John Wyn" (doubtless John Wynn ap Meredith) and another, attest, as justices of the peace, a Deed dated 24th Aug. 33rd Hen. VIII. The deed relates to property belonging to Howell ap Gruffith, whose son Robert married a daughter of Lewis ap Jevan ap David.

[3] Alice vch William.—L.

[4] Plas Newydd signifies *the new Mansion or Gen-tleman's house*; the name is therefore very common in Wales, and it is difficult to determine what Plas Newydd the author alludes to. It should seem that our modern expression of a *Gentleman's Place* is taken from this Welsh term.—B. See *Mona Antiqua* where this Rowland Gruffydd is included in the list of Members of Parliament. W.D.—L. It was Plas Newydd on the Menai, now the property of the Marquis of Anglesea.—W.

[5] Frith is a very common term in Wales, and signifies generally a small field taken out of a common.

L

I find in the records of the Exchequer of Carnarvon, the transcript of an act of resumption enrowled, made in the third yeare of king Henry the Seventh, by which act all king Richard's gifts are resumed, excepting one lease of the frith of Dolwyddelan, granted to Sir Ralph Berkinnet of the countie of Chester, knight, Chamberlaine of North Wales. Haveing purchased this lease, he removed his dwelling to the castle of Dolwyddelan, which at that time was in part thereof habitable, where one Howell ap Jevan ap Rys Gethin,[1] in the beginning of Edward the Fourth his raigne, captaine of the countrey and an outlaw, had dwelt. Against this man David ap Jenkin rose, and contended with him for the sovreignety of the countrey; and being superiour to him, in the end he drew a draught for him, and took him in his bed at Penanmen with his concubine, performing by craft, what he could not by force, and brought him to Conway Castle. Thus, after many bickerings betweene Howell and David ap Jenkin, he being too weake, was faigne to flie the countrey, and to goe to Ireland, where he was a yeare or thereabouts. In the end he returned in the summer time, haveing himselfe, and all his followers clad in greene,[2] who, being come into the countrey, he dispersed here and there among his friends, lurking by day, and walkeing in the night for feare of his adversaries; and such of the countrey as happened to have a sight of him and his followers, said they were the fairies,[3] and soe ran away. All the whole countrey then was but a forest, rough and spacious, as it is still, but then waste of inhabitants, and all overgrowne with woods;

There is a market town in Derbyshire called *Chapel in the Frith* which is situated in a valley amongst such inclosures. The term of *frith* is originally Saxon, hence *deorfrid* signifies a forest with its bounds. Chron. Sax. A.D. 1086.—B.

[1] The *Brogyntyn MS.* states, after " Gethin " and before " in the," this—"' a base son of Jenn' ap Rys Gethin."

[2] The tradition is well known, that Robin Hood and the outlawes his followers, were clad in the same livery. As they generally lived in forests, perhaps it might be conceived that they were less distinguishable when dressed in this colour.— B. Holingshed, in his description of Ireland, p. 12, gives an account of Robin Hood and Little John; he says they lived about the year 1189.—L.

[3] See p. 202 of Peter Roberts's *Popular Antiquities.*—L.

for Owen Glyndwr's warres beginning in 1400, continued fifteen
yeares, which brought such a desolation that greene grasse grew
on the market place in Llanrwst, called Bryn y botten, and the
deere fled[1] into the church-yard, as it is reported. This desolation
arose from Owen Glyndwr's policie to bring all things to waste,
that the English should find no strength, nor resting place. The
countrey being brought to such a desolation, could not be re-
planted in haste ; and the warres of York and Lancaster happen-
ing some fifteen yeares after, this countrey being the chiefest
fastness of North Wales, was kept by David ap Jenkin, a captaine
of the Lancastrian faction, fifteen yeares in Edward the Fourth
his time, who sent diverse captaines to besiege him, who wasted
the countrey while he kept his rocke of Carreg y Walch ; and,
lastly, by the Earle Herbert, who brought it to utter desolation.
Now you are to understand, that in those dayes, the countrey of
Nantconway was not onely wooded, but alsoe all Carnarvon,
Merioneth, and Denbigh shires seemed to be but one forrest
haveing few inhabitants, though of all others Nantconway had
the fewest, being the worst then, and the seat of the warres, to
whome the countrey about paid contribution From the towne of
Conway to Bala, and from Nantconway to Denbigh,[2] (when
warres did happen to cease in Hirwethog,[3] the countrey adjoining
to Nantconway), there was continually fostered a wasp's nest,
which troubled the whole countrey, I mean a lordship belonging
to St. Johns of Jerusalem, called Spytty Jevan, a large thing,
which had privilege of sanctuary. This peculiar jurisdiction, not
governed by the king's lawes, became a receptacle of thieves and
murtherers, who safely being warranted there by law, made the
place thoroughly peopled. Noe spot within twenty miles was
safe from their incursions and roberies, and what they got within
their limits was their owne. They had to their backstay friends

[1] " Fed in the church-yard of Llanrwst."—Bala
MS.—L.

[2] All this tract of country is mountainous, though
not very rocky ; it may therefore have been formerly
covered with wood, according to the account,
though there is at present little or none to be seen.
—B.

[3] Hiraethog.—L.

and receptors in all the county of Merioneth and Powisland.[1] These helping the former desolations of Nantconway, and prey- ing upon that countrey, as their next neighbours, kept most part of that countrey all waste and without inhabitants. In this estate stood the hundred of Nantconway when Meredith removed his dwelling thither, being (as I guesse) about the four and twentieth yeare of his age, and in the beginning of King Henry the Seventh his time. Being questioned by his friends, why he meant to leave his ancient house and habitation, and to dwell in Nantcon- way,[2] swarming with thieves and bondmen, whereof there are many in the kinge's lordship and townes in that hundred; he answered, " that he should find elbowe roome in that vast coun- trey among the bondmen, and that he had rather fight with outlawes and thieves, than with his owne blood and kindred ; for if I live in mine house in Evioneth,[3] I must either kill mine owne kinsmen or be killed by them." Wherein he said very truly, as the people were such in those dayes there; for John Owen ap John ap Meredith, in his father's time, killed Howell ap Madoc Vaughan[4] of Berkin, for noe other quarrell, but for the mastery of the countrey, and for the first good-morrow ; in which tragedie Meredith had likely beene an actor, if he had lived there, for the reasons aforesaid. He and his cosen the heire of Bron y foel were both out of the countrey, Morys ap John ap Meredith and Owen ap John ap Meredith were alsoe growne old men, soe as there was none in the countrey that durst strive with John Owen ap John ap Meredith, but Howell ap Madoc Vaughan of Berkin,[5] which cost him his life.

---

[1] Powisland formerly included a large district of country, chiefly Montgomeryshire. The *Reguli* of this part of North Wales are said to have been buried at Myfod in that county, which is situated on the river Vurnwy.—B.

[2] Nantconway signifies the valley situated on the Conway.—B.

[3] Evioneth is a hundred in the S. Western part of Carnarvonshire: it is supposed to have obtained this name from its being watered by a great number of small rivers. The same etymology is given by Leland to the province of Aquitane in France.—B.

[4] Howel ap Madog Vaughan was re-feoffed of lands, &c., in Evioneth, by deed dated on the next Monday after the Festival of St. Katherine the Vir- gin, 4 Hen. VIII. The Original deed is at Pen- iarth.

[5] Berkin (or Aberkin) is situated in the parish of

Howell ap Madog Vaughan his grand mother, was Jevan ap Robert ap Meredith his sister, soe he was cosen german's sonne to Meredith. John Owen that killed him was cosen german to my grandmother, being the daughter of Morris ap John ap Meredith. In respect of the feude of my grandfather he could not abide any descended of Owen ap John ap Meredith, neither could she abide any of his kindred of Berkin. I write it but to show the manifold divisions in those days[1] among soe private friends.

Howell ap Madog Vaughan haveing most valiantly fought out with his people, received his deadly wound in the head. Being downe, his mother being present, clapped her hand on his head, meaning to ward the stroke, and had halfe her hand and three of her fingers cut off at the blowe.

David Llwyd[2] Gruffith Vychan,[3] my uncle, told me, that his father dwelling at Cumstrallyn in Evioneth, hearing of the affray, but not of his cosen's death, (for Howell ap Madog Vychan out-lived the fray certaine dayes), sent him, being a child, to see how his cosen did; and he coming to Berkin found him layd in his bed, and his wounded men in great number lying in a *cocherie*,[4] above the degree near the high table, all in breadth of his hall, all gored and wallowing in theire owne blood. He likewise saw the gentleman's milch kine brought to the hall doore, and their

---

Llanistindwy.—B. Berkin, or Aberkin, was sold about the year 1822, by William Wynne of Peniarth, Esq., to whom it had descended from Howel ap Madoc Vaughan, to Thomas John, second Lord Newborough. Some of the Berkin plate is still at Peniarth.—W. (1872.)

[1] " This Griffith " (he was of Talhenbont, and grand.uncle to Howel ap Madog Vaughan), " was slaine by Morris ap John Meredith, his cousin german, as thus. He called him forthe & bid him looke up & with a knife stabbed him in the belly." *Harl, MS.* 1969. I cannot, however, make out that they were cousins german.—W.

[2] See also p. 63. This person was not *uncle* to Sir John Wynn, but first cousin to his grandfather; a relation that even now (1872) would be styled, amongst the humbler classes in Wales, " uncle," as would the first cousin of a father or mother.—W.

[3] David Llwyd ab Gruffith Vychan.—L.

[4] This term seems to be derived from an old French word *coucherie*; it may therefore signify a long boarded bed, placed with a proper inclination from the side of the room, which was the common dormitory of the servants. A shelf of boards thus disposed might answer the purpose of what in England was formerly called a *pallet*, and slanting shelves of this sort are sometimes used in barracks for the soldiers to sleep upon. As for what is mentioned of its being *above the degree near the high table*, it is well known that the principal table in an ancient hall is always raised a step or two, as it ocntinues to be in most colleges.—B.

milk carried hot from the kine, to the wounded men, by them to be druncke for the restoring of their blood.

Howell Vaughan, upon his death-bed, did say, "that this quarrel should never be ended while his mother lived; and looked upon her hand." Which was true indeed; for she persecuted eagerly all her time, and John Owen was kept in prison seven years in Carnarvon Castle, for soe long she survived her sonne, and his life was saved with much ado. After her death the feude was *compounded for*.[1]

John Owen and his followers were exceedingly sore hurt in that bickering; soe that returning to his father's house from the fray, and his aged father sitting or walking before the doore of his house, and seeing his son and his company all hacked, wounded, and besmeared with their owne blood, he said unto them, *Drwg yw'r drefn yma, a wnaethoch chwi eich gwerth;*[2] which is as much as to say, "You are in an ill-favoured pickle. Have you done nothing worthy yourselves?" "*I*,[3]" said the sonne, "I feare me we have done too much." "If that be soe," said Owen ap John ap Meredith, "I was this morning the best man in my countrey," meaning Evioneth, "but now I know not who is."

You are to understand, that in Evioneth of old there were two sects or kindred, the one lineally descended of Owen Gwynedd, Prince of Wales, consisting then and now of four houses, viz. Keselgyfarch, y Llys ynghefn y fann, now called Ystimkegid. Clenenny, and Brynkir, Glasfrin or Cwmstrallyn; the other sect descended of Collwyn, whereof are five houses or more; viz. Whelog, Bron y foel, Berkin, Gwnfryn, Talhenbont, and the house of Hugh Gwyn ap John Wynne ap Williams[4] called Pennardd,[5] all descended of their common ancestor, Jevan ap Einion[6]

---

[1] Such compositions were common in Wales before the statutes of Henry the Eighth.—B.

[2] Gwerth in *Brogyntyn MS.*

[3] *I* is probably used here for *ay*, as it is throughout the folio editions of Shakspeare.—P.

[4] "Ap Williams" should be John Wynne ap William.—W.

[5] Also Plas du, Bodvel, Boderda, Madrin, Penyberth, Rhosgyll, Bodean, Coytcay, (in *Hengwrt MS.* folio 48 of this History.)

[6] "He" (Enguerrard de Coucy, son-in-law of Edw. III., in his expedition against the Duke of Austria, under pretence of demanding the dower due to him—Enguerrard—in right of his mother) "was likewise accompanied by Jevan-ap-Eynion-ap

ap Gruffith.[1]   His brother was[2] Howell ap Einion ap Gruffith,
that worthy gentleman called Sir Howell y fwyall,[3] who be-
haved himselfe so worthyly at the field of Poitiers,[4] (where John
the French King was taken by the Blacke Prince),[5] that he received of the Prince in guift the constableship of Cricketh castle,
and other great things in North Wales, alsoe the rent of Dee
milles in Chester ; and, what was more, a messe of meat to be
served before his battle axe or partisan forever, in perpetual memory of his good service.[6]   This messe of meat was afterwards
carried downe to be given to the poore,[7] and had eight yeomen
attendants found at the King's charge, which were afterwards
called yeomen of the crowne; who had 8d. a day, and lasted
till the beginning of Queene Elizabeth's time.   Sergeant Roberts
of Havod y bwch, neare Wrexam, was, at his beginning, yeoman of the crowne.   He maried Sir William Gerrard's halfe-sister
by the mother, as did Robert Turbridge of Caervallen, neare Ruthyn, Esq., another : to whom he told, "that being yeoman of
the crowne, he had heard it by tradition in the King's house,
that the beginning of their order was upon the occasion as is
afore remembred."   This did Robert Turbridge relate unto me,

Griffith, a Welsh hero, not less renowned than himself, who had defended Henry[8] of Transtamare,
and the throne of Castile, against the Black Prince.
An ancient Swiss song, in which most of these
details are preserved, also mentions a duke Ysso de
Callis (Wales), with his gold cap, who commanded
the English Cavalry." Simonds' *Switzerland*, Vol.
2, p. 152.

[8] Annis 39 and 40, E. 3.   See Sandford p. 185.

[1] [Howell ap Griffith in Mr.. Robert Vaughan's
Collections.] In parenthesis in *Hengwrt MS.* 350,
folio 48 of this History. He certainly was Howel
ap Griffith, and was uncle to Jevan ap Einion ap
Gruffith.—W.

[2] In *Brogyntyn MS.* for "his brother" is "whose
brother."

[3] i. e. The axe.—B.

[4] This circumstance hath been before mentioned

by the author. See p. 29.—B.

[5] It seems probable however, that Sir Howel y
Fwyall *was* a captor of the French King. He
first surrendered himself to Denis de Morbecque,
"but there was a struggle for the possession of the
captive King, one saying ' I took him,' and another
making a like assertion." Afterwards, the King
was taken from Morbecque by "some English
Knights," and they were quarreling as to whose
prisoner he was. . .   The earls of Warwick and
Suffolk ordered these knights to release their prisoner, took him under their protection, and carried
him and his son Philip to the Prince of Wales.
Longman's Edw. III. Vol. 1 pp. 392, 395.

[6] Our author here repeats what hath before been
stated, of which there are some other instances when
the matter was particularly interesting.—B.

[7] " For his soul's health." *Bala MS.*—L.

upon the creditte of the other man. The countrey people, grounding upon the songes, which say, " that he bridled the French King," will have it, that he took the French King prisoner: a matter unlikely, as the one served on foot, and the King on horseback.[1] But the foot captaine is a brasen wall of the army, and may be said truly to winne the field.

After Meredith [2] had lived certaine yeares at Dolwyddelan castle,

[1] Notwithstanding the author's doubts with regard to this tradition, it seems scarcely to admit of a cavil, as such an extraordinary and expensive establishment could not have been granted by the crown, but for most meritorious services. As for the impossibility relied upon, that a soldier on foot could not take the French King on horseback, this circumstance is most fully accounted for by a MS. given to the Lord Treasurer Oxford by Mr. Hugh Thomas, and now deposited in the British Museum. —— " Sir. Howell ap Fwyall, ap Griffith, ap Howell, ap Meredith, ap Einion, ap Gwgan ap Meredith Goch, ap Colhwyn, ap Tangno, called Sir *Howell y Fwyall*, or Sir *Howell Pole Axe* from his constant fighting with that warlike instrument.—It is said he dismounted the French King, *cutting off his horse's head* at one blow with his battle axe, and took the French King prisoner; as a trophy of which victory it is said that he bore the arms of France, with a battle axe in bend sinister, argent.". *Harl MSS.* N° 2298. p. 348. —the reference in the printed catalogue to p. 21. of this number being inaccurate.

The conqueror anciently had a right to quarter the arms of his prisoner. This appears by a treatise on heraldry, printed by Wynken de Worde, without date, in which there is the following passage: " We have armys by our meryts, as very playnly it appeareth by the addycyon of the arms of Fraunce to those of Englonde after the taking of K. John of Fraunce in the battayle of Poyctiers, the which certayn addition was lawfull and ryght, and wyselye done. And on the same manner of wyce a poor archer might have taken a prynce or noble lord, and so the arms of that prisoner he may put to him and his heyrs." *Book of St. Albans*, by dame Julian Berners.

The author seems also to have forgotten some Welsh verses which are inserted in the margin of the MS. commemorating the grant of the mess of meat to be served at Sir Howell's table, whilst the battle axe followed.

Segir fy seiger wyall doeth honn garr bron y brenin, Gwedyr maes gwaed ar y min; i dwysaig ai dewiswr Al diod oedd waed a dwr. [Kowydd* i Jevan ap Meredith O Ceselgyfarch Howell ap Reignalt ai cant. †] " Place on the table my *sewer*, (bearing the axe which came from the presence of the king, with blood on its edge) the two dishes which I have chosen. The drink must be blood and water." " The poem in praise of Jevan ap Meredith of Ceselgyfarch, by Howell ap Reinalt the Bard."—B.

* Cowydd (or distich) was inserted in the margin by a different hand from that of the copier: it is said to be very incorrect, and consequently not perfectly intelligible. The above translation is supposed to be nearly the sense of it.—B. A fragment cannot be easily made out without the whole poem The Bard lived about 100 years after the battle of Poitiers, which was fought September 19. 1356. W. D.—L.

† Flourished from 1460 to 1490.—L.

[2] I find that the aforesaid Meredydd Wynn ab Iefan ab Rhobert went twice to Rome; and that at his death, by his will, dated the fourth of March, 1525, he left his Estate to certain trustees, to be divided amongst his four sons, viz., John Wynn, Rhys Wynn, Humffrey Wynn, and Cadwalader Wynn. To John Wynn he gave Gwydyr, and his lands in Nantconway, Dolwyddelan, and Llanfrothen. (Rhys Wynn dyed before the partition.) To Humphrey Wynn he left Cessailgyfarch, &c., and to Cadwalader Wynn he gave Wenallt, who was several times Member of Parliament. Meredydd ab Iefan ab Rhobert, after he had done great service to the King, abroad in his wars, in France, where he was a considerable commander, at the siege of Tourney, and at home in extirpating of outlaws and banditti which infested Wales, and were called *Herwyr* and *Gwylliaid*, and thereby had contributed very much to the civilizing and quieting this country,—purchased the seat of Gwydyr from Dafydd ab Howell Coytmor, (a descen-

he builded the house in Penanmen, being the principal best ground in Dolwyddelan, and also within certaine yeares after, he removed the church of Dolwyddelan from a place called Brin y

dant from Iarddur of Llechwedd) and began to build the lower house : he finished that part which is called Neuadd Fredydd, (or the Hall of Meredydd), and the adjacent lodgeing ; and then, leaving his paternal seat of Cessailgyfarch, and also his other house of Penanmen, he removed and settled at Gwydyr, where, in peace and honour, he departed this life, on the eighteenth day of March, 1525, aged about sixty-five, and was interred at the church which he himself had built at Dolwyddelan, leaving behind him a very numerous issue, that is to say, By his first wife, Alis vch William Gryffydd ab Robin o Gochwillian, he had Sion Wynn 2 ab Mered. of Gwydyr, who married Elin the daughter of Mawris Sion ab Meredydd o Rhiwaedog: Rhys Wynn 3 ab Mered. was never married. He had also by Alis two other sons, William 1 ab Mered. and Rhydderch 4 ab Mered. but both died before their father, sans issue. His daughters by her were these :—

Sionet 1 vch Mered = Edmund Gryffyth of Caernarfon : 2dly, Syr John Puleston, Knight.
　　Marget 2 vch Mered. three times, — Rhys ab Dafydd ab Gwillym o Lwydiarth,
　　　　　　　　　　　　　　　　　　— Evan ab Sion ab Meredydd o Bryncir.*
　　　　　　　　　　　　　　　　　　= Rhobet Vaughn o Bronhaulog. O. S. P.
　　　Catrin Llwyd 3 vch Mered = Rowland Gryffyth o Plasnewydd yn Môn.
　　　Catrin Gwynion 4 vch Mered. = Lewis ab Ief. ab Dd. o Pengwern yn Festiniog.
Lowri 6 vch Mered. = Rhydderch ab Dd. ab Mered. o Bala, ancestor o Lewis Gwynn of Bala, and alsoe
　　　　　　　　　　　　　　　Brigadier James Wynn.
　　Marali 6 vch Mered. = Tomos Gruff. Siencin o Coed y Rhygyn yn Trawsfynydd, and also of
　　　　　　　　　　　　　　　Clynnog fawr yn Arfon.†
　By his second wife Gwenhwyfar vch Gruff. ab Howell y Farf o Treiorwerth yn Mon, and relict ot　bo
Gryffyth of Plasnewydd, Meredydd had issue as followeth :—
　　　　　　　　　Elin 7 vch Mered. died unmarried.
　　Elsbeth 8 vch Mered = Sion ab Rhob. ab Lln. ap Morgan o'r Penllech.

By his third wife Marget vch Morus Sion ab Meredydd o Rhiwaedog, Meredydd had issue,— Humffrey ab Mered. on whom he settled Cessailgyfarch, and most of his lands in Evionydd, and who married Catrin, da. and heir of Iefan Gryffydd ab Meredydd ab Gwylim Powis o Cwmbowys yn

　　Elin 9 vch Mered. = Edd. Stanley, constable of Harddlech castell.
　　　Sian 10 vch Mer. = Cadwalader Prys o Rhiwlas.
　　　Agnes 11 vch Mer. = Rhobert ab Rhys Wynn Salsburi.
　　　Alis 12 = Tomas ab Rhys Benned o Bodlewyddan.
　　Gwen 14 vch Mer. = Owen ab Reynallt o Glynn Lligwy.
　　Marget 15 vch = Sion Gryff. o Cichley 3 ab Syr Will. Gryff. o'r Penrhyn.
　　　Eurlliw 16 vch Mer. = Sion Hooks o Conwy.

Ffestiniog. Cadwalader ab Mered. to whom he gave Wenallt in Nanhwynen, and the rest of his lands in Evionydd: he = Sionet vch Tomos ab Morus ab Gryffydd ab Iefan o'r Plâs du.

The daughters of Meredydd by his third wife were these :—

Besides these 20 children by his wives, Meredydd had the following by diverse women :—by Sionet vch Siencin Gryffydd Vychan he had Sir Robert, a Priest ; 2d. Sion Coytmor, from whom descend Syr Edmund Williams, Bart. Syr John Williams of the Isle of Thanet, and Syr Morris Williams, Knight ; and third, Catrin vch Mer. = Sion Dd. o Tregaron, father of Tomos Jones, commonly called Twm Sion Catte, (a great antiquary). And by Catrin vch Sion ab Heilyn o Benmachno, Meredydd had Evan and Huw, (who had issue Rhobert ab Huw, and Reinallt ab Huw of Flintshire). Meredydd had also by a dau. of Howell ab Rhys ab —————, Lewis, and Marget vch Mer. = Dafydd Owen A.M. father of

Morris Kyffin, consecrated Bish. of St. Asaph, 1603. And, lastly, by Gwenllian vch Gwylym ab Evan Llwyd, he had Catrin vch Mer. who = William ab Tomas Gronwy, by whom she had Syr Tomas ab William the famous physic. to Qu. Eliz. that made the Welsh Dictionary, and in whose MS. of Achau I found this hanes of Meredydd's children by his three wives, which agreeth with a catalogue of them in Lewis Dwnn's visitation MS. signed and attested by Owen Wynn of Caermelwr 4 ab Sion Wynn ab Mered. and grandson to Meredydd ; dated the 14 of June, 1588. H. Bangor, October 18, 1699, 1700.—L.

* Party to a deed on 5th Aug., 1525.
† Party to a deed on 1st Oct., 15 Hen. VII.

M

bedd, to the place where now it is, being parte of the possessions of the priory of Bethkelert. He also there new-built the same as it is now, one crosse chapell excepted, which my uncle Robert Wynne built. It should seeme, by the glasse window there, that it was built in anno 1512; but whether it was in that yeare glazed, (which might be done long after˜ the building of the church), I am uncertaine. The church, which is very strongly built, the castle, and his house of Penanmen stand three square, like a trivett, either a mile distant from each other. Questioning with my uncle, what should move him to demolish the old ·church, which stood in a thickett, and build it in a plaine, stronger and greater than it was before: his answer was, he had reason for the same, because the countrey was wild, and he might be oppressed by his enemies on the suddaine, in that woodie countrey; it therefore stood him in a policie to have diverse places of retreat. Certaine it was, that he durst not goe to church on a Sunday from his house of Penanmen, but he must leave the same guarded with men, and have the doores sure barred and boulted, and a watchman to stand at the Garreg big, during divine service; being a rock whence he might see both the church and the house, and raise the crie, if the house was assaulted. He durst not, although he were guarded with twenty tall[1] archers, make knowne when he went to church or elsewhere, or goe or come the same way through the woodes and narrowe places, lest he should be layed for: this was in the beginning of his time. To strengthen himselfe in the countrey, he provided out of all parts adjacent, the tallest and most able men he could heare of. Of these he placed colonies in the countrey, filling every empty tenement with a tenant or two, whereof most was on the Kinge's lands. Many of the posteritie of these tenants remaine until this day. One William ap Robert of Iscorum, being one of his followers, he .placed in a tenement of the towneshippe of Gwedir, called Pen-

---

[1] *Tall* at this time often signifies *stout*, and is used by Shakspeare in that sense.—P.

craig Inko, now worth £. 30. per annum, who paid for the same onely a reliefe to the King or lord, which was 10s. 4d.

Such were the lawes in those days, and are still, that if the King's tenant holding in freehold, or freeholder holding under any other Lord, did cease for two years to do his service to the King or Lord, the said may re-enter. The writte is called *Cessavit per biennium;* the exactions were, in those dayes, soe manifold, that not onely the bondmen ranne away and forsooke the Kinge's land, but alsoe freeholders their owne land.

Here to lay downe in particular the Welsh customes would make the volume too great.

Owen ap Hugh ap Jevan ap William, great grandchild to the said William, enjoyeth the land to this day; though in my grandfather's time it was in sute, by the contrivance of John ap Madog ap Hoshell, but it is now recovered by the meanes of my grandfather. Einion ap Gruffith ap Jockes, a freeholder of Festiniog and Llanvrothen, he placed in the King's frith at Bryntirch, of whom are descended many in Nantconway, Festiniog, and Llanvrothen. Howell ap Jevan ap Pellyn, a Denbighshire man, and a tall archer, of whom are descended the race of the Pellyns, he placed in the tenement of Garth. He alsoe placed Gruffith ap Tudor, a Denbighshire man, in Rhiw Goch; as likewise Jevan David ap Ednyfed, an Abergeley man (who felled, in one day, eighteen oakes, towards the building of a parte of Penanmen-house), in Bwlch y kymid. Lastly, he placed Robert ap Meredith in Berthios, whose sonne John ap Robert was dayry-man there, untill the beginning of my time.[1]

In Ddanhadog he found Rys ap Robert, a tall stout man, who being originally (as they say) a Vaynoll Bangor[2] man borne, and a freeholder, killed a man there, forsook his land, and fled thither. Rytharch and Richard ap Rys ap Robert were my father's fosters;

---

[1] "And manie others, too long to be repeated." *Bala MS.*—L.

[2] So called from being near Bangor, to distinguish it from other places bearing that name.—B.

and from the said Richard ap Rys ap Robert is lineally descended
Humphrey Jones[1] of Cravelyn, Gentleman. Diverse other tall
and able men dwelt in the countrey, which drew to him, as to
their defender and captaine of the countrey, soe as within the space
of certaine yeares, he was able to make seven score tall bowmen
of his followers, arrayed, as I have credibly heard, in this manner. Every one of them had a jacket or armolett coate, a good
steele cappe, a short sword and a dagger, together with his bow
and arrowes; most of them alsoe had horses, and chasing slaves[2]
which were to answere the crie upon all events.

Whereby he grew soe strong that he began to put back and to
curbe the sanctuary of thieves and robbers[3], which at times were
wont to be above a hundred, well horsed and well appointed.

It is to be noted likewise, that certaine gentlemen and freeholders dwelt in the countrey, but not many, who were to answere the crie, and to come also upon the like distresse.

The Issue of MEREDITH[4] ap JEVAN ap ROBERT[5] of Keselgyfarch
Gwedir[6] com. Carn.

By his first wife Alice[7], sixth daughter[8] of William Griffith ap Robin
of Cochwillan, he had,

I. William Wynne, who died without issue.

[1] Receiver General of North Wales, and ancestor to Mawris Jones of Ddôl. The heiress of Ddôl
in Edernion married Mr. Parry of Llanrhaidr,
from whom the present Richard Parry, Esq., of
Llwyn-ynn and Plas newydd, is lineally descended.
—L.

[2] Q. Staves i. e. hunting spears.—P.

[3] This was before described to be Yspytty Evan
which belonged to the Knights Hospitalers, and is
not far from Dolwyddelan, where this chieftain
resided. These knights had St. John for their
patron, and hence it is possibly called Yspytty
Evan [or rather Iwan which signifies John]; it is
now a small village situated on the Conway. Dr.
Davies renders Yspytty hospitium.—B.

[4] In the Brogyntyn MS. the whole of this, down
to and including "A.D. 1525," (p. 87), is in the
more modern hand referred to previously.

[5] Meredith Wynn ap Evan ap Robert after he
had done great service to his King abroad in his
wars in France, where he was a considerable
com'ander in the siege of Tournay, and at home in
extirpating the outlaws & banditi which infested
Wales, & were called Herwyr & Gwilied, and
thereby had contributed very much to ye civilizing
& quieting this country, purchased the Seat of
Gwyder of One of the descendants of Howell
Coytmore & began to build the lower House he
finished that part which is called Neuadd Fredydd
or the Hall of Meredith & the adjacent Lodgings,
And then leaving his paternall Seat of Kesailgyfarch as also his other house of Penanmen, He
removed & setled at Gwyder where in peace &
Hon'r he departed this life on the Eighteenth day
of March 1525, aged about 65, & was interred
in the church which he himself had built at Dolwyddelan leaving behind him a very numerous

II. John Wynne ap Meredith of Gwedir.[9]

III. Rees Wynne.

IV. Rytherch.

V. Margaret, wife first of Rees ap David ap Guillim of Angle-sey,[10] then of Jevan ap John[11] ap Meredith of Brynkir, and after him of Robert ap Meredith of Bronheulog.

VI. Jonet, wife first of Edmund Gruffith, son of Sir William Gruffith the elder Knight, after him of Sir John Puleston, Knight.

VII. Catherine Lloyd, wife of Rowland Gruffith of Plas-newydd.[12]

VIII. Catherine Gwinniow, wife of Lewis ap Jevan[13] ap David of Festiniog.

IX. Lowry, wife of Rytherch ap David ap Meredith of Bala.[14]

issue. (From a Gwydir Pedigree at Wynnstay, which appears to have been compiled by H. Humphreys, Bishop of Bangor, in the year 1700, from Sir John Wynn's *History of the Gwydir Family*.) I find that this Meredith Wyn ap Evan ap Robert made two journeys to Rome, & that att his death by his will dated 4. May 1525 he left his estate to certain Trustees to be divided among his 4 sons. John Wyn Rees Wyn Humphrey Wyn & Kadwalader. To John Wynne Gwyder & his lands in Nanconway Dolwyddelan & Llanfrothan (Rees dy'd before ye partition) to Humphrey Kesail-gyfarch &c : &c : Cadwalader (who was several times member of parliam't) Wenallt &c. (From a note in the handwriting of Humphrey Humphreys, Bishop of Bangor, afterwards of Hereford, in a MS. of Sir John Wynn's *History of the Gwydir Family* at Wynnstay.)

Meredith ap Jevan ap Robert died 18 Mar. 1525, aged about 65. (i. e. 1525-6.)

In the South part of the East window of Pen-morva church are the pictures of Meredith ap Evan ap Robert and his last wife—Marg[ta]. verch Maurice, with the inscription following under them :—

Orate pro Merydyt ap Evan ap Robert et Margerta verch Maurice uxorem ejus—qui hanc fenestram fecerunt.* (From another MS. Vol. of notes relating to the Wynn family at Wynnstay, and which

appears to have belonged to Bishop Humphreys.)

* A portion of this inscription remains in the West window of Penmorva church, formerly a doorway, to which some fragments of the old glass have been transferred.—W. (July, 1870.)

[6] In first edition this reads " and Gwedir."

[7] Alice could not have been his first wife ; for, by his monument at Dolwyddelan, it appears that they both died on the same day, 18 Mar. 1525.

[8] She was an illegitimate daughter.

[9] Died in 1559; will proved at Doctors' Commons.

[10] Whose will is dated 10 Dec. 1519.—*Penrhos MS.*

[11] Jevan ap John ap Meredith party to a deed 5th Aug. 7th of Hen. 7. (1492.)

[12] He is party to a deed in which he is styled " Roland Gruffith son and heir of Robert Gruffith of Porthamal," dated 6 Feb. 27th of Hen. 8. His father [Robert Gruffith of Porthamal] was probably then living, as he is not said in the deed to be deceased.

[13] He is witness to a deed dated 24th March, 33rd Hen. 8, and died in 1551.

[14] Who was a Justice of the Peace for the Co : of Merioneth on the 17th Aug. 2nd and 3rd of Philip and Mary.

X. Margaret, wife of Thomas Griffith Jenkin.

By his second wife Gvenhover, daughter of Gruffith ap Howell y Farf, relict of Robert Griffith of Porthaml.

XI. Elizabeth, wife of John ap Robert ap L'ln [1] of Penllech.

XII. Elen.

By his third wife Margaret, daughter of Morris ap John ap Meredith, he had,

XIII. Humphrey Meredith, of Keselgyfarch.[2]

XIV. Cadwalader[3] of Wenallt, father of Thomas, father of Cadwalader, father of John Vaughan, father of Cadwalader, M.A.[4]

XV. Elen, wife of Edward Stanley, Constable of Harddlech.[5]

XVI. Jane, wife of Cadwalader ap Robert ap Rees of Rulas.

---

[1] This contraction is for Llewelin.—B.

[2] He was living 4th June, 1578.

```
              ........ - Humphrey,Mere-  ⊤ Catherin d.&h.
                   d. of . . .   dith, of Kesel-    of Evan ap Gr.
                                 gyfarch.           ap Meredith ap
                                                    Gwilym Powys
                                                    of Cwmbowy,
                                                    in Festiniog.
```

```
John Wynn  ap - Catherine, dau. of ⊤ Evan Lloyd, of   Gwen, wife of    Margaret, wife of
   Humphrey.     Wm. Wynne ap  |   Havod llwddoc.     Evan ap Robert   Wm. Jones, of
                 Wm. of Coch-   |                     ap  Evan  ap     Castell March
                 willan.        |                     Iorwerth,  of    in Lleyn, Esq.
                                |   Thomas, married    Tanybwlch.
       ⊤ John Lloyd.            |   Marred, d. of
       |                        |   Ellis ap Wm.
       |                            Lloyd, of Rhiw-
       |                            goch.
       |
    Jevan Lloyd.
```

(From a pedigree lent to me by Edw. Breese, Esq., written about the year 1703; and *Hengwrt* *MS.* 419, fol. 94.—W.)

[3] "Wmffre ap me'd p'ter' voc' pen yfed et Kesaylgy-farch, xiij⁸ . . Kadwaladr ap me'd p'ter' suis et aliis—xix⁸· ⱴ ᴸ." (From the assessment referred to after the " Jones pedigree " in appendix to this vol.)

Cadwalader was living upon Nov. 5, 1563. His daughter, Marselie, was married *about* the year 1578, to Maurice ap Robert Wynne, of Glynn, in the county of Merioneth. Cadwalader was dead before the 4th June, 1578. His widow is stated to have been of the age of 60 years 29th Dec. 34 Eliz. (1591). His son John Cadwalader was of the age of 30 at that time.

[4] Degrees were at this time considered as the highest dignities, and it may not be improper to observe, that a clergyman who hath not been educated at the universities, is still distinguished in some parts of North Wales, by the appellation of *Sir* *John, Sir William,* &c. Hence the Sir Hugh Evans of Shakespeare is not probably a Welsh Knight, who hath taken orders; but only a Welsh clergyman, without any regular degree from either of the universities.—B.

[5] Sheriff of Merioneth 1545 and 1560.

XVII. Agnes, wife of Robert Salisbury.

XVIII. Alice, wife of Thomas ap Rees ap Benet of Bodel-widdan.

XIX. Gwen, wife of Owen ap Reinalt, of Glynllygwy.

XX. Margaret, wife of John Griffith, of Kichleu.

XXI. Elliw, wife of John Hookes of Conway.

By Jonet, daughter of Jenkin Gruffith Vaughan, he had,

XXII. Mr. Robert, a Priest.

XXIII. John Coetmor, father of William, father of John Williams,[1] goldsmith in London; who had issue Sir John Williams of the isle of Thanet,[2] Bart. Sir Edmund Williams,[3] Bart. &c. From him alsoe came Sir Morris Williams, Physician to the Queene.

XXIV. Catherine.[4]

By a daughter of Jevan ap John ap Heilin of Penmachno he had

XXV. Hugh.

XXVI. Jevan.

[5] He died A.D. 1525.

---

[1] This John Williams, goldsmith, was an antiquary of considerable eminence, and furnished Drayton with many of the particulars relative to Wales, which he hath taken notice of in the *Polyolbion*. Bishop Nicholson therefore need not have been surprised, "that it should contain a much truer account of this kingdom, *and the dominion of Wales,* than could be well expected from the pen of a poet." *Hist. Libr.* p. 5. Mr. Bagford also in his letter to Hearne prefixed to the First 'Volume of Leland's *Collectanea* says, that John Williams the goldsmith furnished Drayton with Leland's papers.—B. John Williams was founder of a chapel in Nanhwynen, and endowed it with £5 per ann. the chapel is now in ruins.—E. It should seem from this, that Nanhwynen was probably the place of his birth.—B.

[2] Of Minster, in the Isle of Thanet, created a baronet 22 Apr. 1642.

[3] Of Marnehull, in Dorsetshire, created a Baronet 19 Apr., 1642.

[4] Catherine = John David

Tom Sion Catty, the Antiquary.
(From the Gwydir Pedigree at Wynnstay).

[5] "And Lastly by Gwenllian Daughter of Gwilim ap Evan Lloyd (his concubine) he [Meredith ap Jevan ap Robert of Gwydir] had Catherine who maried to Wiliam ap Thomas Gronwy by whome shee had Sʳ Thomas ap Wiliam the famous Physitian that made the Welsh Dictionary, and in whose Booke of Pedigrees I found this catalogue of Meredith's children by his Three wives, which agreeth also with the catalogue of them which is in Lewis Dwn's Visitac'on Book signed and Attested by Owen Wynn of Caer Melwr, (4th son of John Wynn ap Meredyth, & grandchild to Meredyth) Dated the 14th June 1588. H: Bangor, 1700." (From a MS. at Wynnstay, containing a pedigree with the armorial bearings, and inscriptions in a roofn at Gwydir in 1690, and upon the monuments of the Wynns of Gwydir.)

THE ANCIENT MANSION OF [UPPER] GWYDIR,
As it was in 1684, when the Duke of Beaufort, in his Progress through Wales,
lodged there.

MEMOIRS, &c.

PREFACE.

THE History of the Gwydir Family, by Sir John Wynn, has long been out of print; and an object of curiosity and interest to persons connected with the Principality of Wales, and, indeed, to most antiquaries. The Lives which accompany it in the present volume are the work of the same accurate Historian; and, in the Editor's opinion, no less deserving of publicity than the private feuds of a single family. She laments that it is not in her power to add to them those of the other Divines, natives of the Principality, whose virtues and learning are still affectionately borne in mind, by all who are able to appreciate the beauty and accuracy of our vernacular translation of the Holy Scriptures and Liturgy. Extended fame was not to be expected by men whose labours were confined to a narrow district, and to a Language long treated with undeserved neglect by the great body of European Scholars. But the benefit which they conferred on their own little country, and the renewal by their means of genuine religion in those regions where it had lingered latest, may secure, it is hoped, no unfavourable reception for this humble tribute to the Fathers of the Reformation in CYMRU.—L. in edition of 1827.

MEMOIRS, &c.

THIS Country, in Queen Elizabeth's time, produced six that were Bishops in sundry places; and the last in order and the first to be remembered (as the course of this History leadeth), was Henry Rowland, Bishop of Bangor, born at Meullteyrn,[1] in Llûn, son to one Roland ab Rhobet, an ancient Esquyre, who sat in that See eighteen years. He was sufficiently learned, for he preached twice, with approbation, before king James; and was a good provident governour of his Church and Diocese, a great repairer of his decayed Cathedrall Church, and a great builder upon the glebe of diverse other Churches which he had in commendam. In housekeeping and hospitality, both to rich and poor, the greatest that hath been in our time, and yet dyed rich. And though he were in the commission of the peace continually, and in other commissions that came into the country, yet he would put them off as much as in him lay, having no will to deal but in his own element.

He left an Alms-house for six poor men in the town of Bangor. He hath left lands for two Fellowships in Jesus Colledge in Oxenforde, and other lands for the maintenance of a Free School in Llyn Bodtwnog, being the place that he was brought up himself at school, and liberally left money to build it. He, with the volun-

---

[1] Of which place he became Rector in 1572; advanced to the Deanery of Bangor, August 21, 1593, from whence he was preferr'd, anno 1598, to the Bishoprick. He died July 6, 1616.—L.

tary contribution of his clergy, whereof he had the command in good will more than any before him, bought three fair bells for the steeple of the Cathedral Church of Bangor, they having but one before. He erected a monument there in the Church, with fair statutes of himself and of his cousin, the next precedent Bishop, Doctor Richard Vaughan, with the following inscription:

Piæ memoriæ duorum Episcoporum in hac Ecclesia proxime succedentium, qui fuerunt contigue nati, Coetanei, sibi invicem cari Condiscipuli, Consanguinei ; et illustri Familia Vaughanorum de Talhenbont in Evionydd: Prior Filius Thomæ ab Robert Vachan Generosi de Niffryn in Llyn, Qui Sedem hanc per Biennium tenuit, deinde Cestrensem per Septem Annos; Postea Londinensem per Triennium tenuit, ubi vitam mensis martii ultimo An. Dom. 1607, immatura morte commutavit. Cujus Virtus post funera vivit: Posterior Henricus Filius Rolandi ab Robert Armigeri de Melteyrn in Llyn et Elizabeth filia Griffini ab Robert Vachan, Armigeri, de Talhenbont, qui annum Consecrationis suæ jam agit decimum octavum multosque agat feliciter ad honorem Dei & Evangelii propagationem, mutuo amore alter ultrique hoc struxit monumentum mense maii, Anno Dom. 1616.

Orimur, Vicissim morimur,
Qui non precesserunt sequuntur.

Next to him in that See preceded Richard Vaughan,[1] D.D.

[1] Of the same name, but not of the Talhenbont tribe, was Rhys Vaughn (the faithful follower of Richard the Third), who ought to be mentioned with respect while fidelity is rewarded as a virtue. Richard was a tyrant, and the vilest of men ; but he was Rhys Vychan's benefactor, and Rhys Vychan was grateful. The following well attested fact I translated out of an old MS. at Caerwys : "Rhys Vychan was owner of great lands and possessions in Môn, Caernarvonshire, and Flintshire; he was Squire of the body unto Richard the Third, and did attend him in his Privy Chamber, and by patent was free Denizen within England. He had purchased from the king three goodly manors near Whitchurch, and had purchased Aber, Cemmis, and Wig, and diverse other things, which were all taken from him by Henry the Seventh. When Richard saw that Stanley was become a turncoat, and that the Welshmen had all revolted from him, he called for a (Boule) bowl of wine, sitting on horseback in his complete armour, and when the wine was brought him, he called unto Rhys Vychan, and drank unto him in these words, 'Here, Vychan, I will drink to thee the truest Welshman that ever I found in Wales,' and, having drunk, threw the bowl over his head, and made towards his enemies, where he was immediately slain." Hereupon Rhys Vychan lost all his lands (which was begged by new Courtiers) before he could obtain his pardon. He married Margaret Conway and left two sons.—L.

Qu : If Rhys Vychan be the "nameless Page" alluded to by Horace Walpole, in his Historic

born also in Llyn, descended of the Vaughns of Talhen-bont, an ancient house of Esquyres. He sat there two years, but never was at the Bishopric in all that time, for that the means and demesnes [1] (demains) of the Bishopric was not able to find him being. A worthy housekeeper, and a liberal minded man, as the proof did manifest while he lived at Chester, whereto he was translated. He was an excellent and a rare scholar, a discreet and temperate man, and very industrious in his vocation, which shortened his days. He was translated from Chester to London by King James, in whose good grace and favour he lived as any other Bishop (whatever) whatsoever. He dyed a poor man, for he respected a good name more than wealth.

Next before him was Nicholas Robynson, D.D. [2] born in the town of Conway, in Caernarvonshire, was of honest parents and wealthy, whose father I knew bailiff of the town, being chief officer, having by their charter authority to keep courts, with sergeants and under officers. He was an excellent scholar, and would have preach'd exceeding well, especially when he did it without premeditation, for then he exceeded himself; but upon meditation (in my conceit) not so well, for I have heard him at both; at St. Paul's in London, in time of Parliament, once, and in the country often; whereof I can attribute no occasion, but that he was extreme choleric, and fearful withal, which, in my judgement, put him out of his natural bias; withal he was a very wise man. He dyed

---

doubts, as having made Richard the Third acquainted with Sir James Tyrrel's character, when Syr Robert Brackenbury refused to murder the young Princes in the Tower?—L.

[1] Sir John Wynn evidently alludes to Arthur Bulkeley, Bishop of Bangor, who granted a lease of all his lands in the hundred of Llyn, by indenture dated 1547, ann. prim. 6, to Gryffydd ab Madoc Vychan for a term of 99 years, at a reserved rent of nine pounds per ann. It is worthy of remark that this lease expired the very year [1646] that the Parliamentary Commissioners were engaged in making a survey of the Bishop's lands, which is perhaps the reason that these lands (which must be of very con-

siderable value) have not been since recovered. The Commissioners confess, that not having time to take the actual survey, they applied to William Lloyd of Plas-hên, who referred them to his steward Huw Lloyd, by whom they were informed, that the manor of Edern was leased by William, late Bishop, and William Lloyd of Plas-hên, for three lives, for the sum of nine pounds. vid. Survey of 1647.—L.

[2] Made Dean of Bangor March 3, 1556, and consecrated Bishop thereof on October 23, 1566. He died February, 1584-5, and was buried in the Cathedral Church, near the altar, leaving five sons and one daughter, by his wife Jane, daughter of Randal Brereton.—L.

rich, and left many hopeful children, for whom he had well provided.

This county,[1] anon after the beginning of Queen Elizabeth's reign, produced three that were Bishops at once, born within or near the town of Conway. The one, Richard Davies, first of St. Asaph, after translated to St. David's, where he govern'd like himself, and for the honour of our nation (loving entirely the North-wales men), whom he placed in great numbers there, having ever this saying in his mouth (myn y firi Faglog), his familiar oath, " I will plant you, North-wales men, grow if you list." He kept an exceeding great post, having in his service younger brothers of most of the best houses in that country, to whom, with his own sons, Thomas, Peregrine, and Jerson, which I knew at Oxenford, both born at Geneva, he gave them good maintenance and education. He did stoutly confront Sir John Parrot, Knight, in those days an inward favourite of the Earl of Leicester, who afterwards was Lord Deputy of Ireland, and one of the Lords of the Privy Council, a man of great possessions in that country, (who would have wrong'd him). He called to him William Salusbury of Plasisa, near Llanrwst, in the county of Denbigh, and divers others, Welshmen, profound scholars, and skilful linguists, and translated the New Testament, the Psalms, and Book of Common Prayer into the Welsh tongue; and was very far onward with the Old Testament,[2] and had gone through with it if variance had not happen'd between him and William Salusbury (who had liven with him almost two years in that business), for the general sense and etymology of one word, which the Bishop would have to be one way, and William Salusbury[3] another, to the great loss of the old

---

[1] Caernarvon.—L.

[2] Dr. Richard Davies translated the Old Testament from Joshuah to the end of Samuel into English, besides several of the Epistles. His father was David ab Gronw, who married Jonet, daughter of David ab Richard, descended from Ednoweh Bendew. They had other children besides Richard.—L.

[3] William Salusbury was born at Plasisa, near Llanrwst (descended from the Salusbury's of Lle-weny). He composed a Welsh treatise on rhetoric, which was afterwards revised and published, by Henry Perry, B.D. He translated, and first published in print, the Epistles and Gospels for the whole year, in King Edward the Sixth's time. He published also the whole New Testament in Welsh, at the command, or by the direction, of the Bishops of Wales, to which Dr. Richard Davies prefixed an excellent prefatory Epistle that does him great credit.—L.

British and mother tongue; for, being together, they drew Homilies, Books, and divers other Tracts in the British tongue, and had done far more if that unlucky division had not happen'd, for the Bishop lived five or six years after, and William Salusbury about twenty-four, but gave over writing (more was the pity), for he was a rare scholar, and especially an hebrician, whereof there was not many in those days. This worthy Prelate, Richard Davies,[1] was a poor Curate's son, who serv'd at Cyffin, within half a mile of the town of Conway, born at a place called Plas y Person. In Queen Marie's time he was fain to flee with his wife to Geneva; where being an exceeding poor man, and living upon the contribution and alms of the fugitives there, he was so industrious that in three years time, or somewhat more, he attained the country language spoken in Geneva, which I think to be French. He served a Cure there, and preached; and in the latter end lived well thereby. Oh! how my heart doth warm by recording the memory of so worthy a man! He dyed poor, having never had regard to riches.

Thomas Davies, L.L.B.[2] and Chancellor of the Diocese of Bangor, born within three miles of the town of Conway, some say that he was born within the town, son to Davies[3] of Caerhyn, Gent., was, after Richard Davies's translation, elected Bishop of St. Asaph, where he sat many years. He had at one time one brother called Gruffith Davis, high Sheriff of the county of Caernarvon, and another brother of his Coroner, and another brother Escheator in the said county.

In Queen Marie's time sat William Glynn[4] in Bangor; a great

---

[1] "Was Vicar of Burnham, and Rector of Maidsmorton, Co. Bucks, of which preferments he had been deprived in Queen Mary's reign, as it seems for being married: became nominated to the See of St. Asaph by Queen Elizabeth, 1559. On May 21, 1561, he was translated to St. David's, where he died 1581, at his episcopal palace at Abergwille, in the parish church of which place he was buried." Browne Willia.—L.

[2] Consecrated Bishop of St. Asaph, May 21, 1561. He died about Michaelmas, 1573, and was buried

at Llanbedr, Co. Caernarvon. He dyed rich, and settled a scholarship on Queen's Coll., Cambridge. —L.

[3] The Davies line ended in an heiress, who married the Rev. Hugh Jones of Brynhyrddyn, Mona; their daughter and heir Catherine married Ralph Griffith, in whose family Caerhun remains at this day.—L.

[4] Consecrated Bishop of Bangor, 1555; died aged 54, May 21, 1558, and was buried at his own Cathedral, near the Communion Table. He was a descen-

scholar, and a great hebrician, as by quotation of his books do shew, being rare in that time. He was a good and religious man, after the manner of that time. He was born in Hen-eglwys[1] parish, in this county of Caernarvon: he was a Priest's son, as I have heard. Qu. of what kindred and house.

Another William Glynn, L.L.D.[2] of the house of Glynnllifon, being an ancient house of Esquyres, proceeded before him as Suf.fragan to Bishop Skevington,[3] being Abbot of Bermondsey, who never came into the country, but yet bestowed great costs on the Cathedral Church of Bangor, for he built the body thereof, and the bell tower, and furnished the same with bells, which were sold by the Bishop, Dean, and Prebends in King Edward the Sixth's time, when, as it was expected, that all the bells in England should have rung in the Courtiers purses; which likely had been so if the Duke of Somerset had stood longer. This man, i.e. Glynn, was of a stirring spirit, and a great housekeeper; spent all, and had a hand in all the great temporal affairs of the country as well as the spiritual. Qu. whether there was any before him of this county, that were Bishops of Bangor?

William Morgan, D.D.[4] born at Dolwyddelan, in the comot of Nant Conway, and county of Caernarvon; descended of the race of the bondmen of that town, servants (both he and his ancestors) to the house of Gwydyr, where he was brought up in learning. His first preferment was with myself, and by my means; he was first made Bishop of Landaff, and afterwards translated to St. Asaph,

---

dant from Einion ab Gwalchmai of Treveilir, a celebrated Welsh Bard, who flourished about the year 1240. Treveilir continued in the possession of his lineal descendants till the last owner sold it, in 1775, to William Evans, Esq.—L.

[1] Hen-eglwys is in Anglesey.

[2] He was Archdeacon of Merioneth, and afterwards of Anglesey, and died 1537.

[3] Thomas Pace, alias Skevington, born at Skevington, in Leicestershire, succeeded as Bishop of Bangor, by papal provision, dat. 7 Cal. Mar. 1508. He died in June, 1533, and was buried in the Choir of Beaulieu church, Co. Northampton, of which place he was Abbot. See Browne Willis.—L.

[4] "That incomparable man for piety, industry, zeal for religion and his country, was the son of John Morgan by his wife Lowry, daughter of Gwylym ab John, descended from Marchudd. He was educated at St. John's College, Cambridge, and was (first) Vicar of Welsh Pool, 1575, and thence preferred to the Vicarage of Llanrhaidr ym moch-nant, Co. of Denbigh, and diocese of St. Asaph, 1588."—P. B. Williams. Consecrated Bishop of Landaff in 1595. He published his Welsh Bible in 1588.—L.

where he dyed[1] after he had sat there some two or three years.
He translated the Old Testament into the Welsh tongue before he
was Bishop, and while he was Vicar of Llanrhaidr yn moch-
nant, in the county of Denbigh, whence he had the benefit and
help of Bishop Davis and William Salusbury's works, who had done
a great part thereof; yet he carried the name of all.   He repaired
and slated the Chancel of the Cathedral Church of St. Asaph, which
was a great ruin.   He died a poor man.   He was a good scholar,
both a grecian and hebrician.[2]

In Queen Elizabeth's time lived John Wynn, Doctor of the
Arches,[3] born at Gwydyr, in the said county of Caernarvon,
youngest son to John Wynn (of Gwydyr) ab Meredydd.   In his
youth, being Fellow of 'St. John's College, and Doctor of the University, he arrested John, Duke of Northumberland, who yielded
unto him.   He died without issue, and gathered a great estate,
which he left to Gruffydd Wynn, second brother of that house.
He was a learned man, and a bountiful housekeeper; and never
married.   He founded two Fellowships, and three Scholarships at
St. John's College in Cambridge, whereof he had been Fellow.
This small foundation hath God so blest, of fifty years standing at
the most, that it hath produced in our own time the Right Honor_
able John Williams, D. D. Bishop of Lincoln, and Lord Keeper
of the Great Seal of England.

Owen Wynn, D.D. son to Gruffydd Wynn, and brother to the
said founder, now master of that College.   God grant that his
mercy may follow the same society for ever.

James Ellis,[4] Doctor of the Civil Law, and Chancellor of Peter-
borough, in Queen Elisabeth's time; son to Ellis Mauris, born in
Cleneneu, Co. Caernarvon.

---

[1] Was translated from the See of Landaff to St.
Asaph on September 17, 1601, where, dying on
September 10, 1604, he was buried the next day in
the Choir of the Cathedral Church.—L.

[2] The above account shews Sir John Wynn's
pique against Bishop Morgan. Vide Yorke's *R.
Tribes*.—L.

[3] Viz. Advocate in the Arches Court of Canter-
bury.—L.

[4] Living in Jan. 1595.

William Gruffith, Doctor of the Arches, one of the younger sons of William Gruffith of Caernarvon, born in Caernarvon, Judge of the Admiralty in North Wales, in Queen Elisabeth's time.

Mauris Glynn,[1] Doctor of the Civil Law, son to Robert ab Meredydd, born at Glynnllifon, Co. Caernarvon. A younger brother of that house, was Dean of the Arches, died without issue, and what he had he left to religious houses. He lived in King Henry the Eighth's time, before the ruin of Monasteries.

Grûffith Williams, D. D.[2] born at Treveilian, in the said county, of ancient freeholders, his mother well descended, being of the house of Penmynydd[3] in Mona; a great scholar, and an industrious preacher of God's word, as appears by divers of his sermons in London, preach'd at St. Paul's Cross, and are extant in print. Also, he was Lecturer in St. Paul's for some eight years together; now Chaplain in Household to the Right Honourable the Earl Montgomery.

Owen Meredydd,[4] sometime fellow of Alls Souls, in Oxenford, B. D.; an honest man, and a good scholar; son to Meredydd ab Tomas Gruffith, of Clynnog, Co. Caernarvon.

Edmund Griffith, B. D.[5] and now Dean of Bangor, born at Llyn, in the same county, and a younger son to Gruffydd[6] ab Sion Gruffydd of Cevenamlwch, of an ancient house, and a worthy gentleman in Divinity.

William Bryncir[7] Bachelor in Divinity, born at Bryncir, in the comot of Evionydd, in the said county, a younger son to Robert Bryncir.

The county of Caernarvon also produced Sir William Jones,[8]

---

[1] He died in 1525.

[2] A folio volume of his works was printed in his life-time: its principal object seems to be the refutation of Popery.—L.

[3] Owen Tudor was of that house.—L.

[4] Buried at Llanwnda 23rd Nov. 1612.

[5] Became Dean of Bangor in 1623. Sir John Wynn dying in 1626, did not live to see him consecrated Bishop of Bangor, February, 1632. He died May 26, 1637, and was buried in his own Cathedral. —L.

[6] Gryffydd 2 ab Sion married Catrin, daughter of Sir Richard Bukeley, of Baron Hill. Edmond was their fourth son.—L.

[7] Entered at Oxford in 1599. Living in 1616.

[8] Sir William Jones married Marget, daughter of Gryffydd ab Sion. They had four sons.—L.

O

now living, who was Chief Justice of the King's Bench in the
Realm of Ireland: and now is one of the Judges of the Common
Pleas at Westmynster. He was born in Llyn, at his own house
called Castellmarch, which is a very ancient house of gentlemen.

In King Henry the Sixth's time, there was also a Judge of Common Pleas, Jeffrey Coytmor,[1] born in the hundred of Nant Conway,
in this county of Caernarvon, of the Coytmors there, which were
very gentlemen. His grandfather Howell Coytmor,[2] lieth buried
under a fair monument in Llanrwst church, in the county of Denbigh. He was captain of a hundred Denbighshire men, with the
Black Prince, at the field of Poytiers, where John, King of France,
was taken. He lived at Henle upon Thames.

William Thomas,[3] son and heir to Rhys Thomas, born in Caernarvon; captain of two hundred men out of North Wales; went
with Robert, Earl of Leycester, to the Low Countries, where, finding Sir Thomas Morgan, and Sir Roger Williams[4] and Sir Martyn
Shink, the most forward of that army, associated himself with them
and especially with Sir Martyn Shink, and with him put himself
and his company into Berke upon Rhyn; whereas, the Prince of
Parma, with all his army, did invest him, and besieged them for a
great time, omitting nothing that was to be perform'd for the win-
ning of the same; but, in the end, he was fain to give it over;
after which time, both Sir Martyn Shink and he came to the Earl
of Leycester, to the camp before Suttroin, where, in that great
skirmish, Sir Phillip Sidney was hurt to the death, and slain; a
brave, courageous, wise gentleman as any in this country produced
in his time, or for many ages before. He had been Page to the
Duchess of Somerset, and was brought up under the same Tutors
as her son the Lord Edward Somerset was, who was not much older
than he. He could speak Latin, Italian, and French. It was

[1] I find "John Cotesmore" a puisne judge of
the Common Pleas 15 Oct., 1430, and Chief Justice of the same Court upon 20 Jan., 1439. Jeffrey
and John were then the same name.—W.

[2] Dafydd, son of this Howel Coytmor, sold his

paternal property, Gwydyr, to Jevan ab Meredydd,
ancestor to Sir John Wynn, the historian.—L.

[3] Slain in Flanders 1586 (*Peniarth MS.* 47, p. 100)

[4] Of Penrhos, Monmouthshire.—L.

thought that his Language was the occasion of his death; for it is reported, that he yielded himself in the Italian tongue. [He who took him] envious that he should possess such a prisoner, kill'd him in cold blood. These are reported, and whether true or no I cannot say; but there he died.

Gruffydd Wynn, born at Gwydyr, second son of John Wynn ab Meredydd, serv'd in his youth Sir Edmund Knivett, Knight, Lord of the castle of Buckname, in Norfolk; who, having had a quarrel in those days with the Lord Fitzwalter, son and heir to the Earl of Sussex, for his mother in law, the Earl's wife, with whom it was thought he was too familiar, retained a great many of our country gentlemen, on whom it was thought he did most rely for his safety. There served him at one time four of the house of Gwydyr, viz. next Gruffydd Wynn, Cadwalader Wynn ab Meredydd, John ab Rhys Wynn, and David Lloyd ab Rhys Wynn, brethren. Thomas Williams, father to Sir William Williams, Baronet, and one of the younger sons of William Williams the elder, of Cochwillan, and Edward Williams his brother, which also was a man at arms at Bullen, and servant to Lord Paget. Qu. whether he was his man or no.

Sir Edward Knivet, being a very gallant forward gentleman, was the first that, of the King's side, did set upon the rebels of Northfolk, who lay in the neighbouring village 500 strong, with thirty horse of his own servants, where he kill'd five or six of the rebels; but there he receiv'd a blow, which afterwards, was 'the occasion of his untimely death. From thence he rode to the Court to advise the state of the rebellion, and to get the King's pardon for those that he had kill'd. From the Court he return'd in great credit and authority with the Marquis of Northampton, the Lord Sheffield, and diverse other noblemen. Gruffydd Wynn was with Sir Edmund, and was of his Chamber, and with him in all places, and at the battle that was fought within the city of Norwich between the Marquis of Northampton, General for the King's forces,

and Kett, wherein the King's men were put to the worst, and the
Lord Sheffield and many other gentlemen kill'd.   I have heard
himself often reported, that his master and he were as forward as
the Lord Sheffield; they were armed with white armour, capapee, [1]
&c. &c. and that he receiv'd such a blow at that time on the head that
he staggar'd, and one of his horse ears were cut off with a gleeve [2]
and thrust through the wythers ; and if it had not been for the
goodness of his horse he had never come off, who brought him to a
park near the city, and there fell under him dead.   And he did
verily believe that the cause of the Lord Sheffield's death was the
reason that he was in guilded armour, and therefore they sought
after him more than others.[3]   Sir Edmund Knyvet's Lady was
fain to flee by night from her house to Fremingham castle, where
the King's daughter, the Lady Mary, then lay.   The rebels came
to Buckingham castle and burnt it, and made havoc of all that they
found therein, for the people were all fled.   The Marquis, and Sir
Edmund, and the rest that survived, returning to the Court, the Earl
of Warwick, and diverse other noblemen, as appeareth by the
Chronicle of that time, and Sir Edmund, were sent down against
the rebels, with a great army, where they fought with and overthrew
them ; and Kett was slain, whose nag and saddle being of russet
velvet, Gruffydd Wynn brought home with him to Gwydyr, and
the nag was call'd "Glâs Kett,[4]" by his former master's name,
while he lived.

After Sir Edmund's death, Gruffydd Wynn became servant to
William, Earl of Pembroke, with whom he serv'd as a man at arms
at Wyatt's field, in ranks that day with old William Mostyn, Esq.
who serv'd the Earl also.   His younger brother, Doctor Gwynn,
made him his heir, and thereby advanc'd his estate much.   He was

---

[1] Polished steel was so called.—L.

[2] A glaive, an ordinary cutting and thrust weapon of the Infantry, being a large blade on the end of a pole. See Dr. Meyrick's very valuable work upon ancient armour.—L.

[3] Many instances occur of persons having been put to death for the sake of their armour.—L.

[4] i. e. Kett's Grey.—L.

the most bountiful housekeeper, both to rich and poor; a religious, stout, and wise man; and was high Sheriff of the two counties of Denbigh and Meirionydd. I bought him a commission to be Justice of the Peace in the counties of Caernarvon and Meirionydd, but he refused them. At his death, his living was worth a thousand pounds p. ann. and was wealthy withal.

Robert Wynn, born at Gwydyr, in the said county, third son to John Wynn ab Meredydd, serving Sir Phillip Hobbie, Knight, in his Chamber, (being one of the council of King Henry the eighth, and a great commander of his army), was with the King and his master at the siege of Bullen, where he receiv'd a shot in his leg, whereof he was long lame: notwithstanding all the surgery the King's men could afford, it was strange that the surgeons could not find it at first and have it out, but it remain'd in that place for the time beforementioned; it was wont, sometimes in four years, sometimes in six years, to grieve him, drawing an inflammation to his leg, which by repercusives being driven back, he should be well again. First, he married Dorothy, daughter of Sir William Gruffydd, of Penrhyn, Knight, Chamberlain of North Wales, and widow to William Williams the younger, of Cochwillan, who was a woman in years, and with whom he lived till he was past three score and six years old. Afterward, he married a young gentlewoman, daughter of James Dymoc, of Willington, in the county of Flint, who, in his old age, brought him many children. Some six years after his last marriage, his wonted inflammation took him in the leg with an extraordinary vehemence, so that he supposed it would endanger his life; in the end it grew to a heat, and he that was of his Chamber found with his probe a hard thing in the orifice, which he supposed a great scale of his shin bone: fearing least the same should rot, he being at my house at Gwydyr, I brought him to his chamber, desiring that I might see his man dress his leg afore he went to bed; being unbound, and the sore open, I found with my nail a hard thing in the orifice, and of a great length; so I call'd for the probe, and with the same search'd the wound deeper than his man durst, for fear of hurting him, and found that it was no bone, but the lead that had lain so long in his flesh; and so sent for a surgeon to cut the dead flesh and skin and pull it out, which he did, and he was well recover'd, and felt no pain at all while he lived.

He was at the rummage and burning of Edenborough and Leith, in Scotland, and the memorable journeys mention'd in the Chronicles in King Henry the Eighth and Edward the Sixth's time, excepting Marlborough field,[1] in Scotland, whereat I did hear him say he was not. In the latter part of King Edward the Sixth's reign, his master was sent Ambassador to the Emperor Charles the Fifth, who was then in Hungary, with the greatest army that the Christians ever had, to confront Solyman the Turk, that came with 500 thousand men to conquer Christendom; at which service both his master and he was. His master being revoked by Queen Mary, and another placed in his stead, by reason of his religion being a protestant, found the Queen's countenance averted from him; whereupon after he had kept his house for a while very privately, he desired of the Queen license to travel, which she granted with this addition, that she would give him leave, and all of his opinion, to travel out of the land and never return. He travelled not, but within a while after died in his own house, of melancholy and grief of mind. Robert Wynn, his servant, return'd home, and anon after married as aforesaid, and built a goodly house[2] in the town of Conway, in this county of Caernarvon, where he kept a worthy plentiful house all his time; and lieth buried in the church there, having two monuments, the one for himself, and another for his first wife.

Hugh Griffith,[3] son to Griffith ab John of Cefnamlwch, a very proper man, of a comely tall personage, was by his father put an

---

[1] Qu. If Musselborough ?—L.

[2] This house still exists, opposite the Inn, and retains many proofs of the fanciful decorations of the period.—L.

[3] He was third son of Griffith ab John, by Catrin Bulcley [Bulkeley], and brother to Edmund Gryffydd the Bishop of Bangor. Page 97.—L.

apprentice to a merchant adventure in London, whom he serv'd
very honestly and well untill his years were out, and became fac-
tor, both for his master and others, in the parts beyond the seas :
and passing from London towards his place of trade, with twelve
hundred pounds, which he had taken up upon his own credit,
was taken by the Dunkyrks and there imprisoned, and thence deliver'd by the means of Hugh Owen, who was the private council
to the Prince of Parma. This Hugh Owen was born in this county, a younger brother of an ancient gentleman's house call'd Plâs
dû; he serv'd in great credit with the Earl of Arundel, and was a
chief actor in the Duke of Norfolk's action, and was thought to be
the wisest man amongst them ; and when he saw that his counsel
was not follow'd, travers'd his ground in time into Brussels, where
he continued privy councellor to that state forty years, and until
the end of his days. This Hugh Griffith being by his means re-
leased, and having paid his ransom, and having lost his credit ir-
revocable, gets a letter of mark, and furnish'd himself to sea, and
proves there the worthiest, the most valiant captain of any nation
that was at sea. In the end, within the straights lighting upon
the ship of war of the King of Spain, that carried the King of
Spain's treasure out of Italy into Spain, resolved either there to
die or to win it, which, in the end, he did, after a most admirable
fight for four or five days continuance, having slain the most
valiant captain, being a Dutchman, and a great number of the soldiers, but having received a great loss by the other, himself being
sore hurt, and his company so weakened that he was fain to be
taken himself to Argier[1] for refuge; where, either he died of his
hurts, or was poisoned, and his goods seized upon to the Turk's use.
Robert Powell, one of his followers, returned home full of double
pistolets, who was searched, tortured, and beaten, to make him
confess, as he told me himself. He also told me, that in the fight,
which was long, fierce, and admirable, both parties would rest at
times, and the captains parly, and drink one to another.

[1] Qu. Algier.—L.

For martial men, our age hath produced out of this county Sir Mauris Griffith, Knight, born in the town of Caernarvon, and one of the younger sons of William Griffith. He served in the realm of Ireland all his youth, and was captain there; and for his good service received his degree: and liveth at this time in conachtat castell, which himself built, and is called Bala me Rusk: and he is one of the council of the province.

Captain Pritchard, born at Madryn isa, in Llyn, in the said county of Caernarvon, younger brother to Griffith ab Richard, heir of that house; commanded with great credit 100 men, under the states of the Low Countries, in Queen Elizabeth's time.

Sir Richard Wynn, of Caernarvon, Knight, of the house of Bryncir, captain of a hundred men in Ireland, provost martial of Flushing, under Sir Phillip Sydney, sometime page to captain Ronelall, who was slain in the North of Ireland, whose armour he brought to Sir Henry Sydney, then Lord Deputy of Ireland, whose follower he was all his life time after: and after his death, and for his sundry good services, being knighted; and after having got the widow of captain Thomas aforementioned in the country, lived at Caernarvon all the rest of his time. He was one of the council of the marches; keeping a very worthy house, being a religious, honest, and true-hearted man to his friend, having always in his mouth this saying, "Duw a diwedd da," which in English is, "God and a good end," which no question God did hear, for he made a christian and a good end, as Gryffydd Williams,[1] Doctor in Divinity, now living, being his ghostly father at his end; and respecting which, also, the Rev. Father, Lewis, now Bishop of Bangor, preaching the funeral sermon of William Glynn, of Glynnllifon, Knight, did remember persuading all to the imitation of him

The memorable services of John Wynn ab Hugh,[2] born at Bod-

---

[1] See page 97.—L.

[2] John Wynn ab Hugh was Sheriff of Caernarvon in 1551; and married Elizabeth, daughter to Sir John Puleston; by her he had Hugh Gwynn Bodvel, Sheriff of Caernarvon in 1597, grandfather to Sir John Bodvel, Knight, likewise Sheriff of

TABLE No. IV.

TABLE IV.

Sir John Wynn, of Gwydir,=Sidney, da. of Sir William Gerrard,
Bart. so created in 1611. | Lord Chancellor of Ireland.
a

| 1 Sir J. Wynn,=Marget, da. | 2 Sir Rich. | 3 Sir Owen Wn=Grace, da. | 4 Rbt. Wn. | 5 Wm. Wn.=A da. & | 6 Morris Wn. | 7 Ellis, a 8 |

1 Sir J. Wynn,=Marget, da.　2 Sir Rich.　3 Sir Owen Wn=Grace, da.　4 Rbt. Wn.　5 Wm. Wn.=A da. &　6 Morris Wn.　7 Ellis, a 8
d. in his father's | of Sir Thos. Wn. Bart. Sheriff for Den- of Hugh O.S.P. Esq. Pro- heiress of O. S. P. student
life-time. at | Cave. mar. a dau. bighshire in Williams, thonotary Thomas *g* of the law
Lucca, in 1621. of Sir *c* 1656 ob. 1668, of Wig. of Wales. Lloyd, of at Gray's
b Francis aged 68. *e* *f* Gwern-y- Inn. o. s. p.
One da. who died an infant. D'arcie Brechtyn. buried in Whitfo
O. S. P. *d* Church. *h*

Sir Richard Wynn, of=Sara, da. of Sir Thomas　　Edward Thel-=Sidney Wynn,　　Sir John Wynn, Bai
Gwydir, Bart. *l*　Myddelton Bt. of Chirk　wall, Esq. *n*　only da. and　mar. Jane, fh. Eyty
Castle. *m*　heir. *o*　Evans of Watstai.
O. S. P. *p*
1st wife
Mary, da. of
Visc. Bulkele

Mary Wynn,fh.=Robert Bertie, Duke　Sir Wm. Williams, Bt. of Llanvor.=Marget, fh. Watkyn Kyffin　Rich. Mostyn,=Chai
she died in 1689. of Ancaster. *r*　da, Spr. of the House of Commons, of Glascoed.　of Penbedw.　fch.
son of Hugh Williams, D.D.　*t** Digl
ob. 1700.　Goat

Peregrine Bertie, 2d Duke of Ancaster.=　Sir William Williams,=Jane, only da. and heir, born
He married Jane, da. of Sir John Brown- Bt. of Llanforda. 25 Dec. 1665, mar. in 1689. *t*
low, Bt. Peregrine died in 1742. b. 1684, d. 1740. *s*

w

Brownlow, 5th | Peregrine Bertie,= Sir Watkyn Wms.=Frances, da. | Rbt. Williams,=Miriam, fch. | Rich. Williams=Anna Bella, fh.
duke, 1780. = 3d duke of Ancas- Wynn, b. 1691, ob. of George of Erbystoc. Arthur Wil- married 1st *x* Edd. Lloyd, of
ter, ob. 1778. 1749. His 1st wife Shackerley. *v* liams of Charlotte, fh. Tre-newydd, ob.
was Ann, fch. Ed. of Gwersyllt Ystym Colwyn. Rich. Mostyn, 1795. *s*
Mary Elizabeth. Vaughn of Llan- 2d wife. O. S. P. of Penbedw.
gedwyn. above named, O. S. P. *y*

Rbt. Bertie, | Priscilla Bar- | Georgina | Sir W. W. W.=Charlotte, da. | Watkyn Wms.=Elisabeth, | William | Anna Bella=Rev. Philli
4th Duke, bara Elizabeth Charlotte married 1st to the Rt. Hon. M.P. for the fch. Col. Wms. esq. fh. d. 1824. Puleston,
ob. 1779. Baroness Wil- Bertie. The Lady H. G. Grenville, boroughs of Stapelton, O. S. P. Lloyd,esq. D.D. of Pic
loughby, of Somerset, da. & sister to Flintshire, ob. of Bodrhy- 1803. cill, Vicar c
Eresby, wife of to the Duke of the Marquis of 1808. S. P. ddan, died Ruabon &
Peter Burrell, Beaufort. Buckingham. April, 1825 of Worther
Esq. created · *aa* *bb*
Baron Gwydir,
of Gwydir,
May 28, 1796.
See the Peerage.

Sir W. =The Lady | Right Hon=Mary, da. | Right Hon.=Hon. | Anna=Ed. Lloyd | Eliz- =Wil-
W. Wynn Harriet C.W.Wynn of Sir F. H. W. Wn. Hester Bella Lloyd,esq. abeth. *hh* liam
dd Clive, da. to Pres. of the Cunliffe, Ambassador at Smyth, *ff* of Pen-y- Wynn
the Earl of Board of Bart. the Court of da. to lan. *gg* Esq. of
Powis. Controul, M Denmark. Lord Pen-
Daughters married. of the Privy Caring- niarth.
See the Baronetage. Council, &c. ton. *ii*
ee

Hennetta. | Watkyn. | Herbert | Charles Watkyn Charlotte. Mary. Harriet. | Sidney. Sons & Daughters. | William Watkyn | Phil
ij | Watkyn. | Watkyn. Henry. | *ll* | Edward Wynne. | a
kk

* The Heiress of this ancient Family, Ann, daughter of John Puleston, of Emeral, Esq. married Richard Pary Price, Esq. of Bryn-y-P
the name of Puleston. Created a Baronet in 1813.

Wn.=Catrin,   Sir Roger=Mary   Sir John==Elizabeth
fh. Ellis   Mostyn, | Wynn   Bodvill,   Wynn.
Lloyd, of   Knt. *j*   Knt, *k*
Rhiwgoch.

ir Thos. Mostyn, Knt.=   Sidney, wife of Sir Rich=
ar. Eliz. da. of Sir Jo. | Grosvenor, of Eaton, Bt. |
Vhitlock, kt. C. Justice. | who died in 1664. *q*

         2d wife
=Sir Roger Mostyn,=Prudence, da. of Sir   Roger=
created a Bart. in | Martin Lumley, Bt.   Grosve-
1660.   nor, ob.
                               1661.

Sir Thos.=Bridget,   Jane, w. of Ro-   Sir Thomas=
Mostyn, | fh. Darcy   ger Puleston,   Grosvenor,
ma. (at 11 | Savage of   Esq. of Emeral,   Bart. ob.
years old), | Beeston.   com. Flint. *   1700.
in 1662.

Sir Roger Mostyn,=The Lady Essex   Sir Robert=
Bart. ob. 1749. | Finch, da. of the Earl   Grosvenor,
            of Nottingham.   Bart.
                               died 1765.

Jane, ob.=Robert   Sir Thos=Sara, fch.   Rich. crea=
821. | Lloyd,   Mostyn, | Robert   ted Lord
cc   Esq.   Bt. born | Western,   Grosvenor
      of Swan   1704, ob. | of London.   in 1761.
      Hill.   1758.   See the
                               Peerage.

a=Edward   Jane=John   Sir Ro=Margt.
,   Gatacre,   2 fch.   Wn.   ger M. | fh. Rev.
.   Esq. of   Eyton   b. 1734, | Hugh
     Gatacre.   Esq.   died at | Wynn,   Daugh-
                of   Mostyn, | D. D.   ters
                Leeswood.   in 1796. | of Bod-   married
                              scallen,
                              ob.1792.

ston Ed. Gatacre.   Ann Bella.   Sir Thomas Mostyn,
       mm   *nn*   Bart. only son. *oo*

lintshire, by whom she had one son, Richard, who took

---

a See Table III. after page 48.
He died on Thursday, 1 March, 1626-7 and was buried on Friday, 2 March.

b In his elegy, by Cadw. Cesail he is stated to have died in 1614.

c Sir Rich. mar. Anna dau. of &c.

d " D'arcie " of Isleworth "O. S. P." 1649 at 61.

e " 1668 " read 1680. Ob. 13 Aug.

f Died 24 Oct., 1664.

g Will dated in 1671, proved at London. Marriage Articles dated 20 Mar., 1648. (A copy of *Ben Jonson's Works* at Peniarth, fol. 1640 contains Morris Wynne's autograph, also a copy of *Laud against Fisher.*)

h Died 20 Nov., 1619 aged 20.

i Died 27 July, 1671, in his 69th year.

j Born in 1567, died 18 Aug., 1642.

k

           " Sir John=" Elizabeth Wynn "
           Bodville | married 2ndly John
           Knt." | Thelwall of Gray's
                       | Inn, Esq.

     Mary wife
     of Hugh,
     Viscount
     Cholmondeley.

l Died before 13 Apr. 1675 (Qy. did he not die the end of Oct. 1674?)

m She died 16 June 1671.

n Died 12 Dec. 1679.

o Married in June 1664.

b Sir John Wynn died 11 Jan. 1718-9 aged 91.

The Seal of Sir John Wynn of Watstay 21 July 1684. 1 Owen Gwynedd. 2 Gr ap Cynan. 3 the three heads, necks encircled by snakes. 4 Collwyn ap Tangno. 5 Llowarch ap Bran. 6 Salisbury. (To a letter at Brogyntyn).

q They were married in 1628.

r Married at Westminster Abbey 30 July 1678.

s In MS. "b. 1684" is struck out, and there is added; Marriage settlement dated in 1686.

[TURN OVER.

t In MS. the word "only" (dau.) is struck out, and a note is added to the effect that the dates* do not agree with those below:—

Wm. Wynn of Garthgynan ;=Jane Lloyd of Gwern-y-brech-
ob: Oct 24, 1664. He was Pro- | dyn. Marriage covenants dated
thonotary of North Wales. | March 20, 1628.

Rd. Wynn of Garth-=Cath de dau : of Rich. | Richard William } ob : inf. | Sidney wife of Edw.
gynan Esq. Living Viscount Bulkeley, | Mary [bapt. } | Thelwall ot Plasy-
3 June 1639. buried at Llan- | at King's Norton 3 | ward Esq. ob :
drillo, 5 Sep. 1706, | June 1639] | 15 June 1683.
aged 69. | Thomas [bapt. at
| King's Norton 1 Feb.
| 1636]

Simon Jane, wife of Sir | Mary wife of Edw. | Sidney wife of Cad- | Mariana born
Edward Wm. Williams, | Vaughan of | waladr Wynne of | 8 May 1673
William Bt. born 25 Dec. | . . . . born 20 | Voelas, Esq, born
John 1664, ma. 1684* | Nov. 1671.* | 16 July, 1670.*
mar. settlement at
Wynnstay dated
1686.

[Salusbury MS. (Mr. Morris' transcript) at Wynnstay]

t 3rd son, ob. 1735, æt. 76.

u For "Charlotte" read Charlotta Theophila and strike the ' a ' out of "Goathurst."

v ob: s. p.   w For "Miriam, fch." read Meryel dau: of.

x For "1st" read 2ndly, and for "Charlotte" Charlotta.

y Strike out "O.S.P." and add—He died 14 Mar. 1740, leaving a son Richard who died 19 [Feb. 1745-6 in his 16th year.

z For "Edw" read Charles: add 3rd wife after date.

aa Died 1832.   bb Died 1801.   cc For "1821" read 1820.

dd Died 1840.   ee Died 1850.

ff Married, secondly, Major Gen. T. Molyneux, K.H. who assumed the name of Williams. She died in 1862.

gg Assumed the additional surname of Williams.

hh Died 1822.   ii Died 1834.   jj Should be Henrietta.

kk "Watkyn Henry" should come first, with died young after his name. "Charles W." second.

ll ———
  "Sidney."
  Emma
  d. young.

mm For "Ed. Gatacre" Ed. Lloyd Gatacre.   nn For "Ann" Anna.

oo Add died unmarried.

fel, in Llyn, in the said county, whereof he was Lord, he now in this tract is not to be forgotten. He was standard-bearer to John Earl of Warwick, and afterwards Duke of Northumberland, in the great field fought between him and Kett, and the rebels of Northfolk and Suffolk near Norwich, in Edward the Sixth's time, his horse was slain under him, and himself hurt, and yet he upheld the great standard of England. There is mention of this shot made at the standard of England in the Chronicles of that time, for the which service the Duke of Northumberland bestowed upon him two fine things in Llyn, viz. the Isle of Bardsey, and the Demesne House of the Abbot of Bardsey, near Aberdaron, called the Cowrtwith. The honourable mention made of his good ser‐ vice in the grant, which I have seen and read, a rare matter to find so good a master.

Caernarvon 1623, whose daughter and heir, Sara, married Robert Roberts, son of Lord Viscount Bodmyn, and their son, Charles, was created Earl of Radnor—L.

[1] Kett's rebellion, referred to on pp. 99, 100, oc‐ curred in the year 1549.

FINIS.

INDEX.

ADDITIONS AND CORRECTIONS.

Page xvi. *Howel Coetmore.* "Hic Jacet Howel Coetmor ap Gruff Vychan ap Coruff." Howel Coetmor and his brother Robert were executors of the will of Griffith Vaughan ap Griffith ap David Goch, as were Res Gethin and Gruff. Lya, and were living 11 Mar. 21 Rich. II., being Monday in the third week of Lent.—*Public Records,* "Welsh Plea Rolls."

Page 2, note 8. There are several copies of the *Great Extent of North Wales,* as it is called. Two of them are in the British Museum, and two in the Hengwrt Collection. The whole, with the exception of that of Merioneth, were made in 26 Edw. III. The Merioneth "Extent" is of 7 Hen. V. They are printed in the *Record of Carnarvon.*

Page 19, Note 4. *Einion ap Seisylt:*—"Et etiam (Juratores) dicunt quod quidam Eignion ap Seysyllt fuit seizitus in dominico suo ut de feodo de tota terra que fuit & est inter Aquas de dyvi & dewlas tempore Llewelyn ap Jorwerth nuper principis. Et quod terra illa tunc fuit pars & parcella Comoti de Estimaner in Comitatu Merioneth & adhuc de iure esse debet. Et quod idem Eignion ap Seysyllt terram illam tunc tenuit de Llewelyn vawr ap Meredith ap Kynan & Llewelyn vychan fratre eius dominis de Merioneth in capite Et quod idem Eignon propter discentionem & discordiam inter ipsos Llewelyn vawr & Llewelyn vychan et ipsum Eignion tunc habitam fugit ad Owenum Kevelock dominum de Powys & devenit tenens eius de terra predicta &fecit homagium & fidelitatem suam sibi pro terris predictis. Et sic hucusque terra illa tenta fuit. Et est parcella dominiorum de Powys iniusta, &c." (Extract from the Record of an Inquisition held at Bala, on the next Monday after the Festival of St. Michael the Archangel, 6 Hen. VI., in *Hengwrt MS.* 119).

Page 32. For note 7 read 6, for note 6 read 7.

Page 33, note 2. For "Now called Ystymcegid," read "Part of the tenement now called Ystymcegid."

Page 36, note 2. Mr. Barrington's note as to the long possession of Porkington by the Owen family, is incorrect. That estate came into possession of the Owens by the marriage of John Owen, secretary to the famous Sir Francis Walsingham, and a younger son of Owen ap Robert of Bodielin. in Carnarvonshire, with Ellin, eldest grand daughter and heiress of Sir William Maurice, Knt., of Porkington; and of Clenenney in Carnarvonshire. She was born, 7 Oct., 1578, married secondly to the Hon. Sir Francis Eure, Chief Justice of North Wales, a younger son of Wm. Lord Eure, and died in 1626. Her first husband was buried at Whittington 20 March 1611-12, and Sir Francis Eure was buried at. Selattyn 11 April 1621. *Bledh.* (Bleddyn), referred to in the note at page 36, was one of the sons of Owen Brogyntyn or de Porkinton, Lord Dinmael and Edeirnion, who was an illegitimate son of Madoc ap Meredith, Prince of Powis.

Page 37. *Marriage of Robert ap Meredith.* This statement differs from that on page 56. The following is from a Pedigree in the autograph of the eminent Welsh Genealogist, Griffith Hiraethog, in *Hengwrt MS.,* 428, folio 73 :—

> Robert ap Meredith=Angharad, dau.
> of David ap
> Llewellyn ap
> David by Margaret   dau :
> Rydderch ap
> Jevan Lloyd,
> of the South.

Page 38, note 4. Read as follows:—"9th of Hen· IV., Hen. V. being then Prince of Wales. Amongst the Records of the late Welsh Record Office, is a license for Meredith ap Hwlkyn Llwyd to build a mill, &c., &c."

Page 45. *Rhobin Ddu,* Robin (Ddu o Von,) an eminent poet who flourished from 1430 to 1470. Several of his poems are preserved in Manuscript, and among them is one written in 1450, from which we learn that he was returning from a pilgrimage to Rome, to Pope Nicholas V., in a ship with a cargo of wine, bound to Anglesey, his native country.—Williams's *Eminent Welshmen,* p. 458.

Page 46, note 2. For "Gruffith Lloyd ap Ellis *and* Gruffith ap Einion" read "*ap* Gruffith ap Einion."

Page 48, note 4. For "the present year" read "that year."

Page 49. Table III. Dr. Rice Wynne, lineal descendant of the house of Gwydir, died in Shrewsbury on 7 Apr., 1847 (?) at the age of 69, and was buried on Apr. 14, in St. Alkmond's Churchyard. He had been a medical practitioner in that town for half-a-century.

Pages 51 and 52. *Robin Vaughan.* The text and the note signed P. are somewhat obscure. The following pedigree, from a MS. in the Hengwrt Collection, in the autograph of the eminent genealogist, Griffith Hiraethog, and another in the hand of the celebrated Merionethshire antiquary, Robert Vaughan, *Hengwrt* MS. 96, will serve to explain it.

Robin Vaughan=Angharad, dau. of
ap David ap   Madoc ap Rees.
Howel*ap*David
ap Gruff.

Angharad married   Rees ap=Catherine.
to Ithel Vychan   Einion
ap Kynric ap   Vychan.
Rotpert.

Gwenhwyvar,   Lleuky=Griffith ap Madoc
dau.&heiress,   Vaughan.
wife of Ro-
bert Salis-
bury.

Margaret, wife of Griffith Vychan ap Jevan ap Robert ap Meredith.

Page 63. *Robert ap Rys.* He was Chaplain to Cardinal Wolsey. His tomb stone is or was in the Church of Yspytty. Amongst the Muniments at Rûg is a receipt dated 3 Nov. 21 Hen. viii. from Margaret verch Elysse to her vnculle (uncle), Master Robert ap Rice, Clerk, for a sum of money in part payment of a legacy, which was bequeathed to her "to my dowry," by her brother Rice ap Elisse. The deed is witnessed by Sir John Gruffith, Sir Richard, parson of Cerrigydruidion, Sir Thomas ap Robert, Priests, ffowke Salysbury, and David ap Res Porthmon. In the same collection is also a receipt of the same date from Gruffith ap Ellis ap Howel ap Res, brother and executor to Res ap Ellysse for 4£ in gold, paid the 5th day of August last, by demand of Res ap Elysse, "then being sore secke to by (buy) all thyngs necessary to his buriall." It is witnessed by the same persons.

Page 71, note 3. The following is an addition to the note, and taken from the same source:—

Though the estate of y⁰ father was divided among y⁰ sons by gavelkind, yet y⁰ estate of a person dying wth out issue was never divided among all his nearest relations in equal degrees (y⁰ being in some cases impracticable) but descended to one next of Kin & senior to y⁰ rest : . . . . . . this answers y⁰ marginal note p. 82, & renders y⁰ argument for y⁰ seniority of Robt. Mredydd unanswerable. (A note to the *Brogyntyn MS.*)

Page 91, Line 5. For "statutes" read "statues" Do. line 4 of Note, for "rewarded," read "recorded."

Page 92. Line 4 of Note 1. For "prim 6." read "prim. Edw. 6." In lines 16, 17, of same note, for "leased by William, late Bishop, and William Lloyd," read "leased by William, late Bishop, to William Lloyd."

Page 104. *Table IV.* Note *l.* The second Sir Richard Wynn died Oct. 30, 1674.

ADDITIONAL SUBSCRIBERS' NAMES.

Causton, H.K.S., Esq., 55 Vassall Road, Brixton, Surrey.
David, J. Esq., Dolgelley.
Evans, Mr. Robt., Smithfield House, Beddgelert,
Phillips, J. Roland, Esq., 133, Finborough Road, South Kensington, London, S.W.
Reveley, H. J., Esq., Brynygwin, Dolgelley.

WOODALL and VENABLES, Steam-Printers and Lithographers, Bailey Head, and Oswald Road, Oswestry. Nov, 1878.

PEDIGREE OF JONES.

PEDIGREE OF JONES,

OF WERN, PARISH OF PENMORVA, COUNTY OF CARNARVON.

Sioned, dau. of Rhys ap═Ievan, 2nd son of John ap Meredith, of Ystymkegid, co. of Carnarvon. (See pages 36, 43, 44, 45.═Moryıdd, or Margaret, dau.
Llewelyn ap Hwikin of | 47, 51, 55, 58, 59, 66 and genealogical table No. II. page 28). Ievan is party to a deed dated | of Meredith ap Ievan ap
Anglesea. | 5 Aug. 1525. He was lineally descended, as is shewn in the *History of the Gwydir Family*, from | Robert of Gwydir.
| Owen Gwynedd, Sovereign Prince of North Wales.

Ellis.

Grace, wife of Robert Evans, LL.B., Dean of Bangor, instituted 12 Dec., 1534, when he resigned the
Rectory of Llantrisant. He was also Rector of for
Aber and Llanrengan, which he was deprived of for
being married, as of the Deanery, but he was re-
instituted, and died in 1570.

Sioned, wife of
Thomas ap Rhys
of Brynmenadd,
in Carnarvonshire.

Ellin, wife of
Robert ap
John ap
Madoc
Vychan.

Gaynor, wife of
Howel ap Griffith
ap Howel of near
TalLlyn Tarddeni
(Llyn Quellyn).

Ellin, wife of
Wm. ap
Hugh ap
David ap
Robert.

1. Margaret, wife, first of Howel ap Madoc
Vychan—see page 76—(icffcient subsequent
to their marriage dated the next Monday
after the Feast of S. Catherine the Virgin,
4 Hen. VIII.), and andly of John Wynn
ap Robert Vaughan.

2. Ellin, wife of Thomas ap Griffith
ap Jenkin ap Rhys, of Trawswynydd.
He is party to a deed dated 14 Hen.
VII. (1499).

3. Lowry, wife of Hugh
ap Madoc ap Llewelyn
ap Morgan ap Ievan ap
Meredith, of Penllech.

4. Angharad, wife of Morgan
ap Robert ap Griffith ap Howel
ap Llewelyn ap Howel of Caer-
gybi (Holyhead).

5. Gwenhwyvar, wife of Ellis ap William
ap Griffith ap Jenkin, of Trawswynydd.
His Will in Register of Arthur Bulkeley,
Bishop of Bangor, folio 170. Robert Lloyd
M.P. for the co. of Merioneth in 1586, 1601,
and 1614, of Rhiwgoch, was their eldest
grandson.

6. Annes, wife of Thos. ap Rhys ap Howel
Vychan. "This Thomas had £1500 per ann"
but he sold most of it and died at Hupsdale"
(Hopesdale in Flintshire). See *Peniarth MS.*
47, p. 144. What would this £1500 per annum
amount to now (1875)?

7. Elizabeth, wife of
David Lloyd Vychan of
Lleyn.

8. Jane, wife of Wm.
ap Morris ap Griffith
ap Ievan, of Bdonedd.

9. Mary wife of Ievan (or
Lewis) ap Jenkin ap Griffith
ap Tudur, of Towyn Merioneth. She died s.p.

2. Robert, son and heir. Party to a deed
upon 5 Aug. 1525. Married Margaret
dau. of Robert ap Griffith ap Rhys, of
Dinmael, and died in 1565.

Morris ap Ievan, died in 1563, buried at Penmorva.═
Will in Reg. of Arthur, Bishop of Bangor, folio 302
It appears by his elegy, by Griffith Hirnaethog, that
he served in the army, in France and Ireland.

Owen.

John Wynn.

Annes, dau. of Rhys ap David ap
Gwilym, of Llwyrfiarth, in Anglesea.
Her father's will is dated 10 Dec, 1539
Her brother, David ap Rhys, was
Sheriff of Anglesea in 1550. She is
mentioned in her father's will.

Rhys.

Rowland.

Rhys. | John ap Morris, born about 1538 joined═Alen, dau. of John ap Richard, of Gwyn-
| with a hundred men, the army sent by | wyrn. The grandfather of John ap
| Owen Elizabeth to occupy Newhaven | Richard was Griffith ap John ap Groun.

Ellin, wife of Robert
ap Richard, of Llech-
iddior, on Carnarvon

Alice, wife of
Rhydderch
ap Lewis

Elizabeth, wife
of Lewis

Ellis. (1590).

son Maurice's name is assessed in the "Estreate" of the hundred of Evioneth of that date.

1. Annes, wife of Ellis ap Robert Wynn, of Trawsvynydd.

2. Sarah, wife of Griffith ap Robert ap Hugh, of Penmorva.

3. Jane, wife of Thomas ap Ievan ap Griffith ap David, of Penmorva.

4. Gaenor, wife of Thomas ap Robt. ap Hugh ap Reinallt, of Fronoleu. He was living 22 Jan. 1625.

5. Mary, wife of John ap Wm. ap Howel ap Robert, of Tredyn, or of Pennant.

2. Ellis. A deputation to "Ellis Jhonnes, gent." and others, from Wm., afterwards Sir Wm. Maurice, Knt., to exercise certain powers under him, as Deputy Vice-Admiral of N. Wales, bears date 20 Oct., 1593.

3. Cadwalader, of Nant Francon, married Catherine, dau. of John ap Evan, of Nant Francon. A warrant from Sir Wm. Maurice, Knt. and Wm. Humffreys, as Justices of the Peace for the co. of Carn., to arrest "Cadw' ap John ap Maurice gent," bears date 13 July 17 James I. He was a housholder in Penmorva, upon 12 Aug., 1617.

4. Evan.

5. Arthur.

6. Richard, married Elizabeth, dau. of John Owen, of Penmorva.

Agnes, dau. and co-heir of David Lloyd, of Wern=Maurice Jones of Wern. Feoffee in a deed of 17 May, 1602, died=Jane, dau. of Rees Bold, and y Dwyrid. This place is close to Wern. 1624. An elegy upon him written by Rd. Phillip. wife, died before her husband.

1. Jane, wife of Thomas Lloyd, of Hendre Urien, co. of Merioneth. He was living in 1637.

2. Dorothy, wife of Howel Lewis, of Waredog (or Gwaredog), co. of Anglesea, Sheriff of that co. in 1666.

3. Gaenor, wife of Hugh ap Ellis ap Lewis of Llanelltyd.

4. Alice, wife of John ap Pierce ap Ellis.

5. Barbara, wife, it is believed, of John Wynne Owen, of Ystymkegid.

6. Mary, married to John, son of Griffith Lloyd, of Carne. His brother, Edmund Lloyd, was inducted to the Rectory of Rhoscolyn in 1663.

John Jones, of Wern, married=Margaret, dau. of Captain Ellis Maurice (2nd son of Sir Wm. Maurice before the death of his father. of Clenenney, Knt.), by Jane, one of the dau'rs of Sir Wm. Mering Appears by a letter dated 16 Jan. to Ellis Anwyl, living in 1655, of Parkie, co. of Carnarvon, son of 163⅓ to have been then living. Morris Lewis Anwyl, a younger son of Lewis Anwyl of Park, co. of Merioneth, mentioned above.

Cadwalader, born probably about 1589, died without issue.

Humffrey,

Thomas, living in 1649.

Ellis.

Maurice Jones, of Wern, a trustee to the will=Frances, dan. of Wm. of Henry Roberts, of Carnarvon, 8 Oct. 1641. Wynne, of Glyn, co. Married on or before 21 Nov. 1646. Cove-Merioneth. Living nants after his marriage dated in 1649. 20 Sept. 1666. Living in 1666. Dead probably several years before 21 May, 1677.

James, went to Barbadoes and married there where he was living upon 21 May, 1677.

Ellin, wife of Wm. ap David ap William, of Cwm mawr, co. of Carnarvon.

Catherine, supposed to have been married to Robert, a younger son of John Vaughan, of Aberkin, co. of Carnarvon.

Other children, who died young.

Elizabeth Jones, heiress of Wern, married to her cousin, William Wynne, 4th son of Robert Wynne, of Glyn, and so conveyed Wern into the Wynne family. He was Sheriff of Carnarvonshire in 1686. He died 31 Dec. 1700, and was buried at Penmorva. She was buried at Penmorva 21 Oct., 1715, and her will was proved at Bangor. There is an elegy upon her by Owen Griffith.

Wern was sold, about the end of the last century (about 1798), by Wm. Wynne, of Peniarth, Esq., the representative of Wm. Wynne and Elizabeth Jones, to a Captain Barlow, by whom it was again sold to Col. Wardle, M.P. of York notoriety.

W.

Notes to Pedigree of Jones.

Robt. Wyn ap Jeu'n ap John
P'terre (sic) suis et al . . . .

Pro terr' voc erw seran	vijs. ixd.	
et p' tenn't voc Tythyn dwy	vjs. iiijd.	
P' ter' voc bodlache	iiijd.	
P' ter' voc' ynys y pandy	vjd.	
P' ter' in tenure (sic) will'm ap madoc ap hoell	vjd.	S'u xvi. . . .
P' ter' voc' drylle y kyente	ijd.	
P' ter' voc' ter' merched gwyne ...	xd.	
P' ter' voc' myr y ty her	vijd.	
P' ter' hughe ap madoc in tenure (sic) Ric' ap gr' ap d'd'	xvd.	

* Robt. Wynn { (brace for above rows) }

freth de pennant in perth deon ... ... iij	iiijd.	
freth de pennant yn Enys y grywyen	xd.	S'u
freth de pennant Keysen y sadd	xd.	ix . . . .
freth de pennant yn meresher	iis.	viiij . . . .
freth de pennant in mwlch rywdyrthen, ...	vijd.	
freth de penna't in ysain	iis.	

Morres ap Jeu'n ap John {

Morres ap Jeu'n ap John p'ter' voc' Kay mawr	xxd.	
Et p'ter' voc' ter' gwyn y pwll y march ...	viijd	
P' ter' voc' ter' Jeu'n ap Eign ap gwas ...	vd.	
P' ter' voc' ter' Luce [qy Luce] yn Penmorva...	vd.	iij . . .
p' ter' voc' ter' Jeu'n ap eign ap gwas yn bryn coch	xijd.	vijd. . . .
John ap Jeu'n ap Robt. pro ter' voc' Kavyn Key veneth	jxd.	

From an assessment of Crown rents, at Brogyntyn, written between 20 July 1538, and the year 1563, inclusive. The dotted lines and figures in italic are, in the original, in a paler ink, slightly more recent.

Award dated 2nd Oct., 1587, contending parties, Wm. Maurice, of Clenenney, Esq., and John ap mores ap Jeu'n (Ieuan) ap John, of Pennyved,. co: Caern: gentleman; Arbitrators, Robert wyn ap Elissa and Lewis Anwyll. They adjudge to be the property of the said John " such quantitie & soe much of the moore & lands called Gwern Virogle sett & leinge within the towneshippe of Penryved as we the said arbitrators shall meere tread out & appointe to be the lands & medowes of the said John ap mores, without interrupcion ejection &c. of the said Wm. Maurice, or his heirs, &c., or by any colloure of encrotchements belonging to the right honorable the L. of Leicester," and the said William is to make and assure by deeds, &c. to the said John " all those parcelles of landes rents & hereditaments &c. which are now in the tenure &c. of the said John in a close called y Kav mawr, and above the hey way of the west and northe syde of the same, within the townshippe of Pennyved, except soe much of the laste resyted premisses adjoining to the sayd hey way, as we shall meere " &c. They award as the property of the said William Maurice " all those parcelles of lands arrable medowe & pasture &c. commonly called dryllie y madu lloyd, within the township of Treflys, in the tenure &c.: of Jonedd verch Robert ap Eign."

(Executed by)

" Robert wynn ap Elissa "
" By me Lewis Anwyll " (and duly sealed).

[From the original at Brogyntyn.]

* The same person as " Robert son and heir " (See " Pedigree of Jones "*a*) He was direct ancestor, in the male line, to the Brynkirs, of Brynkir.—W.

74.

CPSIA information can be obtained
at www.ICGtesting.com
Printed in the USA
LVHW082152110320
649817LV00007B/453